Laudato Si' and the Environment

This volume is a response to Pope Francis environmental encyclical *Laudato Si'*. Published in 2015, the encyclical urges us to face up to the crisis of climate change and to take better care of the Earth, our common home, while also attending to the plight of the poor.

In this book the Pope's invitation to all people to begin a new dialogue about these matters is considered from a variety of perspectives by an international and multidisciplinary team of leading scholars. There is discussion of the implications of Laudato Si' for immigration, population control, eating animals, and property ownership. Additionally, indigenous religious perspectives, development and environmental protection, and the implementation of the ideas of the encyclical within the Church are explored. Some chapters deal with scriptural and philosophical aspects of the encyclical. Others focus on central concepts, such as interconnectedness, the role of practice, and what Pope Francis calls the "technocratic paradigm."

This book expertly illuminates the relationship between *Laudato Si'* and environmental concerns. It will be of deep interest to anyone studying religion and the environment, environmental ethics, Catholic theology, and environmental thought.

Robert McKim is Emeritus Professor of Philosophy of Religion at the University of Illinois at Urbana-Champaign, USA. He specializes in the philosophy of religion and applied ethics, and has published extensively in these areas. He has written the following books: *Religious Ambiguity and Religious Diversity* (2001), *On Religious Diversity* (2012), and *Religious Diversity and Religious Progress* (2019). In addition, he has edited or co-edited the following books: *The Morality of Nationalism* (1997), *Religious Perspectives on Religious Diversity* (2017), and *Climate Change and Inequality* (2018).

Routledge New Critical Thinking in Religion, Theology and Biblical Studies

The *Routledge New Critical Thinking in Religion, Theology and Biblical Studies* series brings high quality research monograph publishing back into focus for authors, international libraries, and student, academic and research readers. This open-ended monograph series presents cutting-edge research from both established and new authors in the field. With specialist focus yet clear contextual presentation of contemporary research, books in the series take research into important new directions and open the field to new critical debate within the discipline, in areas of related study, and in key areas for contemporary society.

Vision, Mental Imagery and the Christian Life
Insights from Science and Scripture
Zoltán Dörnyei

Christianity and the Triumph of Humor
From Dante to David Javerbaum
Bernard Schweizer

Religious Truth and Identity in an Age of Plurality
Peter Jonkers and Oliver J. Wiertz

Envisioning the Cosmic Body of Christ
Embodiment, Plurality and Incarnation
Aurica Jax and Saskia Wendel

***Laudato Si'* and the Environment**
Pope Francis' Green Encyclical
Edited by Robert McKim

For more information about this series, please visit: https://www.routledge.com/religion/series/RCRITREL

Laudato Si' and the Environment
Pope Francis' Green Encyclical

Edited by
Robert McKim

Routledge
Taylor & Francis Group

LONDON AND NEW YORK

First published 2020
by Routledge
2 Park Square, Milton Park, Abingdon, Oxon OX14 4RN

and by Routledge
52 Vanderbilt Avenue, New York, NY 10017

Routledge is an imprint of the Taylor & Francis Group, an informa business

British Library Cataloguing-in-Publication Data
A catalogue record for this book is available from the British Library

Library of Congress Cataloging-in-Publication Data
A catalog record has been requested for this book

ISBN: 978-1-138-58881-3 (hbk)
ISBN: 978-0-429-49206-8 (ebk)

Typeset in Sabon
by codeMantra

Contents

List of contributors　　vii

PART 1
Introduction　　1

1　The challenge and the opportunity: some
　perspectives on *Laudato Si'*　　3
　ROBERT McKIM

PART 2
Implementation　　19

2　*Laudato Si'* and private property　　21
　ERIC T. FREYFOGLE

3　Reading *Laudato Si'* in a rainforest country: ecological
　conversion and recognition of indigenous religions　　38
　ZAINAL ABIDIN BAGIR

4　The cry of the earth and the cry of the poor　　60
　DARREL MOELLENDORF

5　*Laudato Si'* and population　　76
　HERMAN DALY

6　Rethinking our treatment of animals in light
　of *Laudato Si'*　　95
　DAVID L. CLOUGH

7 "We were nowhere. We've got somewhere." Does
   Laudato Si' go far enough, and is the Church on board
   for the climate journey?   105
   PADDY WOODWORTH

PART 3
Scriptural, theological and philosophical aspects   135

8 *Laudato Si'* and the reinterpretation of Scriptures
   in light of the ecological crisis   137
   MARGARET DALY-DENTON

9 Sources of authority in *Laudato Si'*   152
   CRISTINA L.H. TRAINA

10 A constructivist engagement with *Laudato Si'*   167
    KIERAN P. DONAGHY

PART 4
Central concepts   187

11 A new anthropology? *Laudato Si'* and the question
    of interconnectedness   189
    CELIA DEANE-DRUMMOND

12 "Realities are more important than ideas": the
    significance of practice in *Laudato Si'*   202
    GRETEL VAN WIEREN

13 Opposing the "technocratic paradigm" and
    "appreciating the small things"   217
    ROBERT McKIM

Index   239

Contributors

Dr. Zainal Abidin Bagir is Director of the Center for Religious and Cross-cultural Studies at the Graduate School of Universitas Gadjah Mada, Yogyakarta, Indonesia and a founder and Board Member of the Indonesian Consortium for Religious Studies, Yogyakarta. He has a degree in Islamic Philosophy from the International Institute of Islamic Thought and Civilization, Malaysia and a Ph.D. in the History and Philosophy of Science from Indiana University. His research interests include religion and science and religion and ecology. His publications include an edited book, *Science and Religion In A Post-Colonial World: Interfaith Perspectives;* a chapter on Islam in the *Routledge Handbook of Religion and Ecology* (2017); and papers on religious freedom in Indonesia.

David Clough is Professor of Theological Ethics at the University of Chester and past President of the Society for the Study of Christian Ethics. He is the author of *Ethics in Crisis: Interpreting Barth's Ethics* (Ashgate, 2005); co-author of *Faith and Force: A Christian Debate about War* (Georgetown, 2007); co-editor of *Creaturely Theology: On God Humans and Animals* (SCM, 2009) and *Animals as Religious Subjects: Transdisciplinary Perspectives* (T&T Clark/Bloomsbury, 2013); and author of *On Animals*: Volume I *Systematic Theology* (T&T Clark/Bloomsbury, 2012); Volume II *Theological Ethics* (T&T Clark/Bloomsbury, 2019).

Herman E. Daly is Emeritus Professor at the University of Maryland, School of Public Policy. From 1988 to 1994 he was Senior Economist in the Environment Department of the World Bank. He was co-founder and associate editor of the journal *Ecological Economics*. His research interests include economic development, population, resources, and environment. He has published over a hundred articles in professional journals and anthologies as well as numerous books, including *Toward a Steady-State Economy* (1973); *Steady-State Economics* (1977; 1991); *Valuing the Earth* (1993); *Beyond Growth* (1996) ; *Ecological Economics and the Ecology of Economics* (1999); *Ecological Economics and Sustainable Development* (2007); and *From Uneconomic Growth to a Steady-State Economy (2014)*. He is co-author with theologian John

B. Cobb, Jr. of *For the Common Good* (1989; 1994) which received the 1991 Grawemeyer Award for Ideas for Improving World Order. He has received Sweden's Honorary Right Livelihood Award (1996), the Heineken Prize for Environmental Science awarded by the Royal Netherlands Academy of Arts and Sciences; the Sophie Prize (Norway) for contributions in the area of Environment and Development (1999); the Leontief Prize for contributions to economic thought (2001); the Medal of the Presidency of the Italian Republic for his work in steady-state economics (2002); the Lifetime Achievement Award from the National Council for Science and the Environment (USA) (2010); and the Blue Planet Prize awarded by the Asahi Glass Foundation of Japan (2014).

Margaret Daly-Denton is the author of three books including *John: An Earth Bible Commentary: Supposing Him to be the Gardener* (London: Bloomsbury T&T Clark, 2017). She has taught in Trinity College Dublin, The Church of Ireland Theological College and The Milltown Institute in Dublin. Her research interests include the Christian reception of the psalms, the New Testament origins of Christian liturgy and ecological/biblical hermeneutics.

Celia Deane-Drummond is Director of the *Laudato Si'* Research Institute, Campion Hall, Oxford, UK. Previously she was Director of the Center for Theology, Science and Human Flourishing and Professor of Theology at the University of Notre Dame, IN, USA. Her research interests are in the engagement of systematic and moral theology and the biological sciences, including specifically ecology, evolution, genetics, animal behavior, psychology and evolutionary anthropology. She has published over two hundred scholarly theology and scientific articles or book chapters and twenty five books as editor or author. These include *Wonder and Wisdom: Conversations in Science, Spirituality and Theology* (2006), *Ecotheology* (2008), *Christ and Evolution* (2009), *Creaturely Theology* ed. with David Clough (2009), *Religion and Ecology in the Public Sphere*, ed. with Heinrich Bedford-Strohm (2011), *Animals as Religious Subjects*, ed. with Rebecca Artinian Kaiser and David Clough (2013), *The Wisdom of the Liminal: Human Nature, Evolution and Other Animals* (2014), *Re-Imaging the Divine Image* (2014), *Technofutures, Nature and the Sacred*, ed. with Sigurd Bergmann and Bronislaw Szerszynski (2015), *Religion in the Anthropocene*, edited with Sigurd Bergmann and Markus Vogt (2017), *A Primer in Ecotheology: Theology for a Fragile Earth* (2017) and *Theology and Ecology Across the Disciplines: On Care for Our Common Home*, edited with Rebecca Artinian Kaiser (2018).

Kieran P. Donaghy is a Professor of Regional Science in the Department of City and Regional Planning at Cornell University, which he chaired for seven years. He recently served as the Faculty Director of Economic

Development at the Atkinson Center for a Sustainable Future at Cornell and as the Interim Dean of the College of Architecture, Art, and Planning. Much of his research has been addressed to issues of transportation, land use, the natural and built environments, climate change, and globalization and the evolving economic geography of the United States.

Eric T. Freyfogle is a long-time faculty member of the University of Illinois College of Law, where he currently is Research Professor and Swanlund Chair Emeritus. He has taught and written on property, natural resources, land-use, wildlife and environmental law and on conservation thought and economic justice. His extensive writings for scholarly and popular audiences include *Our Oldest Task: Making Sense of Our Place in Nature* (University of Chicago Press), *A Good that Transcends: How U.S. Culture Undermines Environmental Reform* (University of Chicago Press), *On Private Property: Finding Common Ground on the Ownership of Land* (Beacon Press), and *Why Conservation Is Failing and How It Can Regain Ground* (Yale University Press).

Robert McKim is Emeritus Professor of Philosophy of Religion at the University of Illinois at Urbana-Champaign. He specializes in philosophy of religion and applied ethics. He has written these books: *Religious Ambiguity and Religious Diversity* (2001), *On Religious Diversity* (2012), and *Religious Diversity and Religious Progress* (2019). He has edited or co-edited these books: *The Morality of Nationalism* (1997), *Religious Perspectives on Religious Diversity* (2017), and *Climate Change and Inequality* (2018).

Darrel Moellendorf is Cluster Professor of International Political Theory at the Excellence Cluster Normative Orders and Professor of Philosophy at Johann Wolfgang Universität Frankfurt am Main. He is the author of *Cosmopolitan Justice* (2002), *Global Inequality Matters* (2009), and *The Moral Challenge of Dangerous Climate Change: Values, Poverty, and Policy* (2014). He co-edited (with Christopher J. Roederer) *Jurisprudence* (2004), (with Gillian Brock) *Current Debates in Global Justice* (2005), (with Thomas Pogge) *Global Justice: Seminal Essays* (2008) and (with Heather Widdows) *The Routledge Handbook of Global Ethics* (2014).

Cristina L. H. Traina is Professor of Religious Studies and Chair of the Department of Religious Studies at Northwestern University. She is a student of Christian theology and ethics, with emphasis on Roman Catholic and feminist thought. Areas of special interest include childhood, especially child labor; the ethics of touch in relations between unequals; sexuality and reproduction; ecology; justice issues in bioethics; economic and immigration justice; and method. She is the author of *Natural Law and Feminist Ethics: the End of the Anathemas* (Georgetown, 1999) and *Erotic Attunement: Parenthood and the Ethics of Sensuality between Unequals* (University of Chicago Press, 2011).

Gretel Van Wieren is Associate Professor of Religious Studies and Environmental Philosophy & Ethics at Michigan State University. She is author of the book *Restored to Earth* (Georgetown University Press, 2013) and two books in progress, *Food, Farming and Faith in God: Emerging Ethical Perspectives in the United States* (Routledge) and *Spirit of the Woods: An Experiment in Connection with Nature* (Oregon State University Press). Her articles have appeared in a variety of journals including *Environmental Ethics, Conservation Biology, Worldviews* and the *Journal for the Study of Religion, Nature and Culture.*

Paddy Woodworth is an author, journalist, lecturer, cultural and environmental tour guide. He has reported for the *Irish Times,* the *International Herald Tribune, Vanity Fair,* the BBC and NPR. He wrote two acclaimed books on the Basque Country, including *Dirty War, Clean Hands: ETA, the GAL and Spanish Democracy* (Yale 2002). *Science* rated his recent study of ecological restoration projects worldwide, *Our Once and Future Planet: Restoring the World in the Climate Change Century* (Chicago 2013) as "highly readable...[providing] valuable access to the central topics, key developments, and contentious issues bound up in the young and evolving field of ecological restoration". He writes regularly for the Environment Page in the *Irish Times.* He is Research Associate at Missouri Botanical Garden, Adjunct Senior Lecturer at University College, Dublin, a founder member of the Irish Forum on Natural Capital, and a member of the European Cultural Parliament.

Part 1

Introduction

1 The challenge and the opportunity

Some perspectives on *Laudato Si'*

Robert McKim

The challenge and the opportunity

The challenge

The challenge presented by the ways in which we human beings are harming the earth is plain for all to see. We are destroying ecological systems and wiping out numerous forms of life. We are adding carbon dioxide and methane to the atmosphere, and thereby changing the climate. The consequences will include higher temperatures, rising sea levels, the swamping of coastal areas, a major global loss of biodiversity, and more besides.

The scope and consequences of this crisis are difficult to exaggerate. Consider, for instance, the shocking fact that about 50% of all wild animals on earth have been wiped out in the last 40 years (World Wildlife Fund Living Planet Report, September 2014). Reduced populations of wild animals might recover. But we are also eliminating forms of life, a process that will not be reversed. The fact that one species is in the process of wiping out in the blink of an eye a significant portion, maybe as much as half, of all other forms of life on earth is beyond tragic.

Consider the plight of our closest biological relatives, the non-human primates. A recent comprehensive review finds that "about 60 percent of primate species are now threatened with extinction and about 75 percent have declining populations." (https://news.illinois.edu/blog/view/6367/453054#image-1. For the full study, see Estrada et al., 2017.) Paul Garber, a co-author of this study, recently observed that for apes, monkeys, tarsiers, lemurs, and lorises inhabiting ever-shrinking forests, and with their habitat disrupted or destroyed across the planet, "[this] truly is the eleventh hour" (https://news.illinois.edu/blog/view/6367/453054#image-1). The culprit is the expanding human presence. Agriculture, hunting, the illegal pet trade, illegal trade in animal parts, and logging are all contributing factors.

We urgently need to reduce the human impact on the earth. This requires polluting less, consuming less, protecting biodiversity, arresting the major global loss of habitat, and slowing down and then reversing humanly induced changes in the earth's climate.

The task we confront—and here I ever so slightly abuse a motif from Aldo Leopold—is learning to live on this planet without ruining it. This challenge is plain for all to see and it confronts all human institutions. It also provides an opportunity for the religions of the world.

The opportunity

How *might* and how *should* the religions of the world respond to this un-precedented challenge? What should they be accomplishing? What stand-ards should they hold themselves to? In probing these questions, I will consider a number of areas of inquiry. Part of my purpose, of course, is to provide a framework within which what Pope Francis has accomplished in *Laudato Si'* can be considered. But I also want to make some broader ob-servations about religion in general, especially about what it would take for the religions to rise to the occasion and to meet this challenge. Pope Francis says that we currently lack the requisite culture and leadership to do so (53).[1] I want to probe some aspects of what it would take for a religion to fill this cultural gap, and to provide the leadership that is needed.

I will discuss five ways in which the religions can be relevant and, we might decide, *should* be relevant to addressing this challenge. This adds up to a five-part framework within which the relevant resources and the relevant accomplishments of the religions in this area can be considered. In probing these areas, many of my observations are based on what impressive religious communities are already achieving.

Someone might wonder why we should turn to the religions for help with meeting this challenge. The question might even be formulated as an objec-tion: to do so—the objection might go—is to burden religion excessively, to expect it to play a role to which it is not suited.

The answer to this question (or objection), however, is straightforward. The religions exercise considerable influence in the lives of many people. They do not hesitate to try to provide guidance in many other areas of life. Why not in the case of this contemporary crisis? Why shouldn't we turn to them for help in this case? Rita Gross has it right in these remarks in her widely cited essay on Buddhist environmental ethics: "[We] know that all living religions have gone through the major changes required to remain relevant in altered circumstances. There is no reason that the same thing cannot happen in re-sponse to the ecological crisis" (Gross 1997: 334). Moreover, the religions have some relevant resources. And some of the relevant accomplishments of some of them, especially at the local level, have already been impressive.

A thorough exploration of the potential of religion in this regard would require us to ponder what might be the role of religion in the lives of human beings in the future; and who is to say what that will be? However, the predictions of those who have thought that religion would disappear from human affairs have so far proven utterly mistaken though, to be sure, they might yet be proven right if we humans have a long future. In any case, the religions are important now and they aspire to providing guidance and leadership now. And there is a great deal to be said about the guidance and leadership they could provide.

Providing guidance and providing inspiration

The first of the five areas of inquiry I will consider is the extent to which the relevant *teachings* of a religious tradition are environmentally constructive. Here, Pope Francis has much to say to us. As discussed in many of the chapters that follow, Pope Francis writes about the value and significance of each creature, about reverence for life in all of its forms, about the value of other species, and about protecting ecosystems. He says that we have an obligation to be good stewards of the earth; that we should care about the survival and flourishing of other species; that it is not our place to wipe out other forms of life and that we have no right to do so; and that we should take a considerate and merciful attitude toward all beings that can suffer. He says that we should live simply, reduce our impact, and avoid wastefulness. He calls for an ecological conversion, which works best when implemented communally. This ecological conversion has many dimensions, including this one: "simplicity which allows us to stop and appreciate the small things, to be grateful for the opportunities which life affords us, to be spiritually detached from what we possess, and not to succumb to sadness for what we lack" (222). (Additional aspects of this ecological conversion are discussed in Zainal Bagir Abidin's chapter.)

Of course, the category of environmentally constructive religious teachings—that is, environmentally constructive ideas that are available in any religion whatsoever—is a very broad one. It includes teachings that may be difficult to reconcile with monotheism. Perhaps an example of such a teaching is the idea that other animals are our kin. (Interestingly, this is an idea that Pope Francis comes close to endorsing.) It includes too ideas that are not compatible with monotheism such as the idea that whatever sacredness there may be is to be found in nature.

But let's face it: all is not sweetness and light when it comes to the environmental implications of religious teachings. The teachings of a religious tradition can also include elements that are not environmentally constructive and even some that are environmentally obstructive. Ideas such as the following at least run the risk of being obstructive:

> the idea that "the end is nigh" and hence the world and everything in it are not to be taken too seriously or—worse—that the destruction of the world is to be welcomed because this would usher in a new age of some sort;
> the idea that once you have taken the step of having faith about, say, loss of biodiversity, this matter is out of your hands so that having faith is itself an adequate response to the loss of biodiversity;

the idea that any environmental harm that occurs is in accordance with the will of God, perhaps because *everything* that happens is in accordance with the will of God, and hence not something about which we should be unduly concerned;

the idea that the more people there are, or the more of one's co-religionists there are, the better; and

the idea that the most developed human beings have transcended all concern for earthly things and are wholly concerned with an afterlife or liberation from rebirth or the like.

Needless to say, these are complicated matters. For instance, some ideas that have some potential for being obstructive are harmless when taken in context. An example of this sort in *Laudato Si'* is provided by the idea that the earth is a gift to human beings. Pope Francis variously refers to the earth as "given to us," "a gift we have freely received," "the patrimony of all humanity," "a gift to everyone," and "a shared inheritance, whose fruits are meant to benefit everyone" (see e.g., 67, 71, 93, 95, 159). Part of his point in making such remarks is to emphasize that the poor and disempowered have a place at the table and that the earth is not just for the rich and powerful, a point that echoes much traditional Catholic teaching. However, the idea that the earth is a gift to human beings could be environmentally obstructive. The thought would be that *being ours*, we humans can do what we please with the world around us. On the other hand, *Laudato Si'* as a whole obviously is opposed to such thinking. For one thing, it also says that the world is "entrusted to us" (244; also 78), which is to say that human beings have a responsibility to look after it. In the very sentence in which we read that the natural environment is "the patrimony of all humanity," we also read that it is "the responsibility of everyone" (95). And, as mentioned, there are repeated observations to the effect that God cares about all creatures and that we should protect the earth. Eric T. Freyfogle nicely sums up the situation when he writes in his chapter in this volume that, according to *Laudato Si'*, "[the] Earth has been given to us collectively, in trust and with strings attached" (Freyfogle, this volume: 23). Consequently, the potentially harmful effect of the idea that the earth is a gift to human beings need not be a concern—at least when it is considered in the context of *Laudato Si'* as a whole—though perhaps it might usefully have been replaced by the idea that the world is a gift not only to human beings but also to all other forms of life on earth, those that have existed, those that now exist, and those that will exist in the future.

In any case, we have some positive and constructive teachings and some negative and obstructive teachings. And the examples mentioned are all drawn from the extant religions. The situation is that many of the currently existing religions seem to have among their teachings both potentially constructive and potentially obstructive elements. In the case of any particular religion, we can therefore imagine setting about the difficult task of trying to assemble *all* its relevant teachings—for all I have done is provide a few examples—and asking what these add up to overall. Members of a tradition might pursue this inquiry in the case of their own tradition.

My main point so far though is that the first (and most obvious) way in which a religion can be environmentally relevant is in terms of its teachings, and the simple and crucial question is whether those teachings provide adequate guidance in this regard. Although there certainly are aspects of what Pope Francis is saying that may reasonably be questioned and challenged on various grounds—see, for example, the chapters in this volume by Paddy Woodworth, Cristina Traina, Darrel Moellendorf, Herman Daly, and David Clough—it seems to me that *Laudato Si'* comes through with flying colors in terms of what its teachings add up to environmentally.

A second respect in which religion can be relevant is in terms of providing encouragement or, more broadly, serving as a source of inspiration, hope, enthusiasm, fortitude, strength of purpose, encouragement, and the like, thereby combatting indifference or pessimism or despair or demoralization or laziness. Pope Francis addresses this possibility in *Laudato Si'* (216). Indeed, he contends that a commitment to protecting the world "cannot be sustained by doctrine alone, without a spirituality capable of inspiring us, without 'an interior impulse which encourages, motivates, nourishes and gives meaning to our individual and communal activity'" (216). Addressing his fellow Christians, in particular, he proposes that "[the] rich heritage of Christian spirituality ... can motivate [Christians] to a more passionate concern for the protection of our world" (216).

The accomplishments of religious traditions

As we have seen, we can look to the religions for teachings that provide good environmental guidance. And we can ask whether a religion has resources that provide inspiration or encouragement or strength of purpose, helping people to avoid indifference and despair. These areas of inquiry—relevant teachings and sources of encouragement—have to do with relevant *resources* that religions have or could have. An account of its relevant resources can tell us something about what a religion *could* accomplish.

Next, I want to focus on a rather different topic, namely what is actually being *accomplished*. This area of inquiry is very important. It is one thing for a religious tradition to have great resources—to have, say, admirable relevant teachings or a robust capacity to provide inspiration. But it is quite another for it to *implement* the teachings and actually to *inspire*.

First, I will take a "macro-level" approach to this issue, focusing on the accomplishments of entire religious traditions. So we need to consider, for example:

the extent to which a religious tradition actually implements whatever constructive teachings it may possess and
the extent to which sources of inspiration that are available within a tradition actually inspire its members.

To these we can add such elements as these:

> the extent to which good environmental citizenship is a priority for the
> tradition: perhaps it is considered important for, or even partly defini-
> tive of, membership in the religion;
> the extent to which a religious tradition leads the way, providing a
> model for others; and
> the extent to which future leaders in the tradition are being trained for
> leadership in this area.

I want to highlight in particular the question of whether a religion recognizes the nature and extent of the environmental crisis, sets out to inculcate
an appreciation of its nature in its adherents, and encourages them to respond appropriately.

The accomplishments of religious communities

Next, I temporarily shift the focus away from entire religious traditions—
whether we are thinking of their teachings or their inspirational value or
their accomplishments—and in the direction of a more micro-level issue,
namely the performance of particular religious communities. So here the
focus is on individual churches, mosques, temples, synagogues, chapels,
meeting houses, gurdwaras, and so on, and on the communities of worship-
pers or participants associated with them.

One relevant area of inquiry is the extent to which possible accomplishments of entire religious traditions such as those mentioned in the last section are implemented within particular religious communities. The relevant
questions include the following: whether a particular religious community
pays attention to the constructive teachings associated with the larger tradition of which it is a part; whether sources of inspiration made available
by that tradition have been incorporated into the life of the community and
actually serve to inspire its members; whether members actually endeavor
to be good environmental citizens and how energetic are their relevant efforts; the extent to which a religious community leads the way, providing a
model for others; and the extent to which a religious community promotes
awareness that we are in the midst of a crisis.

A second relevant area of inquiry has to do with how houses of worship
are designed and used; so the focus here is on the building and on the
landscape around the house of worship. Part of the focus will be on energy
efficiency and the like. As for the landscape, part of the focus might be on
creating a micro-haven for native species. Together the building and the
landscape tell us something about the sensitivity and concerns of a religious
community.

A third part of this exploration has to do with various practical steps that
can be taken. A house of worship can adopt a local species or local habitat

that is under threat. It can become the guardian of a river or lake or of a local landscape or ecosystem. Support can be provided for environmentally focused activities that are carried on independently of the house of worship. For example, this support might include providing local environmental organizations with space or support, or inviting them to explain their purposes or their local projects.

We can also ask how, on the whole, a tradition is doing at the micro-level, in effect summing up its micro-level activities. At least, this can be done in the case of houses of worship that belong to denominations or traditions or groupings of some sort so that such summing up makes sense. In such cases, performance at the macro-level will be in part a function of micro-level performance so that what we have here is another window into the accomplishments of entire traditions.

New religious practices and rituals

Here is a related area of inquiry. This is the idea of environmentally constructive religious rituals and practices that can be built into regular religious observances. Here are some possibilities to consider. We can imagine dietary requirements or restrictions or recommendations that target eating food whose production and consumption are in one way or another environmentally problematic. We can imagine extending the idea of sacred places so that the sacredness or special significance of such areas bears on whether they are protected or restored. We can imagine a ritual of repentance or mourning in which we focus on species we have eliminated, or are now eliminating. We can imagine an annual religious celebration of, say, the arrival of migrant species. In the case of non-migratory species, the focus might be on, say, the birth of a new generation or the continued flourishing of local communities of forms of life we cherish.

Religions often involve the idea of withdrawing from everyday concerns and living an ascetic life or the life of a mendicant. We can imagine this idea being refocused in a particular way. I have in mind the idea of withdrawing from various worldly concerns late in life so that there is at this stage of life a diminished preoccupation with your own affairs and instead becoming an "environmental elder."

These possible innovations generally extend existing religious requirements or expectations or practices or the like. There might, in addition, be entirely new rituals that are not built on anything already in place anywhere. Innovations in this area are an additional set of possible religious accomplishments.

Meeting the challenge

The challenge that confronts the religions is to play all of the roles mentioned—those that have to do with resources and those that have to do with accomplishments. There are certain steps that can be taken by leaders, and what Pope Francis has done is exemplary in this regard. But there are also steps that only a tradition as a whole can take and the question arises whether the collective accomplishments of his co-religionists, never mind everyone else, will begin to reflect the leadership Pope Francis is providing in the areas of guidance and inspiration. (This is part of the focus of Paddy Woodworth's chapter in this volume.)

Laudato Si' is a challenge to all members of the Church: it speci-fies a path and calls all members of the Church to take it. In addition, it provides a challenge to other religions, raising the question whether they can match this sort of guidance from within their own resources, providing their own equally impressive, equally inspiring, and equally inviting path.

What is under discussion as we consider accomplishments is religion as it actually is, and not religion as it could be or should be or as its adherents wish it to be or claim it to be, or for that matter imagine it to be. The ques-tion is whether a religion, as practiced, actually has the effects mentioned; and whether it has those effects now and not just that they are promised in some future dispensation. And we should acknowledge that while there are impressive local efforts and encouraging local success stories, it is unclear whether any of the religions *will* rise to the occasion, meet the challenge, and lead the way. (For some general, and generally discouraging, observa-tions on developments to date, see e.g. McKibben 2001: 302; Wilson 2006: 10; Taylor et al., 2016: 348.)

Religions are constantly changing as their members face new ways of life, new experiences, new knowledge, new circumstances, and new challenges. Religion that rises to the occasion and provides guidance on this great chal-lenge of our time would be religion that has come of age in a particular respect: it would be religion that helps us to prepare for the ages to come. It would help us and our descendants, not to mention other forms of life, to continue to live and flourish on earth for a very long time. Toward this end, the religions need to demand heroism and not just minimally decent behavior; when we are wiping out other forms of life on a large scale, it is no time for caution, timidity, or business as usual.

Some perspectives on *Laudato Si'*

The chapters that make up this volume represent many disciplines and fields and many religious and intellectual traditions. The book has four parts. Part 1 consists of this introductory chapter. Part 2, which is Chapters 2–7, deals with implementation of the ideas in the encyclical, either with what their implementation would require or the extent to which they are being implemented. Part 3, which is Chapters 8–10, deals with scriptural, theological, and philosophical aspects of the encyclical. And Part 4, which is Chapters 11–13, examines some of its central concepts.

Implementation

In Chapter 2, "*Laudato Si'* and Private Property," Eric T. Freyfogle's main aim is to examine the implications of the encyclical for the institution of private property. He observes that private property has taken, and now takes, many different forms around the world. Thus, it varies in terms of what you may own, who may be an owner, and what rights and obligations follow from ownership. And these matters are settled at local, regional, and national levels, and sometimes internationally. The idea of the *common good* is central to his exposition of the vision of private property that emerges from *Laudato Si'*. Promoting the common good requires respect for individuals and for families. It requires sharing with the poor, respecting the rights of all, and promotion of the welfare of society as a whole. It requires care for future generations, for all of life, and for the earth. The common good, so understood, is to be promoted locally and globally and at all intermediate levels. And property must be owned and used in ways that promote the common good. The rights and liberties of property owners are therefore secondary to, and constrained by, rules designed to foster the common good. A conception of private property that is responsive to Laudato Si' would take account of the presence of moral value all around us so that what people may do with what they own is understood to be constrained by the presence of this value. This includes, for example, the value of ecosystems and the value of individual creatures. Land must remain productive, resilient, and biologically diverse and landowners must limit their activities to those consistent with these goals. Property owners, therefore, have a right to do only what is consistent with an interconnected set of goals and values. Ownership, so understood, should be regulated at various levels, including locally, nationally, and internationally.

In Chapter 3, "Reading *Laudato Si'* in a Rainforest Country: Ecological Conversion and Recognition of Indigenous Religions," Zainal Abidin Bagir observes that saving forests requires saving the people who live in forests, and this, in turn, requires ensuring that their religious practices continue to flourish. Correspondingly, he sees the lack of recognition for indigenous religions, and indeed the failure to even classify indigenous worldviews as religions so that indigenous people are sometimes classified as having no religion, as among the factors that have led to violations of their rights and to degradation of the places in which they live. In explaining these points, Zainal Abidin Bagir provides many examples from Indonesia. He calls for interfaith environmental dialogue that has a more central place for indigenous perspectives and he contends that world religions such as Christianity and Islam need to build theologies that are more friendly to indigenous religious practices and beliefs and that accept indigenous communities as they are. Indeed, he considers this to be central to implementing Pope Francis's idea of ecological conversion. So he makes an environmental case for recognizing the religious traditions of indigenous peoples. He considers some aspects of what this would require and he probes some resources within Christianity and Islam for granting this recognition.

In Chapter 4, "The Cry of the Earth and the Cry of the Poor," Darrel Moellendorf considers how we might best heed Pope Francis's exhortation to hear both of the cries mentioned in the title of this chapter. The Cry of the Earth is loud and clear and we need to hear it both for anthropocentric reasons and because of the intrinsic value of nature. Likewise, the cry of humanity suffering under grinding poverty, which is an assault on human dignity, has to be heard. Indeed, the eradication of poverty is a morally mandatory aim for the global community; hundreds of millions of deaths from malnutrition and disease and other conditions associated with poverty are preventable and must be prevented in spite of the fact that poverty eradication requires huge increases in energy consumption, and hence energy generation. While he questions the type of reconciliation between humans and nature that is proposed in the encyclical, he makes some suggestions about how we might best respond to these "two cries." Central to Darrel Moellendorf's thinking—which he considers consistent with *Laudato Si'* and its proposal that "we are one single human family"—is the idea of an ecological debt that the global rich owe to the global poor. Partly because of this debt, climate policy should safeguard the right of developing and least developed countries to sustainable development. And highly developed industrialized countries must assume responsibility for a transition to a zero carbon global economy. Developing and least developed states must not have their prospects for development diminished by our collective attempts to address climate change though steps toward development that minimize environmental damage should always be sought.

In Chapter 5, "*Laudato Si'* and Population," Herman Daly bemoans the absence of significant discussion of population from the encyclical. He contends that given the global growth in human population—the quadrupling of human numbers within a lifetime—promotion of justice and care for creation may require both birth control and immigration control, and much of his attention in his chapter is on the latter. As far as solutions to overpopulation are concerned, his view is that there are reasons to be cautious about investing too much hope in the demographic transition because increased consumption and an increased ecological footprint are as central to this transition as is reduced population. He defends robust national boundaries, arguing that these are politically and environmentally necessary and indeed presupposed by the Catholic social doctrine of subsidiarity, advocated in *Laudato Si'*. While emphasizing that the rich have a duty to help the poor, including poor migrants, he proposes that rather than open borders and mass migration what is needed is something along the lines of the Marshall Plan and the Care packages made available after World War II combined with refugee resettlement, urgent steps to limit our own ecological footprint and to live within the carrying capacity of creation, and a shift from a "growth" to a "steady state" economy. And he considers this combination of steps to be in the spirit of *Laudato Si'*.

David Clough begins Chapter 6, "Rethinking our Treatment of Animals in Light of *Laudato Si'*," by highlighting three central aspects of how *Laudato Si'* says we ought to look at, and treat, other creatures. First, we ought to cultivate bonds of affection with them; second, we ought to eschew all forms of anthropocentrism that would dull our sense of tenderness, compassion, and concern for other creatures; and third we should recognize that all creatures have a place in God's redemptive purposes. Next, David Clough provides a brief overview of some of the ways in which we currently use animals for food, and some of the consequences. Finally, he contends that although the encyclical provides *the basis* for a compelling critique of current practices and especially of industrial scale animal farming, it fails to provide this critique.

Paddy Woodworth is the author of Chapter 7, which is entitled "'We were nowhere. We've got somewhere.' Does *Laudato Si'* go far enough, and is the Church on board for the climate journey?" The focus of this chapter is partly on what has *already* been implemented. The author expresses appreciation for many aspects of the encyclical. These include the Pope's contention that consumerism, a throwaway culture, the deification of market forces, valuing private profits over the common good, and the paradigm of infinite growth, all contribute to environmental degradation. Paddy Woodworth also appreciates the encyclical's emphasis on the close connections between environmental degradation and poverty. But he has a number of concerns. Like Herman Daly, he considers unsatisfactory the way in which the issue of population is handled in *Laudato Si'*. In particular, he is concerned about its failure to acknowledge explicitly that overpopulation contributes to environmental degradation. He also bemoans the fact that the encyclical fails to specify clearly and forcefully what actions Christians, and people in general, and indeed the church itself and all institutions under its control, should be taking. Instead, it relies on vague and timid aspirational phrases. He also asks whether the encyclical has had much of an impact to date within the Catholic Church. He reports on his own efforts to answer this question and on his conversations with leading Catholic thinkers and activists who are endeavoring to translate the encyclical into effective action and who have plans for how this should be accomplished.

Scriptural, theological, and philosophical aspects

In Chapter 8, "*Laudato Si'* and the reinterpretation of Scriptures in light of the ecological crisis," Margaret Daly-Denton provides an interpretation of the Pope's use of various texts that Christians have frequently pointed to as evidence that their Scriptures are ecologically sensitive and of his approach to more problematic passages such as the "dominion" remarks in Genesis. She considers the Pope's use of scripture in the context of a new movement within biblical studies that not only looks to the Bible for advice about how we might live on earth but actually sets out to read the Bible ecologically, and she provides a brief history of this new "ecological hermeneutics." Central to this new movement is the idea that believers should reinterpret their Scriptures in light of current realities, thereby gaining new insights. By way of explaining what this involves she writes as follows about an earlier phase in scriptural interpretation in which a particular social context and set of challenges led to new insights:

> [From the 1960s onwards], the quest for social justice in the basic Christian communities of South America led to the reading of the Book of Exodus in a new way. People deprived of their fundamental human right to land and housing recognized their story in that of the landless Israelites journeying through the desert. This challenged an 'official' church, accustomed to being allied with the rich and powerful, to make 'a preferential option for the poor', and consequently to work out a whole new way of being church. Nowadays, something similar is happening as Christians become more and more engaged in the care of our common home.
>
> (Daly-Denton, this volume: 149)

In Chapter 9, "Sources of Authority in *Laudato Si'*," Cristina L.H. Traina identifies four sources of authority that Pope Francis relies on in *Laudato Si'* and discusses how these sources of authority are used. These four sources are earlier encyclicals and church documents, scripture, theology, and science; she devotes most attention to scripture. She compares the role of these sources of authority in this encyclical with their role in Pope John Paul II's 1995 encyclical *Evangelium vitae*. She notes that Francis takes a "decentralized" and "collegial rather than hierarchical" approach to papal and episcopal magisteria. For example, he relies on episcopal conference statements from around the world rather than on papal teachings. She says that Francis's use of scripture closely resembles that of John Paul II in *Evangelium vitae*: both seek a devotional reading of scripture that involves private contemplation of scriptural passages and a personal encounter with the text, with a view to finding guidance relevant to your own situation rather than a definitive and universally authoritative reading or a reading that draws on a systematic consideration of relevant scholarship. However, this sort of scriptural interpretation will reflect the reader's perspective and this can make it harder to appreciate other perspectives: she mentions feminist, anti-racist, and de-colonial approaches in this context. And while she appreciates Francis's inclusive approach to episcopal statements she notes that at points at which he could have cited the work of female authors, only male theologians, philosophers, spiritual writers, and cultural critics are mentioned. And, she observes, Pope Francis cites the bishops of the poor rather than the poor themselves.

In Chapter 10, "A Constructivist Engagement with *Laudato Si'*," Kieran P. Donaghy emphasizes Pope Francis's wish to include everyone in a broad conversation about current environmental problems. He pursues this topic by asking whether a constructivist approach to ethics might yield conclusions about how we should live that are close to those advocated by Francis. Constructivist approaches to ethics endeavor to generate action-guiding principles that apply, and that have a capacity to appeal, to everyone. Such approaches, therefore, do not rely on disputed metaphysical or religious views. Kieran P. Donaghy probes this area of inquiry by outlining Onora O'Neill's constructivist approach to practical reasoning and the action-guiding prescriptions that, in her view, issue from it. He proposes that some of these action-guiding principles are quite close to those recommended by Francis in *Laudato Si'*. So he responds to Pope Francis's aspiration to address a broad audience—to encourage "a conversation which includes everyone"—by exploring a body of reasoning that purports to apply to everyone because it does not build on the perspective of any particular group or tradition or school of thought. Instead it starts from some general assumptions about agents and conditions of action. And yet, he proposes, it can yield prescriptive conclusions that are close to those advocated by Francis.

Central concepts

In Chapter 11, "A New Anthropology? *Laudato Si'* and the Question of Interconnectedness," Celia Deane-Drummond explores some implications of the idea of interconnectedness, which is the focus of much discussion in *Laudato Si'*, for our thinking about what it is to be human and about the significance of being human. She combines reflection about this topic with a focus on another theme in the encyclical, namely the importance of indigenous perspectives, in particular indigenous perspectives on being human. (So one of her topics overlaps somewhat with a theme in Zainal Bagir Abidin's chapter.) Her contention is that an adequate Catholic theological approach to being human must combine its traditional emphasis on human dignity and human uniqueness with a new appreciation of insights from anthropology and other fields. An adequate approach will also recognize that what Christian theology has thought of as uniquely human characteristics are often present in other social animals. She makes it clear that the way forward will involve rejecting human domination of nature and adopting a more holistic way of thinking about the world and humanity's interconnectedness with it. It will also involve a non-tyrannical view that puts emphasis on the personhood of much that is non-human. She is calling for an exploratory process, one that *Laudato Si'* also invites us to pursue but that has barely begun. The best we can do at present is formulate tentative interpretive suggestions and pursue respectful interchange and dialogue among cultures.

In Chapter 12, "'Realities are More Important than Ideas': The Significance of Practice in *Laudato Si'*," Gretel Van Wieren examines some respects in which practice and lived experience are central to the encyclical.

She takes Francis's remark that "realities are more important than ideas," (110) to bespeak a recognition that norms and ideas are often best understood as emerging from wrestling with situations and problems rather than solely from theoretical or abstract reflection. If this is so, we should look to practice and lived experience for ethical insights as to how we should act in relation to the natural world. With this in mind Gretel Van Wieren surveys a number of environmental problems and practices that are emphasized in *Laudato Si'*, including pollution, climate change, and loss of biodiversity, in each case proposing that the encyclical incorporates practices and lived experience in its response. For example, she contends that the encyclical focuses heavily on the lived experiences of the poor as it examines the problems associated with the world's water crisis, how these problems should be understood, and how we should respond.

Finally, in Chapter 13, "Opposing the 'technocratic paradigm' and 'appreciating the small things,'" I ask what exactly is the "technocratic paradigm" that Pope Francis sets out to oppose and what are his main reasons for opposing it. I ask what is meant when Francis says that to be in the grip of the technocratic paradigm is to treat everything around us as if it were "something formless, completely open to manipulation," to ignore or forget "the reality in front of us"(106) and to disregard "the message contained in the structures of nature itself" (117). The best way to interpret such discourse, I suggest, is as saying that we need to take account of the value of various things that have value. What is prohibited therefore is dealing with other humans, other animals, other species, ecosystems, and the entire world around us while neither restrained nor guided by the value of such things. There are many additional dimensions to the target that Pope Francis has in his sights when he opposes the technocratic paradigm. These include the relentless pursuit of profit and letting technology dictate how we conduct ourselves. In turn, the solution to this interconnected set of problems is also multifaceted. It includes an emphasis on the common good and on ecological sensitivity. It includes the cultivation within ourselves of attitudes such as sobriety, care, generosity, a spirit of sharing, and humility. There is also a set of dispositions and attitudes that, Pope Francis says, we should exhibit toward the world around us. These include awe, wonder, fraternity, a friendly hand, a sense of place, and "an attention full of fondness and wonder" (97). The Pope's emphasis on the individual, the small, and the local, and on what individuals can accomplish wherever they may find themselves, is especially important.

Note

1 References in this book are to section numbers in *Laudato Si': On Care for Our Common Home* unless otherwise indicated. The version released by the Vatican is available at: https://w2.vatican.va/content/dam/francesco/pdf/encyclicals/documents/papa-francesco_20150524_enciclica-laudato-si_en.pdf

References

Estrada, Alejandro, et al. 2017. "Impending Extinction Crisis of the World's Primates: Why Primates Matter" *Science Advances*, Vol. 3, 18 January. https://advances.sciencemag.org/content/3/1/e1600946

Francis, Pope. 2015. *Laudato Si': On Care for Our Common Home.* https://w2.vatican.va/content/dam/francesco/pdf/encyclicals/documents/papa-francesco_20150524_enciclica-laudato-si_en.pdf

Gross, Rita. 1997. "Toward a Buddhist Environmental Ethic" *Journal of the American Academy of Religion*, Vol. 65, No. 2, Summer, 333–353.

McKibben, Bill. 2001. "Where Do We Go From Here?" *Daedelus: Journal of the American Academy of Arts and Sciences*, Vol. 130, No. 4, 301–306.

Taylor, Bron, Gretel Van Wieren and Bernard Zaleha. 2016. "The Greening of Religion Hypothesis (Part Two): Assessing the Data from Lynn White, Jr, to Pope Francis" *Journal for the Study of Religion, Nature and Culture*, Vol. 10, No. 3, 306–378.

Wilson, Edward O. 2006. *The Creation: An Appeal to Save Life on Earth.* New York: W. W. Norton & Company.

World Wildlife Fund Living Planet Report, September, 2014. www.worldwildlife.org/press-releases/half-of-global-wildlife-lost-says-new-wwf-report

Part 2
Implementation

2 *Laudato Si'* and private property

Eric T. Freyfogle

Laudato Si' may contain only a few overt references to private property as a social institution, but its broad principles, developed at length, bear directly and critically on this familiar arrangement of public-private power. When drawn together, the pope's comments and principles supply something like an outline for states and communities to use as they go about reconsidering and reforming this influential institution. Private property—the laws and norms that govern property rights—prescribes the rules on who can use nature, in what ways, and with what limitations and obligations. Inevitably, the institution underlies and intertwines with the environmental declines, grave inequalities, and human suffering that *Laudato Si'* so passionately decries.

For a state or community to take the encyclical's guidance to heart, it will need to give critical thought to private property as locally crafted and implemented. It will need to probe for ways to reform the institution in response to the pope's concerns. Likely this will mean, as an outcome, re-calibrating private rights, shoring up the institution's moral foundations, adjusting it to local circumstances, and otherwise enhancing its contributions to overall welfare.

The vision of private property that emerges from *Laudato Si'* is, to no surprise, a distinctly progressive one, quite far from popular neo-liberal, free-market, and libertarian understandings. In the hands of progressives, private property is an evolving social construction, controlled, tailored, and revised over time by lawmaking communities to meet their needs, hopes, and felt responsibilities. It is also a morally complex arrangement in that it can, and too often does, empower property owners to dominate and exploit both people and nature. As nature degrades, as injustice grows, the reform of private property for progressives is not merely a legal and cultural possibility: it is a moral duty.

Property's complexity and flexibility

Before taking up the elements of *Laudato Si'*, it helps to look quickly at private property as an institution to steer clear of simplistic thinking.[1] Private property can take and has taken many different shapes and forms around the world and over time, in terms of what a person can own, who can own, and what it means to own. Private property is not a one-size-fits-all arrangement that a state or community simply pulls of the shelf to put to use. States, that is, are not limited in their options either to embrace private property or to choose instead a socialist or communist alternative. The variations and options are many.[2]

As one digs into the details of various, real-world property arrangements, a quite considerable diversity emerges. Particular systems, for instance, differ on the parts of nature (the natural resources) that one acquires by buying land (does land include subsurface resources? water rights? wildlife? geothermal rights? wind power?). Similarly, how complete is an owner's power to exclude outsiders from entering land (for instance, hikers, hunters, or foragers)? How intensively and in what ways can owners use their property? Can they leave productive resources unused? Are they obligated to take good care of particular structures or places (historic buildings or rare wildlife habitat, for instance)? Widely differing legal rules are used by lawmakers to resolve the inevitable conflicts that arise among neighboring or competing property owners, some that seek to forestall problems *ex ante*, others that operate more *ex post* and with differing types of remedies (money damages, injunctions) available to redress violations. Property rights almost always include durational limits, if only in the form of abandonment or forfeiture rules. Similarly, legal variation characterizes the powers owners have under various systems to transfer or divide their rights or shift to differing resource-uses. Many property systems allow for transfers of private rights without the owner's consent through some form of adverse use or squatting. Further, governments typically retain powers of expropriation (termed eminent domain in the United States) upon payment of just compensation whenever property is needed for an important public purpose.

Wide variations also exist among property regimes in terms of the ways private rights are embedded in governance systems: in public governance systems, in private versions, and in governance systems that mix public controls with private ones.[3] Land- and resource-use rules are often prescribed at local or regional levels but nation-states, too, can play lead roles. Land titles may also be embedded in various ways in private arrangements in which neighboring owners, acting together, can assert control over what they each do.[4] In many settings, a public body oversees or manages a particular landscape even as those who use the publicly owned landscape are mostly private rather than state actors, people who may enjoy considerable legal security in their resource-use rights.[5] Further, land-use controls set at the local level are, in turn, commonly subject to oversight or guiding instructions emanating from governing bodies working at higher levels and broader spatial scales. Often the end result, in terms of governance and lawmaking, is that a given landowner is subject to laws set by various levels of government and by independent regulatory agencies.

A full reconsideration of private property would pay attention to these many issues and to the flexibility lawmakers have, as they define property rights, in resolving them. *Laudato Si'* raises overtly only a few of these many property-related issues. Yet its broad principles—the role of the common good, for instance; the social function of property; its comments on inequality, housing, and biodiversity—touch upon nearly all of private property's constituent elements.

As the final sections of this chapter note, the encyclical implies (rightly) that private property is a morally complex institution, an arrangement long used (when lawmakers allow it) as a tool of domination and exploitation of people and nature. At the same time, a well-structured, updated scheme of private ownership can yield many tangible benefits, not just for owners but for entire communities and non-owners as well. There is thus much at stake in the labor of framing and updating the rules of private ownership, legal work that, according to *Laudato Si'*, is long overdue.

The encyclical's guidance

Private property and social limits

Laudato Si' expressly endorses private property with a quote from a teaching of Pope (now Saint) John Paul II, "the Church does indeed defend the legitimate right to private property" (93) The encyclical does not explain the nature or content of this "legitimate right" to property. It adds only a later reference to "a natural right to possess a reasonable allotment of land where a [farmer or peasant (*campesino* in Spanish)] can establish his home, work for subsistence of his family and a secure life" (94). This narrow, particular right to property fits well with the encyclical's strong concern for the poor and its calls for states to foster small-scale food production systems and to support "small producers and differentiated production" (124–129).

These few express comments about property rights are embedded in and illuminated by broader comments that explain and limit the proper role of humans in nature, comments that imply needed limits on the kinds of rights owners might possess and how they might use what they own. "The Earth is the Lord's" the encyclical instructs, quoting Psalm 24 (67). "Thus God rejects every claim to absolute ownership" (*Id.*). The Earth has been given to us collectively, in trust and with strings attached. "The gift of the earth with its fruits belongs to everyone" (71); it is "essentially a shared inheritance, whose fruits are meant to benefit everyone" (93). Given God's overriding claims, given also the shared nature of our ownership, it follows that all private property is subordinate to "the universal destination of goods"—an amorphous concept that empowers the public to insist that property owners respect the common good. "Christian tradition has never recognized the right to private property as absolute or inviolable." To the contrary, we are told, all private property is invested with a "social purpose" and encumbered by "a social mortgage" (93)—language that reiterates how private use must support overall welfare, of people today, future generations, and other life forms. Like all citizens, landowners bear a duty "to cultivate and maintain a property relationship" with neighbors, whose care and custody is also their concern (70). Cited in support of these social limits on property are the biblical stories of the Jubilee year (every 49 years) as a time of debt forgiveness and biblical injunctions to landowners to leave produce in the field "for the poor and the sojourner" to glean (71).

Scattered throughout the encyclical are other comments that propose limits on what and how much an individual can own. Its many statements on moral value in nature, all highly pertinent, are taken up below. Beyond those, the encyclical questions property systems in which resources can "end up in the hands of the first comer or the most powerful," an ownership arrangement at odds, we are advised, with "the ideals of harmony, justice, fraternity and peace" (82). It similarly questions the private ownership of "places of particular beauty" when the effect is to leave non-owners cut off from them (45). A particular need exists, we are instructed, "to protect those common areas, visual landmarks and urban landscapes which increase our sense of belonging, or rootedness, of 'feeling at home' within a city which includes us and bring us together" (151); a need appropriately translated, it would seem, into limits on what can be owned and on an owner's ability to tear down and replace. As for "makeshift shanty towns" that have sprung up around urban areas, the appropriate response to them entails "developing those neighbourhoods rather than razing or displacing them" (152)—not, one assumes, simply ignoring the rights of the titled landowners but nonetheless requiring such owners to facilitate the land-use changes. Finally and without elaboration, we have the encyclical's charged comment on "the land of the southern poor," often "rich and mostly unpolluted," where "access to ownership of goods and resources for meeting vital needs is inhibited by a system of commercial relations and ownership which is structurally perverse" (52). As readers we are left to consider what structural perversity entails and how to deal with it.

These various comments hardly set a legislative agenda for reforming property rights systems. Rather, they supply the raw materials for critical thought, inviting readers to reflect on the systems around them and to imagine better ways.

Moral value

Supplementing these provocative comments on ownership and resource control are *Laudato Si*'s many teachings on moral value in the universe and where it lies. A private property system that recognized such moral value would necessarily limit, in various ways, what a person can own and how an owner might use what is owned.

For starters, the Earth as a whole—an interconnected whole based on interrelations and interdependence—is itself infused with moral significance. All living creatures, humans included, "are linked by unseen bonds and together form a kind of universal family" (89). Nature is not "something separate from ourselves"; it is not "a mere setting in which we live." Rather, "we are part of nature, included in it and thus in constant interaction with it" (139). Nature's systems as such "have an intrinsic value independent of their usefulness" (140). Our charge is to use the earth as a whole and its various systems in ways that sustain their healthy functioning, that maintain "each ecosystem's regenerative ability" (140). Moral value reaches beyond systems to individual creatures as such and to species as collections of living creatures. "Each organism, as a creature of God, is good and admirable in itself; the same is true of the harmonious ensemble of organisms existing in a defined space and functioning as a system" (140). Species as such "have value in themselves," and we have no right to bring about their disappearance (33). Thus, we must "respect the laws of nature and the delicate equilibria existing between the creatures of this world" (68).

Moral value—of a unique type—also resides in humans, as individuals (41, 81) and as families and communities. Future human generations are part of this larger moral community and their interests play a particularly strong role in our moral duty to tend the Earth to keep it fertile, diverse, and beautiful (159). Even as it honors individuals as such (humans and other living creatures), the overarching principle of *Laudato Si'*—the "central and unifying principle of social ethics"—is the principle of the common good (156). The common good has to do with respect for the human person as such, endowed with basic and inalienable rights, with "the overall welfare of society," and with the "development of a variety of intermediate groups," above all the family, "the basic cell of society" (157). The common good calls for social peace, which requires in turn attention to distributive justice—a major consideration in shaping and reforming private property norms. A duty to promote and defend the common good rests on society as a whole and on "the state in particular," an admonition that, again, has direct bearing on the state's role in creating, shaping, allocating, and enforcing property rights (158).

Central to the common good, and to due respect for moral value, is the duty we all face collectively to care for the Earth; it is our collective good, our patrimony, to administer for the good of all life (human and non-human) and to keep healthy and beautiful for future generations (71, 95). We are mistaken, the encyclical instructs, when we think that biblical passages dealing with human dominion over the land and other life forms gives us God-like powers to rule and exploit. *Genesis* passages that instruct humans to keep the land and till it mean "caring, protecting, overseeing and preserving" the land and other life forms, not ruthlessly exploiting it. "This implies a relationship of mutual responsibility between human beings and nature," allowing us to take from the Earth what we need for subsistence but imposing "the duty to protect the earth and to ensure its fruitfulness for coming generations" (67). Our dominion over the land "should be understood more properly in the sense of responsible stewardship" (116).

Cultural ills and their reform

Private property is as much a cultural institution as it is a legal one. It embodies and puts to work many of the central cultural assumptions that shape a society: the ways people relate to one another and how they perceive, value, and exploit the natural world. *Laudato Si's* criticisms of modern culture are thus, in many respects, critiques of private property as commonly understood, especially property regimes that maximize landowner liberty and thereby facilitate the ecological degradation and social injustice that the encyclical condemns.

The cultural criticisms of *Laudato Si'*, as I have explained elsewhere, track closely the dominant cultural criticisms of the major conservation voices of the United States, including those of Aldo Leopold and Wendell Berry.[6] One of modern culture's primary flaws is its excessive tendency to fragment nature into distinct pieces and to assess the worth of these pieces based entirely on market valuations. By this measure, most parts of nature are valueless. Nature in this all too familiar view is chiefly a warehouse or stockpile of resources, awaiting human use and consumption. This perspective entails an insensitivity to ecological connections and an unwillingness to see and value natural communities and systems as such. The market, of course, places no economic value on the vast majority of species and living creatures; much less does it recognize and respect moral value in them. Guiding our use of nature—another cultural deficiency—is an arrogant tendency to charge ahead despite the vast gaps in our knowledge about nature; a desire to maximize profit in the short term; a belief that human cleverness can solve all problems that arise; and, in general, an instrumental, technocratic view of nature that imposes few limits on manipulation and consumption.

Laudato Si' counters these cultural assumptions with far different ones, drawing upon the moral principles set forth above. We need a new definition of progress, it says; new ways to see nature in ecological, holistic terms; new respect for the moral value that infuses the universe and that we are duty bound to respect. We must use nature responsibly, recognizing duties to future generations and accepting the call to responsible stewardship, understood ecologically. This includes sharing with the poor and respecting the rights of all.

Implications for private property

In combination these various teachings of *Laudato Si'*—along with other passages dealing with state duties and the need for sound land planning—present the elements or raw materials to construct a more morally sound property regime, one that respects owners and their rights yet sets clear expectations for responsible property use.

A tool to promote the (local) common good

The place to start is with the overarching ideal of the common good, set forth in paragraphs 156 to 158 of the encyclical. It helps to put this papal teaching first because it addresses what has long been a central question in discussions of private property: Is property chiefly a tool that empowers individuals as such to protect and exercise their liberties, free of undue governmental or social interference, or is it instead a legal and cultural arrangement that a society crafts, implements, and updates over time for the dominant purpose of promoting the welfare of all? With the first option, the aim is to maximize the individual liberty subject only to duties to avoid overt harm to neighbors and other living people; this broad liberty, proponents claim, encourages and rewards initiative, promoting the prosperity of all.[7] With the second option, all rights are tailored instead to respect the common good, defined in ways that include but go well beyond economic enterprise to consider social justice, environmental degradation, and other moral and social concerns.[8] By giving such primacy to the common good, *Laudato Si'* implicitly endorses this second, more communal understanding of private property. In it, the law would define and limit each specific power of landowners so that their exercise would not transgress this central, communal value. Property law might well limit also who can own land and natural resources and to what extent. The rights and liberties of landowners would thus be secondary to, and derivate of, rules designed to foster the common good.[9]

Echoing and strengthening this central role of the common good are the terms of *Laudato Si'* that speak to the social purpose of all forms of private property and to the social mortgage that encumbers all private rights. The "social purpose" language implies that property rights are subject to limits designed to promote social aims; the "social mortgage" language similarly implies that property rights are encumbered or burdened by social claims, much as the rights of owners indebted to banks are encumbered by mortgages that secure such debts. It is telling that the three paragraphs in which these themes—social purpose and social mortgage—are introduced (93–95) appear in Chapter Two of the encyclical, "The Gospel of Creation," not in one of the later chapters dealing with more secular matters. The implication here is that these ideas of social purpose and social mortgage are somehow embedded in the created universe itself, which has been (as noted) entrusted to humans subject to duties to tend it with care for the benefit of all generations. Thus, these moral limits, in a sense, were put in place before humans took custody of nature, which is to say they constrain not just the rights of individual property owners as such but the powers that states and communities wield as they go about defining, allocating, and enforcing private rights; that is, the social-purpose and social-mortgage limits constrain private rights even when human lawmakers have not yet expressly embedded them in their property laws.

The social purpose language of *Laudato Si'*, when the encyclical appeared, likely resonated with readers in some parts of the world (South America, Italy, elsewhere in Europe) from its prior use there.[10] The language likely drew a more quizzical response from readers elsewhere (including those in the United States) for whom it was unfamiliar. Where used, the language's meaning tends to remain amorphous and aspirational. In content, it overlaps considerably with the moral claim that private property is legitimate only when it generates widely distributed benefits for people throughout society, including those who own no property. Both framings suggest an overriding social claim by society on all private property rights. The social mortgage language of *Laudato Si'* would seem mostly to reinforce both of these phrasings. It too, as noted, suggests that all property is encumbered with obligations to use it in ways that benefit society, with society perhaps including, in the encyclical, other life forms as well as future generations.

As noted above, the only distinct reference in *Laudato Si'* to private property as an individual right, a right that might impose duties on lawmaking communities, is the claim that each individual has a right to sufficient land for subsistence living. This is an older kind of personal right to property, understood as a right of the landless to lay claim to a parcel of land. It differs from the more modern, capitalist, often neo-liberal understanding of property as a kind of private power that an owner can use to keep government at bay. Property as right-of-access imposes duties on states and societies to make land available to those in need, even if it requires pruning the rights of existing landowners who have more than enough. Though few are familiar with it, this was the dominant understanding of the right to property at the time of the American Revolution.[11] It was the particular right that Thomas Jefferson, for instance, sought to implement by pushing his home state of Virginia to give to all young adult males 50 acres of land if they lacked it.[12] It was the right that Congress repeatedly sought to honor with various homestead statutes. Private property, to be sure, does vest owners with reasonably secure rights and limits government's ability to confiscate things owned without payment. But such rights, in a system designed to foster the common good, are tailored so that exercise of the rights by owners does not frustrate the common good. Owners thus possess, not the maximum power consistent with the avoidance of obvious harm to others (the libertarian ideal), but only such power as is consistent with a social order in which all might flourish and the land itself remains healthy.

The ideal of the common good is, of course, one that shifts over time with changing circumstances and evolving values and understandings. A property system can continue fostering an evolving common good only if lawmakers regularly update the norms governing property ownership to reflect these changes. This requires a property system that is dynamic in terms of its elements, which requires, in turn, lawmakers or norm-setters who pay attention to evolving factors and step in to implement needed reforms.[13] It is not the case, that is, that property rights are fixed in content when a land parcel is first allocated for private ownership or when someone first acquires, for instance, a right to use a particular water flow or other natural resource. Lawmakers do need to exercise care as they go about updating ownership norms; otherwise, they can diminish the benefits that a well-functioning property system generates for state or community. But static property systems soon get out of date. As they do, their overall net benefits can decline. Particularly as resources get scarcer and rents escalate, property can too easily become an illegitimate tool of domination and exploitation.

By taking this stance—viewing property as chiefly a dynamic tool to benefit society overall— *Laudato Si'* implicitly calls into question the efforts of global market players to impose, at the international level, limits on the ability of states and communities to update their norms of ownership. Such efforts include the insertion of provisions into international trade treaties that curtail the powers even of nation-states to define what it means to own private land within their borders. Outside investors, of course, want security when they buy resources in foreign lands; they want assurances that legal changes will not undercut their investments. Such valid concerns, however, need to be assessed in light of the corresponding need for lawmaking communities to tailor the elements of ownership to meet local needs and hopes and to insist that anyone who chooses to own land or resources within their borders behave as a responsible member of that local community.

When *Laudato Si'* refers to the common good, it surely means, first and foremost, the common good of the people who live in a given place or region, the local common good, even as the teaching also puts out a call for planet-wide measures to address climate change and other ills. It is not enough to assert that secure, market-friendly property rights promote the overall economic output of the entire world, not when they leave local people landless and suffering. Politics, we are told, must not be subject to the economy (189, 190), a policy preference that would seem to require local lawmakers to retain adequate control over the legal rights and responsibilities of ownership.

As for what can be owned, the encyclical says little directly. It includes language about a human right to clean water (30), a right that likely imposes limits on water hoarding. As noted above, the encyclical also mentions needs for green spaces in cities and for public access to places of particular beauty (44, 45). Finally, there are the moral values that infuse the natural world and give standing to future generations. In ways that need elaboration, they too surely limit what can be owned as well as the powers owners might gain.

Sharing

Perhaps the strongest challenges to conventional private property in the encyclical are posed by its many statements that the fruits of lands and natural resources must in some way be shared. The only illustrations offered come from ancient biblical texts, stories of gleaners who collect harvest residues and of debt-forgiveness mandated (or at least proposed) every half-century. Such examples no doubt were offered to stimulate thought and discussion rather than as workable modern solutions.

Sharing can mean a division of the income or produce generated by land and resources. That division could come through widespread ownership itself. It could come instead by levying taxes or severance charges on private property, in effect diverting part of the yield for local distribution. Sharing can also come by rules insisting that lands and resources be worked by local labor that is paid a fair wage. It can come by rules requiring that produce be sold first to meet local needs with only the excess available for export. Matching such rules could be others requiring that sufficient lands and resources be devoted to the satisfaction of local needs, not the wants of distant markets.

On this subject, the encyclical raises a flag, without elaboration, in its provocative claim that the globe's poorer lands are often burdened by "a system of commercial relations and ownership which is structurally perverse" (52). The criticism offered here, one assumes, is of arrangements where land and resources are owned by absentees, and in large holdings, likely with the lands devoted to outputs to meet foreign rather than local needs. Land-grabbing is a major global challenge, even when well-intended.[14] This is particularly true when state and local governments side with those doing the grabbing. State and local lawmakers, we are instructed, themselves face duties to oversee lands and resources to foster the local common good, including the duty "to adopt clear and firm measures in support of small producers and differentiated production" (129). To favor outside investors, without an honest, accurate effort to assess and satisfy local needs, is to fail at these duties.

Readers of *Laudato Si'* in the end are left to consider for themselves possible ways to promote sharing to meet the needs of the poor. This may mean limits on ownership by outsiders. It may mean limits on the amount of land or resources any owner might hold. Both such limits have appeared in property systems over time; they are familiar to legal historians and to students of communal and tribal property systems. (Homestead laws in the United States, for instance, almost always included acreage limits on landholdings.) Sharing might also come about by some means to capture the rises in land values that happen as communities prosper, as land scarcity increases, and as rents go up. As American political economist Henry George made clear in the late nineteenth century (and as today's economists confirm), it is the growing community as such that gives rise to such increasing land values.

In George's view, embraced by many since him, the community should gain at least a share in the land value increases that communal activities have generated.[15] Similarly, they might demand a fair return on infrastructure investments and other communal or taxpayer-supported efforts that enable owners to create wealth on their private holdings.[16]

For those who are the poorest—the people for whom the encyclical expresses greatest concern—sharing might still today come in time-honored ways, in rights to glean, to hunt, and to forage on the private lands of others. Private property can function perfectly well as an institution (and has over time) without vesting in owners an absolute right to keep subsistence-living outsiders at bay.[17] Private lands can be subject to specific public uses so long as the public uses are carefully prescribed and do not unduly interfere with an owner's primary land- or resource-use.

Respecting nature

Much of *Laudato Si'*, of course, has to do with care for the natural environment; with our calling to keep the land ecologically healthy and biologically diverse. This is a broadly phrased injunction. Challenges arise as one tries to move from the broad normative standard to actual, on-the-ground decisions.[18] The challenges are particularly great given that many ecological processes and life forms require protective measures taken at large spatial scales, well above the scale of any village or even region. Then, too, people must use many lands intensively if they are going to produce food for all. The overriding idea, however, is clear enough: land and resources uses should not sap nature of its fertility and diversity; they should not frustrate the ability of natural systems to remain productive and resilient.

Despite the challenges of moving from goal to implementation, it is clear enough in general terms what this all means for a private property system.[19] Land and resource owners must limit their activities to those consistent with these environmental goals. This entails broad limits on property rights and, very likely, more detailed, resource-use rules tailored to local settings and local challenges. It means, for instance, rules protecting valuable wild-life habitat, wetlands, water courses, riparian corridors, and hillsides vulnerable to erosion. It means limits on chemical uses and enforceable duties to restore lands to pre-use conditions when intensive land-uses wind down (mining operations, for instance). It means leaving adequate minimum flows in rivers to sustain river health as well as human navigation. It means protecting coastal areas and mangrove forests to buffer damaging storms.

In many settings, land- and resource-use regulations would have the effect of holding property owners fully accountable for the harms they cause. Such regulations, that is, would operate to internalize costs that landowners are prone to dump on others. *Laudato Si'* endorses such internalization, in quite clear terms (195). But economic internalization can take place when a landowner simply pays money to cover the harms, with the ecological harms themselves left unrepaired. The strictures of the encyclical would not seem to allow that. The payment of money alone hardly helps the living creatures harmed nor does it offset costs to future generations. Rarely would such money, one guesses, end up benefiting the poorest.

The types of rules that seem needed here are familiar enough to those involved in the work of conservation and restoration. It bears repeating that effective rules are necessarily dynamic, responding to new threats, to changed conditions (changing climate, above all), and to shifts in ecological understandings and human values and hopes—all in an effort to respect nature in the ways the encyclical urges. This means, as the next section considers, property rights embedded in governance regimes that wield the power over time to adjust and tailor constraints in the public interest.

Nestled communities

In the neo-liberal mind that trusts the market—in full, or at least more than it trusts government—lawmakers ought to set the rules governing property rights once and for all and then stand back, leaving the market to reallocate resources to their highest and best uses.[20] It is an appealing vision, implying as it does that lawmakers can rest easy after the set-up work is done. Like most conservation-minded observers, Pope Francis disagrees. Government needs to do more than that, he says, and at governing levels from the local to the global. He challenges "the mindset of those who say: Let us allow the invisible forces of the market to regulate the economy, and consider their impact of society and nature as collateral damage" (123). Without denying the power of market forces to harness entrepreneurial energies (and while stressing in particular the need to promote "business creativity" (129)), the Pope nonetheless rejects any "magical conception of the market" as a remedial force (190). No doubt more carefully tailored property rights could help matters considerably; the market might then do better than it now does. But the work of tailoring property rights requires continued action by lawmakers, not continued deference to the market. It requires the kind of attentive, detailed rulemaking that market advocates distrust and oppose.

What Pope Francis has in mind are effective governments, supported by non-governmental organizations (NGOs), operating at various spatial scales from the local to the global. Each level of governance would attend to matters that smaller-scale governments either cannot or do not address, all based on the general principle of subsidiarity; the principle that a problem should be addressed by the lowest level of government, closest to the people, that is capable of handling it (196). The main regulatory actors, the pope suggests, will be the various nation-states, which are responsible within their borders for "planning, coordination, oversight and enforcement" (177). "One authoritative source of oversight and coordination," the encyclical emphasizes, "is the law, which lays down rules for admissible conduct in the light of the common good" (*Id.*). High on the list of lawmaking tasks for states is "the establishment of a legal framework which can set clear boundaries and ensure the protection of ecosystems" (53). Necessarily, such a framework would limit the uses of land and natural resources, in the process updating private property norms and enhancing their moral legitimacy. Such action is unlikely to take place, however—given the "weakening of the power of nation states" (175)—without stimulus from citizens and citizen groups. "Society, through non-governmental organizations and intermediate groups, must put pressure on governments to develop more rigorous regulations, procedures, and controls" (179). They must work to strengthen the institutional effectiveness of government and, in much of the world, reverse the declining respect for the rule of law.[21] "Laws may be well framed yet remain a dead letter. We know, for example, that countries which have clear legislation about the protection of forests continue to keep silent as they watch laws repeatedly being broken" (42).

Supplementing state-level action should be more local action, by governments, social communities, and individuals. At the local level also—the "regional and municipal" as well as the national—citizens need to regain control of political power (179). Local legislation, the Pope reminds us, can be particularly effective in dealing with environmental ills "if agreements exist between neighbouring communities to support the same environmental policies" (179). At the same time, solutions will vary from place to place. "There are no uniform recipes," we are advised; "each country or region has its own problems and limitations" (180). In any case, collective action is needed, by government and community networks. It is not enough to rely on "the sum of individual good deeds" (219), by private property owners or others.

In part due to the weaknesses of many states and disrespect for the rule of law, in part due to the global scale of many challenges, *Laudato Si'* repeatedly brings up the need for binding international agreements to curtail destructive practices, by property owners and others. The deeper problems simply "cannot be resolved by unilateral actions on the part of individual countries" (164). "Interdependence obliges us to think of *one world with a common plan*" (*Id.*). "Enforceable international agreements are urgently needed," we are told, given the limits on the powers of states and local governments (173). "Global regulatory norms are needed to impose obligations and prevent unacceptable actions" (*Id.*). Global agreements, however, depend upon, and require for their implementation, stronger global institutions. Here, too, the encyclical presents a strong plea for reform. "[It] is essential to devise stronger and more efficiently organized international institutions"; indeed, there is "urgent need of a true world political authority" to protect the environment, regulate migration, and promote food security and peace (175).

What emerges from these comments on subsidiarity and multi-tiered governance is a vision of property ownership that is defined by laws emanating at once from multiple levels of government. To own land in a given place is thus to be guided and bound by a blend of norms and rules, all presumably dynamic in nature and with higher-level rules typically taking priority when they clash with lower-level rules. The danger here, of course, is that higher-level governing bodies will be dominated by economic interests that use global-level power to frustrate state and local efforts to address environmental and social ills, much as the federal government of the United States today (2019) labors to curtail efforts by California and other states to address climate change. The example of the United States is worth studying on this issue because concentrated economic power has largely undermined the ability of the federal government there to deal with many environmental ills. Hope lies, many believe, in expanded state and local efforts, although they are, in the end, no substitute for strong, broadly applicable national and global standards.

An open invitation

The scattered comments on private property in *Laudato Si'* raise the question: Might Pope Francis offer further, more particular guidance on private property, given the institution's central role in bringing about the many ills that his encyclical condemns? The topic is worthy enough to merit separate treatment, and it needs attention drawn to it. It is too easy now, not just for states but for non-governmental organizations and well-meaning citizens, to take property, as currently understood, for granted; to assume that the institution as they know it is an institutional given that they simply must work around. Private property today is much in need of reconsideration. Too many of its norms date from a time when resources seemed abundant, open lands provided opportunity, and the main aim of lawmakers was to stimulate industrialization. On its own, *Laudato Si'* only introduces the topic. Yet it does so in ways that are highly suggestive and that usefully outline the work that lies ahead. It is, in a sense, an invitation for all who read it: Absorb the broad teachings and scattered specific comments and pursue with others the task of reassessment.

This quiet call for attention to private property is itself an important message in *Laudato Si'*. And it is a timely message, for developed nations as well as those undergoing development. In the United States, to use a pertinent example, private property is wrapped up in national culture and self-identity; it is far more than a legal and economic arrangement. In this country, as elsewhere, the extra-legal, cultural elements that infuse ideas of private property tend to insulate it from serious reconsideration. They divert reformers toward solutions to particular ills that do not tamper with existing entitlements and understandings. Here, one might cite the massive misuse of fresh water in California. Holders of water rights there are obligated by law (the state constitution, no less) to limit their water uses to those that are "reasonable." Given droughts and ecological ills, it is far from reasonable, socially or economically, to use massive water flows to irrigate low-valued agricultural crops in desert areas, especially crops (corn, cotton, alfalfa) in oversupply nationally. Meanwhile, high-cost efforts are in the works to desalinate sea water and otherwise craft high-tech ways out of water shortages, adding to energy consumption and unfairly burdening taxpayers and ratepayers while low-valued irrigation largely escapes challenge. What chiefly protects it is not any legal stricture. It is the culture of owning; the aura that prompts people to think that lawmakers cannot touch private property rights. It is a widespread inability to imagine tightening limits and demanding more from those who own and control vital parts of nature.[22]

In the end, then, *Laudato Si'* is perhaps most helpful in that it invites a critical look at private property and frames the needed inquiry in useful ways.

- The Earth is our common inheritance, our common home, it tells us. We hold it in trust not just for one another and for the sustenance of all life forms but for future generations.
- Private property is a valuable form of allocating power over nature to private actors. With that private power must come accountability, an obligation to use what one owns in ways that sustain nature and that promote social justice.
- Society through its various governance forms and institutions possesses not just the legal right but the obligation to insist that owners engage in responsible stewardship and that their activities as owners not oppress the poor.
- What this means, necessarily, is active, ongoing governance efforts to tailor private rights to foster the common good. It means that private property is and must be an ongoing social construction with the elements of ownership recalibrated over time—dynamically updated— to keep the institution sound. A hands-off approach by lawmakers, whether due to faith in the market's power or for other reasons, is simply not adequate.
- Private property is morally charged given the ways private rights can dominate, exploit, and degrade. Lawmakers are called, through their reform efforts, to keep it morally sound.

In the end, these are the encyclical's main messages on private property. They come together as an urgent call for action and as a new, more hopeful and morally sound frame for understanding.

Notes

1 A useful survey of property thought in the West is Schlatter 1951.
2 A good sense of the variety of land-holding arrangements is found in Cahill 2010 and Linklater 2013.

3 Evidence is offered in Godden and Tehan 2010 and Mostert and Bennett 2011.
4 The specific case of managing land as a commons is considered in Ostrom 1990.
5 I consider the ways private and public are sometimes blended in Freyfogle 2007a: 83–106.
6 Freyfogle 2017a: 86–111.
7 A much-cited argument is Epstein 1985.
8 Progressive arguments appear in Singer 2000 and Alexander et al. 2009.
9 The moral implications of property, and the theories used to justify this institution, are considered in Becker 1977 and Ryan 1987. The importance of cultural and legal models of ownership is explored thoughtfully in van der Walt 2009. I take up in broad terms the tensions between some conceptions of property and human well-being in Freyfogle 2013.
10 For discussion, see Grossi 1981.
11 Scott 1977: 36–58.
12 Freyfogle 2003: 53.
13 I develop the point in Freyfogle 2013. The many major changes to the meaning of land ownership in the United States occurring between the American Revolution and the end of the Civil War are considered in Freyfogle 2014.
14 Pearce 2012; Liberti 2013.
15 George 1879/1929; Freyfogle 2003: 126–132.
16 The argument is developed in Alperovitz and Daly 2008.
17 Freyfogle 2007b: 29–60 considers the time period in American history when landowners had limited rights to exclude. Public wandering rights in various countries are assessed in Ilgunas 2018.
18 I undertake the task in Freyfogle 2017b.
19 I address the topic in Freyfogle 2003.
20 The idea of land as a marketable commodity, freely traded to the highest bidder, is a relatively recent idea. See Polanyi 1957.
21 The problem is highlighted in Joireman 2011.
22 I develop the point in Freyfogle 2018.

References

Alexander G., Penalver, Singer J. and Underkuffler L. 2009. "A statement of progressive property." *Cornell Law Review* 94:4, 743.

Alperovitz G. and Daly L. 2008. *Unjust deserts: how the rich are taking our common inheritance.* New Press, New York.

Becker L. 1977. *Property rights: philosophic foundations.* Routledge & Kegan Paul, Boston, MA.

Cahill K. 2010. *Who owns the world: the surprising truth about every piece of land on the planet.* Hachette Book Group, New York.

Epstein R. 1985. *Takings: private property and the power of eminent domain.* Harvard University Press, Cambridge, MA.

Freyfogle E. 2003. *The land we share: private property and the common good.* Island Press, Washington, DC.

Freyfogle E. 2007a. *Agrarianism and the good society: land, culture, conflict, and hope.* University Press of Kentucky, Lexington.

Freyfogle E. 2007b. *On private property: finding common ground on the ownership of land.* Beacon Press, Boston, MA.

Freyfogle E. 2013. "Private ownership and human flourishing: an exploratory overview." *Stellenbosch Law Review* 24:3, 430.

Freyfogle E. 2014. "Property law in a time of transformation: the record of the United States." *South African Law Journal* 131:4, 883.

Freyfogle E. 2017a. *A good that transcends: how U.S. culture undermines environmental reform.* University of Chicago Press, Chicago, IL.

Freyfogle E. 2017b. *Our oldest task: making sense of our place in nature.* University of Chicago Press, Chicago, IL.

Freyfogle E. 2018. *Water, community, and the culture of owning.* University of Utah Press, Salt Lake City.

George H. 1879/1929. *Progress and poverty: an inquiry into the cause of industrial depressions and of increase of want with increase of wealth.* Modern Library, New York.

Godden L and Tehan M, eds. 2010. *Comparative perspectives on communal lands and individual ownership: sustainable futures.* Routledge, New York.

Grossi P. 1981. *An alternative to private property: collective property in the juridical consciousness of the nineteenth century.* University of Chicago Press, Chicago, IL.

Ilgunas K. 2018. *This land is our land: how we lost the right to roam and how to take it back.* Plume, New York.

Joireman S.F. 2011. *Where there is no government: enforcing property rights in common law Africa.* Oxford University Press, New York.

Liberti S. 2013. *Land grabbing: journeys in the new colonialism.* Verso, London.

Linklater A. 2013. *Owning the earth: the transforming history of land ownership.* Bloomsbury, New York.

Mostert H and Bennett T, eds. 2011. *Pluralism and development: studies in access to property in Africa.* Juta, Claremont.

Ostrom E. 1990. *Governing the commons: the evolution of institutions for collective action.* Cambridge University Press, Cambridge.

Pearce F. 2012. *The land grabbers: the new fight over who owns the earth.* Beacon Press, Boston, MA.

Polanyi K. 1957. *The great transformation: the political and economic origins of our times.* Beacon Press, Boston, MA.

Ryan A. 1987. *Property.* University of Minnesota Press, Minneapolis.

Schlatter R. 1951. *Private property: the history of an idea.* George Allen & Unwin, London.

Scott W. 1977. *In pursuit of happiness: American conceptions of property from the seventeenth to the twentieth century.* Indiana University Press, Bloomington.

Singer J. 2000. *The edges of the field: lessons on the obligations of ownership.* Beacon Press, Boston, MA.

Van der Walt A.J. 2009. *Property in the margins.* Hart Publishing, Oxford.

3 Reading *Laudato Si'* in a rainforest country

Ecological conversion and recognition of indigenous religions

Zainal Abidin Bagir

The Interfaith Rainforest Initiative (IRI), launched in Norway in June 2017, was unusual in many respects. While Norway is well known for its attention to environmental issues, connecting an attempt to save the rainforest with religion did not seem to have obvious relevance in that secular country.[1] As an interfaith gathering, the meeting in Norway was even more striking for the centrality of the presence of representatives of indigenous communities from tropical rainforest countries including Brazil, Ecuador, Peru, Columbia, Indonesia, and Congo, each with their unique attire. Partly as a follow-up to the IRI, in 2018, mainstream Indonesian religious communities have also joined with representatives of Indonesian indigenous communities to launch a declaration to protect forests.[2]

These events spoke loudly about a few issues which are at the center of this paper. They reflect the growing awareness of the importance of religion in protecting the environment, a trend to which *Laudato Si'* is contributing. As part of the strengthening trend of involvement of religious leaders and organizations in addressing environmental problems, these events are even more significant from the point of view of both the environmental movement and interfaith dialogue because of the inclusion of indigenous communities. *Laudato Si'* also speaks about this. IRI further articulates what scholars have observed and repeated many times recently: saving the forests requires saving the people who live there—and vice versa. And speaking about the people is speaking about their knowledge, skills, culture, including their religious practices and beliefs, all of which are closely interrelated.

A 2014 report on climate change and community forest rights finds that "[w]hen Indigenous Peoples and local communities have no or weak legal rights, their forests tend to be vulnerable to deforestation" (Stevens et al. 2014: 42). Another report issued in the same year finds that the indigenous communities protect the forests where they live many times more effectively than the residents of "developed" areas protect the areas they occupy. "If the protection of tropical forests is to be effective in the long run, it must build on the rights of indigenous peoples and local communities" (Hofsvang 2014: 38).

What are the rights of indigenous people who live in the forests? Some such rights are related to forests, such as the right to enter or pass through the forest, to benefit from the forest's resources, and to make decisions about forest resources (Stevens et al. 2014: 14). Indigenous communities themselves have become advocates for their forest rights. They have joined with other groups to call for better forest governance in their own countries as well as for global initiatives such as REDD+ (Seymour and Busch 2016: 298–300). However, as representatives of indigenous communities from different parts of the world participating in the IRI expressed eloquently, recognition of indigenous peoples should go further than providing them with legal forest rights, but also recognizing that they have their own religious or spiritual traditions, that is, that they do not lack "religion." In some countries, including Indonesia, as I shall show later, this recognition has important social and legal implications. One of my topics in this chapter is this type of recognition.

From the point of view of interfaith relations, the participation of indigenous communities in interfaith dialogue initiatives such as IRI is significant. Certainly, it means adding more participants around the interfaith table and making dialogue more inclusive. In recent years, indigenous communities have become a more important part of the Parliament of World Religions though broader interfaith dialogue remains mainly a gathering of leaders of world religions. So the gathering in Norway was significant in this respect. And when we reflect on the relations between world religions, especially Christianity and Islam, and indigenous religions in the past, the need for this more inclusive approach is apparent. However, a genuine interfaith dialogue also needs to pay attention to unequal power relations between world and indigenous religions. And I will argue that a more meaningful inclusion of indigenous communities requires a change on the part of world religions where this includes building a theology more friendly to the indigenous religious practices and beliefs.

Herein lies the importance of Pope Francis's encyclical *Laudato Si'* (2015), which is a rare religious text that responds to what is arguably the most important issue of our time. In its breadth, the text does not speak only to Catholics. Its analysis and recommendations could easily find an audience among other religious communities, and it encourages inter-religious conversation. The Pope draws on the work of scientists, environmental anthropologists, scholars of religious studies, and international bodies concerned with the ecological crisis in recognizing the important role of indigenous communities, especially when it comes to conservation of forests. He takes up the topic under the subtitle "Cultural Ecology" (143–146). Further, his notion of "ecological conversion" may be connected to my argument about the need for a theology that is more friendly to indigenous religions.

After a general discussion about indigenous communities, in this chapter I will consider what *Laudato Si'* has to say about the dominance of the technocratic paradigm which, Pope Francis contends, has contributed centrally to the current ecological crisis. Next, I discuss the role of indigenous communities in conservation of the environment, considering the issues of environmental and ecological justice. After discussing the complex relations between the environment, world religions, and indigenous religions, I will take up examples from Indonesia to illustrate the problems and show the difficult decisions, highlighted very well in *Laudato Si'*, that (world) religious communities need to make.

As an Indonesian Muslim, I welcome the special attention that *Laudato Si'* gives to indigenous communities. Indonesia has more Muslims than any other country, and my response to the text may naturally find the connections it may make with Islam. So I will ask how much of *Laudato Si'* resonates with Muslims' beliefs. At the same time, Indonesia is also one of the largest rainforest countries and hosts many indigenous communities living in the forests. Because of past policies concerning development, culture, and religion, many of these communities have been marginalized and threatened with extinction, with some world religions having some share in this situation. In addition to focusing on a specifically Islamic response, in this chapter, I choose to focus more on indigenous communities, mostly because they have not received the attention they deserve in religion and ecology discourse. My ultimate concern is to motivate reflection on what is required from world religions to help rectify the situation—that is, to contribute to protecting the earth for this generation and for future generations. I contend that world religions, especially Christianity and Islam, need to undergo a kind of ecological theological-conversion to facilitate a fuller recognition of indigenous communities, which includes their religions.

Indigenous communities and nature

A central feature of indigenous religion, in general, is its close affinity with nature (lands, forests, mountains, rivers, or seas). Indigenous communities are associated with nature conservation because their practices and beliefs show reverence for nature. The magnitude and extent of this reverence are often contrasted with the practices and beliefs of followers of world religions which are often accused of dominating, controlling, and exploiting, instead of revering, nature. These are surely very general statements which have to be qualified, as I will do later in this section and in the last section of this paper. For one thing, this contrast is best understood not to refer to particular world or indigenous religions, but to ideal types and to the different orientations within religions.

One way to understand this is to see religions, following Robert Doran (as discussed in Ormerod and Vanin 2016: 341–343), as exhibiting three cultural types/dimensions: anthropological, cosmological, and soteriological. The cosmological constructs a symbolic system understood as mirroring the cosmic order, while the anthropological constructs meanings from a world-transcendent source of reason. In (today's) world religions, the anthropological dominates; while among the indigenous religions, the cosmological is prominent (Ormerod and Vanin 2016: 341).

Maarif (2015: 45–48) contrasts world and indigenous religions in a different way. In contrast to the world religions, in the indigenous religions, in general, the distinct and strict categories of humans, the natural, and the supernatural tend to be blurred. Both humans and non-humans are persons/subjects and are roughly equal in their significance. And the inter-subjective relationships that humans have with the non-human should reflect this equality. As such, anthropologically speaking, the communities involved in IRI as mentioned in the beginning of this chapter may be called "the peoples of the forests" in a deep sense: They have lived there for generations on what the forests provided them and developed their traditions, their symbolic systems—whether these are called cultures or religions—in ways that reflect their natural habitat; the humans and the natural habitat form an integral part of the cosmic order.

For the indigenous communities represented in IRI and many others, the continuation of that story is broadly similar: despite some acknowledgment of their important roles in forest conservation, they have been pushed to the margins by forces that try to exploit their natural environment and at the same time modernize them. Since for these communities the natural environment and the tradition are inseparable, when one is destroyed, the other is too. When the forests are destroyed and cannot provide their basic needs, they have to leave the place and with it their religions, their practices, and belief systems. Unlike world religions which spread and prospered beyond their geographical origins, the indigenous religions, like the indigenous peoples themselves, require their natural habitat. Many world religions with their missionizing activities of converting people who are regarded as having no religion or at best a "primitive" religion are complicit in this process. As such, to complete the statement "saving the forests requires saving the people," one may add that saving the people requires preserving their religion with its cosmology, which provides a symbolic system on which they depend, as well as their knowledge, skill, and culture.

At this point, two remarks are necessary to avoid over-generalizations about the role of indigenous communities in conservation. *First*, despite some general characterizations above, indigenous communities around the world do not share the same worldview, and their worldviews are not equally conducive to conservation. Many scholars argue that a form of "animism," in the sense of reverence or even personification of elements in nature, as a label to characterize indigenous beliefs, would naturally lead to better care of the earth and ecologically positive attitude and behavior. However, others show that indigenous religions do not always possess these features and question whether there is an inherent and necessary relation between indigenous cosmology and conservation. This debate is portrayed well in Snodgrass and Tedje (2008), who advise us to avoid generalization and over-simplification as the indigenous communities are diverse and within the communities not all members share the same beliefs. Animisms too are diverse; some lend themselves more readily to conservation, others may have conservation only as a by-product.

In some communities, the work of conservation may succeed only if there is also the capability to institutionalize their beliefs, practices, and behavior (Snodgrass and Tedje 2008). As there are diverse stories, it is difficult to draw a single conclusion.

Second, even if a link may be established between indigenous communities and conservation, some may contend that today indigenous communities only represent small pockets of marginalized, isolated people, and as such they may not be significant. However, if nothing else, understanding how these communities can be harmed by environmental changes provides an opportunity to understand a more general point about how environmental changes may affect everyone, every community. The fact that indigenous communities generally live quite close to their natural environment, such that their whole livelihood, traditions, and even their cosmology depend on their environment, means that they are simply the first to be affected when forests are destroyed or seriously harmed. It is only a matter of time for others. This fact does not escape Pope Francis's attention.

Technocratic paradigm and the extent of recognition of indigenous communities

Laudato Si' (LS) starts its analysis of the ecological crisis by pointing boldly to the so-called technocratic paradigm (101). Despite its undeniable benefits to mankind, modern science and technology are not mere instruments that are under our control but have become an inseparable part of our life, even a way of looking at reality, such that—and here the Pope quotes Romano Guardini—this paradigm claims "a lordship over all" (108). Recognizing the origin of the ecological crisis to lie in this technocratic paradigm, the Pope contends that overcoming the crisis requires "a distinctive way of looking at things, a way of thinking, policies, an educational programme, a lifestyle and a spirituality which together generate resistance to the assault of the technocratic paradigm" (111). Partial technical solutions to different expressions of the crisis—be it pollution, loss of biodiversity, destruction of coral reefs, or increasingly severe "natural" disasters—are not the answer and even run the risk of exacerbating the problem. This is because they share the paradigm that created the problems in the first place. What is needed is a "bold cultural revolution" (114).

An important part of this paradigm that the Pope is opposing is an anthropocentrism that prizes technical thought over reality, since—quoting again from Guardini—

> the technological mind sees nature as an insensate order, as a cold body of facts, as a mere 'given', as an object of utility, as raw material to be hammered into useful shape; it views the cosmos similarly as a mere 'space' into which objects can be thrown with complete indifference.
>
> (115)

Technology gives humans the means to a Promethean mastery of nature, which, for the technological mind, has lost its intrinsic dignity. The Pope criticizes the mistaken understanding of Christian anthropology in which "dominion" marks the relationship between human beings and the world—instead "dominion" should be understood as responsible stewardship (116).

The next step in *Laudato Si'*, described in the third chapter, entitled "Integral Ecology," is to acknowledge that nature is not just the background conditions in which we live. "We are part of nature, included in it and thus in constant interaction with it" (139). As such, the environmental crisis is at the same time a social crisis; what we are faced with is "one complex crisis which is both social and environmental" (139). Thus, the solution should also be "an integrated approach to combating poverty, restoring dignity to the excluded, and at the same time protecting nature" (139). This statement may be understood as an allusion to the issue of environmental justice and it very much echoes the sentiment discussed above about the connections between saving the forest and saving its people. It prepares the ground for the Pope's next concern, which is the fate of local cultures.

The technocratic paradigm globalizes a certain culture which levels down all other cultures.

> The disappearance of a culture can be just as serious, or even more serious, than the disappearance of a species of plant or animal. The imposition of a dominant lifestyle linked to a single form of production can be just as harmful as the altering of ecosystems.
>
> (145)

It is here that discussion of the indigenous communities enters the picture, not merely as "one minority among others, but... the principal dialogue partners." As their land is not a commodity whose value is calculated relative to human interests, but a sacred space, indigenous communities take great care of their land, yet "pressure is being put on them to abandon their homelands to make room for agricultural or mining projects which are undertaken without regard for the degradation of nature and culture" (146).

This reference to the indigenous communities is indeed brief, yet it is quite an important step considering the history of the Vatican's attitude toward such communities. Attitudes such as those expressed in the Doctrine of Discovery of 1493 (The Papal Bull "Inter Caetera" issued by Pope Alexander VI)[3] have encouraged the idea that lands in which indigenous communities lived were *terra nullius*, nobody's land that can be claimed by Christians. As recently as 2012, the UN Permanent Forum on Indigenous Issues felt a need to address this issue, noting the ongoing impact of the Doctrine, which is still referred to in some courts, including in the United States until recently.[4] A year after the release of *Laudato Si'*, after a meeting with representatives of indigenous communities, the Vatican, which initially contended that the Doctrine was not in effect and hence did not need to be discussed at this point, was said to be reconsidering rescinding it.

In any case the view which underlies the Doctrine is still alive, and not limited to Christianity or Europe. Assaults on indigenous communities by states and corporations are sometimes justified partly by reference to their lack of religion, which is coupled with the view of them as uncivilized, un-modern, or anti-development.

Broadly speaking, there are two issues regarding environment and indigenous communities. In many places, economic development driven by the state and corporations has destroyed their natural environment. When their environment (land, forest, or mountain, but also sea) is destroyed, their ways of life and traditions, including their religious or spiritual systems, which are intimately related to their physical environment, are also destroyed. When the communities are marginalized, their role in the conservation of the natural environment is undermined. Not unrelated to this, theologically speaking, their religions, many of which are a form of "animism," are regarded as backward and at odds with the world religions and especially monotheistic religions. Experiences of many indigenous communities around the world show that the protection of their physical environment and recognition of their legal forest rights are inseparable from recognition of their beliefs and rituals.

As I will shortly discuss, in Indonesia, the marginalization of indigenous communities, along with their spiritual tradition and practices—whether they may be called "religion" or not—came about through a combination of those factors. The modernizing drive, especially since the late 1960s, consists of economic development and "religionization," a kind of forced affiliation with one of the recognized world religions. On both these counts, indigenous communities are disadvantaged; they need to be modernized, which means forced to "develop" and their supposedly primitive, animistic beliefs are to be discarded and replaced with "proper religions." Developmentalism, or what the Pope calls the technocratic paradigm, is not only about economy or technology but also about cultural homogenization, and, in Indonesia, it includes religionization.

While not always clothed in theological terms, this view of indigenous communities, as un-developed or even anti-development and lacking religion, still crops up when there are conflicts between states or corporations and indigenous communities over their land. I illustrate this and make further points with examples from Indonesia and other places in the next section.

Politics of non-recognition: illustrations from Indonesia and beyond

The recent and ongoing story of resistance by the indigenous community of Sedulur Sikep, whose members work mostly as farmers, in Central Java, shows how indigenous communities are marginalized. The Sedulur Sikep community (or Samin people, referring to the name of their ancestor) defended their agricultural area in the mountainous Kendeng region against cement factories and the state since 2005. Based on experiences in other areas, they are worried that the factories will destroy what actually is a protected karst area that serves as the reservoir of water for the agriculture there (Putri 2017; Setiadi, Saraswati and Rosyid 2017). The anti-cement campaign has been internationalized, since it involves some factories operated by companies from other countries such as Germany and China in addition to Indonesian factories.[5] The debate was mostly about scientific and legal issues around the impact of limestone mining on the environment; and in this regard the Sedulur Sikep community have won several times, yet the court decisions have not been enforced. The discourse outside the court, however, is one that portrays the community as backward and "anti-development." In this situation, indigenous religions were seen as an anomaly: the ways of life and beliefs associated with them were thought to be at odds with the sort of development that was understood to be the way to achieve prosperity. Some religious leaders, too, support this portrayal. Religious concerns are rarely expressed explicitly in the pros and cons about cement factories. Nevertheless, such discourse has a marginalizing, "othering" effect: because their religion is "unorthodox" and they resist development, somehow indigenous people do not belong to the society at large.

This process of marginalization has become even worse because the national policy on religion registers indigenous people, literally, as the "other" in the civil administration. The Indonesian religious demography based on the latest 2010 Census shows that 87% of the population of 260 million are Muslim, almost 10% are Protestants and Catholics, and less than 3% are Buddhists, Hindus, and, much smaller, Confucians. The final category is "Others," which is 0.13%. This demography hides many important things. Indigenous religions do not figure in this picture because they do not qualify as "religion" in the Indonesian legal-administrative definition of the term. Some may choose "others," but it is not clear what religions, if any, the people who chose "others" belong to. As religion is recorded in the national ID card, and this card is a central instrument to access citizens' rights, from education to health and marriage registration, not having a recognized religion may mean difficulties in accessing these rights. This registration process also conceals the fact that a portion of the population who are recorded as Muslims, Christians, or Hindus may also embrace a form of indigenous religion. The latter group of people may record their affiliation to the established religions simply for pragmatic reasons because they cannot register their own; or they may consciously embrace one of the world religions and at the same time also believe and practice a local, indigenous religious tradition without seeing that there may be inconsistency between them.

The Sedulur Sikep community too shows this complexity. Some may choose one of the recognized religions for their ID card, others may have difficulties in procuring an ID card or may decide not to have an ID card at all. As mentioned, this becomes an obstacle in accessing their basic rights such as education, health, and civil registration (marriage, birth, etc.). Further, as religious education is part of the curriculum in schools, their children also find difficulties because their beliefs are not part of what the state regards as "religion." Thus, the process of marginalization worsens.

It is significant to note that when the Pope talks about indigenous communities in *Laudato Si'*, he speaks about "cultures," and not "religions." Whether the choice of the term was made deliberately or not, this distinction is worth elaborating. "Religion" as we use it today indeed is a modern term that goes back only to the nineteenth century, modeled on modern, Western Christianity, and then applied, mainly during the colonial time, to other "religions" found in countries such as India, Africa, the Middle East, and Indonesia (Smith 1963; Masuzawa 2005). Major religions such as Hinduism, Buddhism, and Islam (which for some time was called Mohammedanism) have had the privilege, if indeed it was a privilege, of gradually becoming part of "world religions" because they somehow fit, or were forced to fit, the template of Western Christianity (Smith 1963). In many parts of the world, what the indigenous people practice and believe is difficult or even impossible to qualify as religion. Recognition as religion carries consequences. In the past, it might determine whether a certain practice (e.g., *sati*, the widow burning in India) is to be prohibited, if it is regarded as belonging to an outdated pre-modern culture, or tolerated, as part of religious freedom that needs to be protected.[6] Indeed, this issue remains relevant today in many policy and academic circles, for example when the reach of the legal concept of freedom of religion is being decided. The K'iche' of Guatemala, for example, rejected mining and hydroelectric projects for what may be understood, in certain definitions of religion, as *religious* reasons related to the protection of their sacred land. But this rejection is not portrayed as violations of their religious freedom in official country reports because their attachment to land does not register legally as religious (Hurd 2015: 49–51). This politics of non-recognition, as Hurd calls it, based on a particular understanding about what qualifies as religion or what is recognizable as religion, is widespread. In sub-Saharan Africa, as shown by Hackett (2015), indigenous religions are religious freedom misfits because the religions could not easily fit the official understanding of religion which reflects world religions' biases. Native Americans experience similar non-recognition. Their attempt to prove that "we have a religion" (Wenger 2009) is similar in many respects to what is experienced by indigenous religions in Indonesia (Atkinson 1983).

In the case of Indonesia, it may seem puzzling at first to find that to be a modern Indonesian citizen is, partly, to have a "proper religion" (Ind. *agama*), which is to say, one of the world religions (Hidayah 2012). Religion has always been an important part of the new nation-state since its independence from Dutch colonialism and even during the colonial era;

to be a citizen is to have a religion. To be modern is not to leave religion, but to opt for a religion that is somehow perceived as supporting modernity. Christianity was brought by the colonials, who excelled in science and technology, while Islam, which came earlier, was also promoted as compatible with modernity. On the other hand, the idea that modern Indonesia has of itself leaves little place for indigenous religions or for animism, which are regarded as primitive. One of the requirements for a belief system to be called *agama* is that it has to exist *not only* in Indonesia, but be present also in other parts of the world. Just as the term "religion" in English, as discussed earlier, was constructed on the template of Western Christianity (Smith 1963), the template of "religion" in Indonesia *(agama)* reflects an Islamic understanding (Maarif 2015: 38). It is a

> peculiar combination... of a Christian view of what counts as a world religion with an Islamic understanding of what defines a proper religion: divine revelation recorded by a prophet in a holy book, a system of law for the community of believers, congregational worship, and a belief in the One and Only God.
> (Picard 2011: 3; Cf. Hefner 2018: 216)

In this framework, indigenous religions are regarded not as religion but as culture, and are administered by the Ministry of Education and Culture, not by the Ministry of Religious Affairs (Maarif 2017).

Another complication in the history that led to this formulation of *agama* is its relation with the purge of Communism after 1965. The attempt to formulate *agama* as a legal-official term started immediately after the declaration of Independence in 1945. The first two decades, when the country was led by the first president Soekarno, was a period of intense nation-building in which many decisions about the form of the Indonesian nation-state were made and written down in the Constitution and in laws, subsequent to debate in the parliament and in public. Triggered by the failed effort at *coup d'état,* allegedly by the Communist party, in 1965, the second president, Soeharto, led Indonesia for three decades with his authoritarian rule. The post-1965 purge of the (suspected) communists provided an opportunity for world religions, supported by the state, to gain more members. Communists were associated with no religion or even anti-religion, and everyone who was regarded as having a dubious religious affiliation, which included many indigenous communities as well as certain types of syncretism found mostly in Java *(aliran kepercayaan)*, were forced to convert to one of the recognized religions—Islam, Protestantism, Catholicism, Hinduism, and Buddhism (See Hefner and Bagir 2016). Though it is difficult to provide numbers, many were converted, especially to Christianity.[7]

At the same time, the New Order, as the regime called itself until its fall in 1998, also promoted massive developmentalism. It was a period of impressive economic growth—Indonesia was hailed as one of the

"Asian Tigers," though the President also earned the title as the most corrupt world leader.[8] This economic growth during the New Order was gained at the cost of exploitation of natural resources, which included massive land conversions from forest to agricultural land, introduction of new agricultural commodities, new ways of doing agriculture, and large-scale change of livelihood. This produced wide-ranging changes among many, especially the indigenous communities. Indonesia was very centralized, and policies in many sectors had to conform to the standard set from the Center in Java. Many aspects of life, from local governance to which food was to be regarded as staple, were homogenized, resulting in the disruption of local cultures. For communities like Sedulur Sikep, the charge of being anti-development and the charge of having ambiguous religiosity were compounded by the stigma of being communist-like, all of which made them even more disadvantaged.

1998, the year when President Soeharto was overthrown by a popular protest movement, marked the start of democratization. It did open up a space of freedom, including for the indigenous communities. In 1999, the Alliance of the Indigenous (*Adat*) Peoples of the Archipelago (Asosiasi Masyarakat Adat Nusantara or AMAN) was established and gained recognition (Hauser-Schäublin 2013). In recent years, a draft law on indigenous communities has been discussed, though the discussions have not gone as fast as hoped for by civil society organizations (Ompusunggu 2018). Yet in general, while there have been significant achievements in terms of legal recognition of *adat* lands, recognition of their "religious" beliefs is harder to get, because in general the paradigm of governance of religion has not changed substantially. They still lack "religion"; what they have is "culture"; as such, as discussed earlier, they have not become full citizens.

Progress in this direction was made in 2017 when the Indonesian Constitutional Court received a petition to review the 2006 law on civil administration, precisely on the options available in the religion column in the ID card. While in other cases related to religion the Court in general tends to maintain the status quo (Butt 2016; Bagir 2018), in this case it made a surprising decision which has the effect of redefining indigenous beliefs as equal in status to the beliefs of adherents of world religions (Sapiie 2017). Nevertheless, that ideal may still be difficult to achieve as there are difficulties in its implementation. Further, a number of established religious communities do not support this decision, as it may potentially disrupt a status quo that is to their advantage. Indeed, this worry is not without reason, as the decision has emboldened some indigenous communities to boldly reassert their past religious identities, and renounce the religions with which they have been affiliated since 1965. (In different places that means Protestantism, Catholicism, or Hinduism). For many indigenous groups, the situation today is significantly better compared to the time of the New Order, or even since the colonial time; yet many challenges remain as old politics of religion and culture are still in play.

Examples of indigenous communities whose cultures and religions were disrupted by developmentalism abound. There are fewer examples of communities that still maintain their ways of life and conserve nature. Others are recently starting to revitalize their traditions, and at the same time trying to prevent corporations and the state from further destroying their place of living. In this situation, established world religions have in some cases been complicit in the process of marginalization, whether supporting the corporations in conflicts over lands, or in not supporting the exercise of the civil, political, social, and economic rights of indigenous people. Genuine commitment to the environmental cause would require changes in how communities of world religions deal with the indigenous religions, probably to the extent that they need to consider a theological rethinking, if not, to use the Pope's term, conversion.

Ecological conversion: what it takes to overcome the ecological crisis

Environmental crises of the scale we are witnessing in our era, now known as the Anthropocene on account of the scale of the human impact on the planet, have many dimensions and require the engagement of many communities and institutions. A central question is how to change the way that we humans lead our lives on this planet, putting ourselves on, to quote the Pope, "the long path of renewal" (202). Speaking about change and renewal that need to be made to overcome the ecological crisis, the notion of "ecological conversion" stands out. This is a term Pope Francis attributes to Saint John Paul II (5). He elaborates on the idea of ecological conversion in the last chapter of *Laudato Si'*.

Ecological conversion requires something deeper than the creation of laws to control action deemed harmful to the environment. It is also deeper than "ecological citizenship," the cultivation of ecological sensitivity and responsibility to protect the environment. Both are praiseworthy and necessary but not sufficient. Overcoming the ecological crisis also requires being connected to the higher reality, personal transformation, and cultivating new virtues to care for the earth. What is needed is nothing short of creating "a new way of thinking about human beings, life, society and our relationship with nature" (215), which cannot be sustained only by doctrines but needs a spirituality capable of inspiring us (216). "The ecological crisis is also a summons to profound interior conversion" (217). Such a change of heart is aptly termed ecological conversion (217). It is not only an individual but also a community conversion (219).

The notion of ecological conversion is potent. In their response to the encyclical, Ormerod and Vanin (2016) note that the term had been in circulation for some time, but lacked precision. LS addresses this problem, yet, for them, the Pope's idea of conversion is still too limited. They expand the definition of "conversion" to comprise four dimensions as elaborated by

Bernard Lonergan and Robert Doran, that is, religious, moral, intellectual, and psychic. "Conversion is a radical shift of one's fundamental orientation, one's horizon, an ongoing process toward consistent self-transcendence and authenticity" (Ormerod and Vanin 2016: 330). They rightly say that a complete ecological conversion should cover all four dimensions. Ecological conversion as religious recognizes the sacredness of creation and builds an intimacy with the natural word (Ormerod and Vanin 2016: 334–335). This conversion goes beyond particular Christian conversion and as such also provides a ground for interfaith relations. Religious conversion prepares one for moral conversion, provides motivation to make moral decisions and to willingly make sacrifices for the sake of the greater good. In turn, religious and moral conversion need to have an intellectual grounding and to be supported with analytical, scientific affirmation. Psychic conversion addresses the affective aspect of our knowledge, decisions, and actions; it is needed to overcome humans' deep biases and habits which are grounded in their personal history and may hinder attempts at personal transformation. Combining all of these elements, a full ecological conversion would "[reorient] our relationship to the natural world in a way that can assist humanity to avoid the most significant social breakdown of our time" (Ormerod and Vanin 2016: 332).

Understanding conversion in that way, Ormerod and Vanin argue that the Pope's treatment is "fairly circumscribed to what we might call the religious, indeed Christian, dimension of such a conversion" (Ormerod and Vanin 2016: 329). This claim seems to reflect a narrow attention on the part of these authors to the particular section titled "Ecological Conversion" (216–221). However, it is also clear that beyond those six paragraphs the Pope explores such a wide terrain beyond Christianity and that he urges a broad and deep "change of heart" which covers the other dimensions. Nevertheless, Ormerod and Vanin's elaboration helps us to further unpack the depth of ecological conversion.

At this point, there are a few difficult questions, to which I do not propose to give full answers, but they will at least stimulate reflection. As Ormerod and Vanin (2016) themselves mention, one such question concerns anthropocentrism. Christianity, like Islam, struggles with finding an alternative to anthropocentrism, since it is difficult for both religions to claim that humans are on a par with members of other species. *Laudato Si'* unequivocally condemns "a tyrannical anthropocentrism unconcerned for other creatures" as having no place in the Bible which, instead, "recognize[s] that other living beings have a value of their own in God's eyes" (69). However, "[a] misguided anthropocentrism need not necessarily yield to "biocentrism" for that would entail adding yet another imbalance, failing to solve present problems and adding new ones. Human beings cannot be expected to feel responsibility for the world unless, at the same time, their unique capacities of knowledge, will, freedom and responsibility are recognized and valued" (118).

It seems, then, that the Pope does not reject anthropocentrism; what he rejects are versions that are "distorted" or "misguided." *Laudato Si'* reframes the discourse—what is central here is not the notion of equality (among creatures), but openness to others in the form of respect, love, and responsibility as a mode of relation with others.[9] An ecologically converted person would embody these characteristics. "We do not understand our superiority as a reason for personal glory or irresponsible dominion, but rather as a different capacity which, in its turn, entails a serious responsibility stemming from our faith" (220). In Ormerod and Vanin's elaboration, while there is no outright rejection of anthropocentrism, it does not mean that ecological conversion leaves it intact. For them, each of the dimensions of conversion makes the subject self-transcending, radically decenters the subject away from her limited horizon, and connects the good of the decentered self to the good of other species. "A commitment to the human good requires a commitment to the whole good for the sake of that whole good, of which we are no more than a part" (Ormerod and Vanin 2016: 351).

As for Pope Francis, in the end he urges us to go beyond both anthropocentrism and "biocentrism" as theoretical or intellectual positions, since his main concern seems much more than an intellectual pursuit, but an affection, a conviction that all things are in deep, universal communion (89–92). Going beyond anthropocentrism, one of the things that ecological conversion entails is "a loving awareness that we are not disconnected from the rest of creatures, but joined in a splendid universal communion" (220). For Pope Francis, an exemplar of a transformed person who embodied "sublime fraternity with all creation," is none other than St. Francis of Assisi (221), whom the Pope mentions at the start of the encyclical and whose influence can be felt at many points in the text. St. Francis communicates the same message of integral ecology that Pope Francis advocates, in particular the inseparable bond "between concern for nature, justice for the poor, commitment to society, and interior peace" (10).

"Animism," Islam and indigenous communities

How is ecological conversion relevant to the changes urged by Pope Francis on the part of world religions as they engage with indigenous communities? In answering this question in this last section, I will restrict my remarks to Christianity and Islam, with more emphasis on the latter, bearing in mind that in the Indonesian examples I give in this chapter, Islam is the main relevant religion.

In the context of this chapter, I understand that ecological conversion should result in a more positive judgment of indigenous worldviews—not as representing a less developed, or even pagan worldview which has no place in world religions, but as an alternative view which needs to be respected if not, to some extent, accommodated theologically. This suggestion parallels something like the acceptance in the Second Vatican Council's Declaration on the

Relation of the Church to Non-Christian Religions (*Nostra aetate*) of religions such as Hinduism, Buddhism, Islam, and Judaism. This amounts to a strong theological affirmation that the Christian God's "providence, evident goodness, and saving designs extend to all men," including non-Christians.

The acceptance of the indigenous cosmology has two inter-related aims. *First*, this would be a theological basis for the acceptance of the communities as they are, not as an object of mission. This is a response to the marginalization of the communities despite their role in conserving their living environment and to the fact that world religions, especially Christianity and Islam, have in the past been a factor in this marginalization. *Second*, the acceptance may even help to facilitate a rethinking of the anthropocentric theology of world religions which tend to put human beings in a dominant position, sometimes at the expense of other beings. In this way, engagement with indigenous communities may help world religions themselves to see possible paths of renewal. Indigenous cosmologies, many of which are often described as "animist," may indeed be anathema to the world religions, yet they actually offer a radical alternative to anthropocentrism when they require seeing other-than-humans also as persons.

The question, then, is whether there is a place for an "animist" cosmology in Christianity and Islam. This question may sound too blunt; a different way to phrase it is to look again at Ormerod and Vanin's analysis of dimensions of moral conversion, especially with regard to cultural types associated with religions. Referring to Robert Doran's analysis, the issue here is how to maintain the balance in the dialectic between anthropological and cosmological cultural types/dimensions. Cosmological culture, which draws meaning from appreciation of the cycles of nature and mirrors the cosmic hierarchy of being, is embodied by indigenous religions. World religions, on the other hand, in general represent the anthropological cultural type with its emphasis on intellectual reasoning and a world-transcendent source of reason. In its development, with the rise of modernization, the cosmological cultural meanings waned. This affected both world religions, in that their cultures become less and less cosmological, and indigenous religions, which are marginalized (Ormerod and Vanin 2016: 341). As such, the issue is not to radically change the (current) theology of world religions, but to strive to repair the dialectic imbalance. This theoretical analysis helps us to understand not only the history of world and indigenous religions but also their future challenges.

Much of what has been discussed so far, from Pope Francis's theological response to the environmental crisis to the discussion about the possibility of acceptance of "animist" theology, resonates very well with a segment of contemporary Muslim scholars involved in religion and ecology discourse. Some of what has been said might even be expressed more strongly by them. By way of example, Seyyed Hossein Nasr, who arguably was the first modern Muslim theologian/philosopher to respond systematically to the environmental crisis, criticized the modernization, or even secularization, of religions, and not only Islam (Nasr 1968). By "modernization," he means the "reformation" of religion to make it conform to the modern mindset, influenced by modern science and colored by the prominence of instrumental reason. That is, to use Doran's terms, the shift from the cosmological to the anthropological. Nasr would criticize the modern mind (which I understand to be quite close to the Pope's technocratic paradigm) and the aspiration of man-made technology to exercise "a lordship over all," which is profoundly at odds with Islam's invocation of the central notion that only God is the true lord (*tauhid*) so that any act of associating lordship with others (*shirk*) is a grave sin that nullifies one's faith. *Tauhid* is simply the most central notion in literature on Islam and ecology; next is the concept of stewardship (*khalifa*), which describes the expected relation between human beings and God's other creatures (Nasr 1968; Haq 2003; Özdemir 2003).

Similar to Christianity, there is also a rejection of the idea that the special status given to human beings may lead to anthropocentrism, which is regarded as detrimental to environment (Afrasiabi 2003). However, there is also a strong current offering different interpretations. One of which sees that human being as *khalifa* stands in a dependent relation to God, just as all other beings (Haq 2003; Nasr 2003). *Khalifa* does not mean that humans own nature, nor does it mean that "the sole aim of nature is to serve human beings and their ends" (Özdemir 2003). Islamic texts (Qur'an and hadith) contain references that value non-humans apart from their usefulness to humans.

The alternative, for Nasr, and here he is more specific than other Muslim scholars, is to return to *the Tradition* (sometimes also called as *scientia sacra* or perennial philosophy), which describes a cosmology shared by many religions, including indigenous religions (Nasr 1988, 2005). Others express this idea through the language of Islamic philosophical mysticism (*tasawwuf* or *irfan*), in which references to nature regarded as living are quite common. An account of *khalifa* goes so far as to say that "every life-form possesses intrinsic value independent of its resource worth to humanity" (Clarke 2003: 76). This resonates well with the theology of *Laudato Si'*.

Mulla Sadra, the most important Muslim mystical philosopher of the seventeenth century, proposed the unity of existence (*wahdat al-wujūd*) and the gradation of existence (*tashkīk al-wujūd*). He contended that everything, by virtue of its existence as manifestation of the Divine Existence, possesses a level of consciousness. "[E]very contingent being, including plants and inanimate things, possesses consciousness, power, and volition, and subsequently life," albeit in different degrees (Akbari 2015: 18). Though human beings are higher than the non-human (animal, plants, and "inanimate" bodies), the difference between them is in degree, not in kind. Moreover, they all are in constant motion toward Perfection. He quotes many Qur'anic verses to show that this idea, though seeming unorthodox, is perfectly in line with the Qur'an, such as "There is not a thing but celebrates His praise; and yet ye understand not how they declare

His glory" (Qur'an 17: 44). Another example is the verse "Verily when He intends a thing His command is "be" and it is" (Qur'an 36: 82), which for Mulla Sadra implies that all existents know and hear—two attributes of conscious life—the Creator, otherwise the command could not be obeyed (Akbari 2015: 19–20).

This kind of metaphysics, abstract as it may appear, is not mere intellectual play with no consequence. Such a metaphysics would naturally be more open to "animism" and may significantly encourage the acceptance of the beliefs of indigenous communities, who, in their relation with the forests, are often accused as performing *shirk*, since they seem to worship things other than the one God.

In his study of the Ammatoans, an indigenous forest-based community in Sulawesi, Indonesia, Maarif (2014) shows how this idea that the people worship trees or stones hinders recognition of their beliefs as legitimate (not "deviant") religion, as well as recognition of their forest and civil rights. The Ammatoans have been Muslims for centuries and have practiced Islam. Yet they also maintain their beliefs and practice rituals inherited from their ancestors. These include sacrificing animals and giving offerings to the forest. The term deviant as attributed to beliefs and rituals rests on the assumption of, first, the absolute distinction between the subject (human beings) as persons and the others as non-person objects. Second, that label is based on the understanding that this act of giving offering involves "worship," that is, of things other than God, and hence constitutes *shirk*. But in the language of the indigenous beliefs, "worship" is not the right term to describe the humans' act of giving offering to the other beings. The relation between them should be described in a different way (Maarif 2015).

World religions answer the questions of who I am, where I come from, who shares the cosmos with me, etc., by positing the supernatural, the natural, and the cultural domains. The relations between them take a hierarchical form: humans (the realm of culture) *worship* God (the supernatural); humans take from nature to fulfill their needs. In this context, when indigenous people bring offerings to a forest or a mountain, followers of world religions may regard them as worshipping the spirits behind the natural objects—hence, the interpretation of animism as worshipping spirits, not God. But in the indigenous religions, since humans as well as non-humans are subjects, the relations between them are inter-subjective, and there is no strict demarcation between the categories of the supernatural, the human, and the natural. For them a ritual such as bringing an offering to a forest is not about worshipping; it is about sharing and keeping the commitment to maintain relations with the non-human subjects/persons. This explanation is part of recent attempts to reformulate animism which criticize the conventional, modernist understanding of the concept. In its reformulation, animism is understood relationally, describing interpersonal relationships between human persons and natural objects, with the latter being seen as non-human persons (Maarif 2015). For Maarif, this reformulation opens the possibility to understand Qur'anic depictions of natural objects (mountains, birds, stars, trees, and so on) as beings which glorify God; this indicates their personhood and that they are, in the Qur'an's own term, *Muslim*. The Qur'an uses this term to refer to an individual who embraces Islam, the religion revealed to the Prophet Muhammad, as well as to the lineage of God's prophets before Muhammad, including Abraham, Moses, Noah, Jesus, and others (Bagir and Martiam 2016). In this way, for Maarif, "being a Muslim in animistic ways" is a possibility.

This discussion has, I hope, shown that paying more attention to indigenous communities facilitates a better understanding of the religious significance of environmentalism, since they help us to, first of all, see more vividly how a way of life and beliefs matter in how one treats and co-exists with the non-human environment. Indigenous communities show not only how religion may contribute to protection of the environment but also how the destruction of the environment leads to the destruction of the tradition. While world religions in general may not be as directly affected by environmental loss, should they not reflect on how and to what extent the missions of religions on earth may be affected when the earth is damaged? The world religions might also reflect on how far the nature-centered indigenous cosmology is theologically acceptable, on which acceptance of indigenous communities may depend to some extent. As the brief discussion of Islam suggests, this kind of reinterpretation seems to be more viable in the mystical dimensions of world religions. The fact that *Laudato Si'* refers to St. Francis centrally is no accident.

Conclusion

When religion is called upon to pay attention to ecological crises, the hope is that, by mobilizing its resources (religious teachings, Scriptures, institutions, and leaders), it may help the ecological cause. But while their normative doctrines are often claimed to side with the ecological cause and, in the case of the monotheistic religions, to require care of this God-given earth, historically religions may contain elements that work in a different direction. If the call to help environmentally is heeded seriously by religions, it may force them to engage in self-critique and to transform themselves. This path to renewal may take the form of reconstruction, or retrieval of old, neglected traditions that may hold a promise of better understanding in light of our ecological knowledge (and crisis) of today. In that case, environmental crises may actually help the religions. Herein lie the challenges as well as the potential benefits for the religions if they engage the ecological crisis. It may help the religions to become more relevant and it may promote interfaith dialogue. Becoming more open, including theologically, to indigenous communities is one of the many steps that need to be taken on this path. As recounted by indigenous participants in the 2017 IRI, and repeated in almost the exact words in Indonesia's religious councils' declaration to save the forest a year later, while they are being recognized as having central roles in forest conservation, recognition of their beliefs is also due. Perhaps it is reasonable to think of this recognition as part of the "ecological conversion" that Pope Francis has called for.

Notes

1 "Harnessing the moral authority of the world's religions to save rainforests" www.unenvironment.org/news-and-stories/story/harnessing-moral-authority-worlds-religions-save-rainforests (19 October 2018).

2 "Umat Beragama Bersatu Deklarasi Lindungi Hutan Indonesia," https://m.republika.co.id/berita/nasional/umum/18/10/26/ph73kk423-umat-beragama-bersatu-deklarasi-lindungi-hutan-indonesia (26 October 2018).

3 The original text and the translation can be accessed at www.gilderlehrman.org/content/doctrine-discovery-1493

4 www.un.org/en/development/desa/newsletter/desanews/dialogue/2012/06/3801.html

5 www.dw.com/en/indonesian-farmer-joins-may-1-rally-to-protest-german-cement/a-38653827

6 The history of the British colonial treatment of *sati* is surely much more complex. See for example Major 2011; a short but helpful essay related to the topic discussed here is Major 2012.

7 Among a few studies of religious conversion during that historical period, which is still a sensitive issue in Indonesia, Nugroho 2008 has to be mentioned for its detailed study of mass baptism in a Javanese village, involving not only those regarded as having no religion but also Muslims who feared anti-communist Muslim militia; some fragments of the story in East Nusa Tenggara are discussed in Kolimon and Wetangterah 2012.

8 https://integritas360.org/2016/07/10-most-corrupt-world-leaders/

9 The Pope's idea resonates with the so-called *critical anthropocentrism* (Fisher 2010). This view reserves a special place for human beings, which is justified with reference to contemporary science. Yet, while maintaining a theological sense of human significance, it is also aware of ecological and environmental concerns.

References

Afrasiabi, Kaveh L. 2003. "Toward an Islamic Ecotheology" in R. C. Foltz, F. M. Denny, and A. Baharuddin, eds., *Islam and Ecology: A Bestowed Trust*. Cambridge, MA: Center for the Study of World Religions, pp. 281–296.

Akbari, Reza. 2015. "Mulla Sadra and the Problem of Other Minds" Working Paper; 10.13140/RG.2.1.1730.3120. Available at www.researchgate.net/publication/287520952_Mulla_Sadra_and_the_Problem_of_Other_Minds

Atkinson, Jane Monnig. 1983. "Religions in Dialogue: The Construction of an Indonesian Minority Religion" *American Ethnologist*, 10: 684–696.

Bagir, Zainal Abidin. 2018. "The Politics and Law of Religious Governance" in Robert W. Hefner, ed., *Routledge Handbook of Contemporary Indonesia*. New York: Routledge, pp. 284–295.

Bagir, Zainal Abidin and Martiam, Najiyah. 2016. "Islam and Ecology: Norms and Practices" in Mary Evelyn Tucker, John Grim, and Willis Jenkins, eds., *Routledge Handbook of Religion and Ecology*. New York: Routledge, pp. 79–87.

Butt, Simon. 2016. "Between Control and Appeasement: Religion in Five Constitutional Court Decisions" in Tim Lindsey and Helen Pausacker, eds., *Religion, Law and Intolerance in Indonesia*. London and New York: Routledge, pp. 42–67.

Clarke, Lynda. 2003. "The Universe Alive: Nature in the *Masnavī* of Jalal al-Din Rumi" in Richard C. Foltz, Frederick M. Denny, and Azizah Baharuddin, eds., *Islam and Ecology: A Bestowed Trust*. Cambridge, MA: Center for the Study of World Religions, pp. 39–66.

Fisher, Christopher L. 2010. *Human Significance in Theology and the Natural Sciences: An Ecumenical Perspective with Reference to Pannenberg, Rahner, and Zizioulas*. Oregon: Wipf & Stock Publishers.

Francis, Pope. 2015. *On Care for Our Common Home: Encyclical Letter 'Laudato Si' of the Holy Father Francis*. Rome: Libreria Editrice Vaticana.

Hackett, Rosalind I. J. 2015. "Traditional, African, Religious, Freedom?" in Winnifred Fallers Sullivan, Elizabeth Shakman Hurd, Saba Mahmood and Peter Danchin, eds., *Politics of Religious Freedom*. Chicago, IL: University of Chicago Press, pp. 89–98.

Haq, Nomanul. 2003. "Islam and Ecology: Toward Retrieval and Reconstruction" in R. C. Foltz, F. M. Denny, and A. Baharuddin, eds., *Islam and Ecology: A Bestowed Trust*. Cambridge, MA: Center for the Study of World Religions, pp. 121–154.

Hauser-Schäublin, Brigitta (ed.) 2013. *Adat and Indigeneity in Indonesia*. Göttingen: Universitätsverlag Göttingen.

Hefner, Robert W. 2018. "The Religious Field: Plural Legacies and Contemporary Contestations" in Robert W. Hefner, ed., *Routledge Companion to Contemporary Indonesia*. New York: Routledge, pp. 212–225.

Hefner, Robert W. and Bagir, Zainal Abidin. 2016. "Christianity and Religious Freedom in Indonesia since 1998: Plurality and Coexistence in an Age of Revival and Democratization" in Allen D. Hertzke and Timothy S. Shah, eds., *Christianity and Freedom: Volume 2. Contemporary Perspectives*. New York: Cambridge University Press, pp. 191–221.

Hidayah, Sita. 2012. "The Politics of Religion: The Invention of 'Agama' in Indonesia" *Kawistara*, 2:2, 105–224.

Hofsvang, Ellen (ed.) 2014. *State of the Rainforest 2014*. Rainforest Foundation Norway. Available at http://stateoftherainforest.regnskogfondet.no/uploads/docs/StateOfTheRainforest_lo.pdf. Last accessed: November 20, 2018.

Hurd, Elizabeth Shakman. 2015. "Believing in Religious Freedom" in Winnifred Fallers Sullivan, Elizabeth Shakman Hurd, Saba Mahmood and Peter Danchin, eds., *Politics of Religious Freedom*. Chicago, IL: University of Chicago Press, pp. 45–56.

Kolimon, Mery and Liliya, Wetangterah. 2012. *Memori-Memori Terlarang, Perempuan Korban & Penyintas Tragedi '65 di Nusa Tenggara Timur.* Kupang: Yayasan Bonet Pinggupir.

Maarif, Samsul. 2017. *Pasang Surut Rekognisi Agama Leluhur dalam Politik Agama di Indoensia*. Yogyakarta: CRCS UGM.

Maarif, Samsul. 2015. "Kajian Kritis Agama Lokal" in Samsul Maarif, ed., *Studi Agama di Indonesia: Refleksi Pengalaman*. Yogyakarta: CRCS-UGM, pp. 21–39.

Maarif, Samsul. 2014. "Being Muslim in Animistic Ways" *Al-Jāmi'ah: Journal of Islamic Studies*, 52:1, 149–174.

Major, Andrea. 2012. "Sati and the Civilising Mission" in Voluntary Action History Society. Available at www.vahs.org.uk/2012/11/sati-major/

Major, Andrea. 2011. *Sovereignty and Social Reform in India: British Colonialism and the Campaign Against sati, 1830–1860*. Abingdon and New York: Routledge.

Masuzawa, Tomoko. 2005. *The Inventions of World Religions – Or, How European Universalism was Preserved in the Language of Pluralism*. Chicago, IL: The University of Chicago Press.

Nasr, Seyyed Hossein. 2005. *The Need for a Sacred Science*. Richmond: Curzon Press Ltd.

Nasr, Seyyed Hossein. 2003. "Islam, the Contemporary Islamic World, and the Environmental Crisis" in R. C. Foltz, F. M. Denny, and A. Baharuddin, eds., *Islam and Ecology: A Bestowed Trust*. Cambridge, MA: Center for the Study of the World Religions, pp. 85–105.

Nasr, Seyyed Hossein. 1988. *Knowledge and the Sacred*. New York: SUNY Press.

Nasr, Seyyed Hossein. 1968. *Man and Nature: The Spiritual Crisis of Modern Man*. Chicago, IL: Kazi Publishers.

Nugroho, Singgih. 2008. *Menyintas dan Menyeberang: Perpindahan Massal Keagamaan Pasca 1965 di Pedesaan Jawa*. Yogyakarta: Syarikat.

Ompusunggu, Moses. 2018. "'Adat' Communities Want Their Own Special Law: Why?" *The Jakarta Post* (11 May 2018). Available at www.thejakartapost.com/news/2018/05/11/adat-communities-want-their-own-special-law-why.html. Last accessed: October 4, 2018.

Ormerod, Neil and Vanin, Cristina. 2016. "Ecological Conversion: What Does it Mean?" *Theological Studies*, 77:2, 328–352.

Özdemir, I. 2003. "Toward an Understanding of Environmental Ethics from a Qur'anic Perspective" in R. C. Foltz, F. M. Denny, and A. Baharuddin, eds., *Islam and Ecology: A Bestowed Trust*. Cambridge, MA: Center for the Study of the World Religions, pp. 3–37.

Picard, Michel. 2011. "Agama, Adat, and the Pancasila" in Michel Picard and Rémy Madinier, eds., *Politics of Religion in Indonesia: Syncretism, Orthodoxy, and Religious Contention in Java and Bali*. London and New York: Routledge, pp. 1–20.

Putri, Primi Suharmadhi. 2017. "The Meaning Making of an Environmental Movement: A Perspective on *Sedulur Sikep's* Narrative in Anti-Cement Movement" *Poer Conflict Democracy Journal*, 2, 297–321.

Sapiie, Marguerite Afra. 2017. "Constitutional Court Rules Indigenous Faiths 'Acknowledged' by State" *The Jakarta Post* (November 7, 2017). Available at www.thejakartapost.com/news/2017/11/07/constitutional-court-rules-indigenous-faiths-acknowledged-by-state.html. Last accessed: October 4, 2018.

Setiadi, Saraswati, Aprilia Rejeki and Rosyid, Nur. 2017. "*Geger Sikep*: Environmental (Re)Interpretation among the Contemporary Anti-Cement Movement in Kendeng, Central Java" *Komunitas: International Journal of Indonesian Society and Culture*, 9:1, 13–28.

Seymour, Frances and Busch, Jonah. 2016. *Why Forests? Why Now? The Science, Economics and Politics of Tropical Forests and Climate Change*. Washington, DC: Centre for Global Development.

Smith, Wilfred Cantwell. 1963. *The Meaning and End of Religion; A New Approach to The Religious Traditions Of Mankind*. New York: Macmillan.

Snodgrass, Jeffrey G. and Tiedje, Kristina. 2008. "Indigenous Nature Reverence and Conservation—Seven Ways of Transcending an Unnecessary Dichotomy" *Journal for the Study of Religion, Nature and Culture*, 2:1, 6–29.

Stevens, Caleb, Robert Winterbottom, Katie Reytar and Jenny Springer. 2014. *Securing Rights, Combating Climate Change: How Strengthening Community Forest Rights Mitigates Climate Change*. Washington, DC: World Resources Institute. Available at www.wri.org/publication/securing-rights-combating-climate-change

Wenger, Tisa. 2009. *We Have a Religion: The 1920s Pueblo Indian Dance Controversy and American Religious Freedom*. Chapel Hill: The University of North Carolina Press.

4   The cry of the earth and the cry of the poor

Darrel Moellendorf

Pope Francis's remarkable encyclical Letter *Laudato Si'* has as a central message the need to turn our ears and hearts "so as to hear *both the cry of the earth and the cry of the poor*" (49). A pro-poor environmentalism is very good news indeed. And while the teaching is, of course, a Roman Catholic one and contains elements that many non-Catholics would find objectionable, the central commitment to social justice and ecological concern is ecumenical and has broad appeal. Moreover, it is offered in the spirit of dialogue, not simply as dogma for all to follow. In this chapter, I critically discuss the reasons offered in *Laudato Si'* for the twin condemnation of global poverty and environmental destruction. Additionally, although I reject the idea that human development can and should proceed in harmony with nature, I consider guidelines for a pro-poor social justice agenda if we take seriously the intrinsic value of nature. The kind of reconciliation suggested by the encyclical is, I think, implausible. Still, the pursuit of poverty eradicating human development should seek to limit the destruction of natural value. To fail to do so is to fail to respond adequately to the value of nature. I offer some preliminary suggestions for how to think about the pursuit of both poverty eradication and the preservation of natural value.

The cry of the earth

The first cry of *Laudato Si'* is the cry of the earth. Industrial production and agriculture as well as mass consumption have exacted a toll in the form of biodiversity loss, pollution, climate change, and other environmental problems. The encyclical recognizes two valid ways to consider this loss of value. The first is at least partially anthropocentric. "Different species contain genes which could be key resources in years ahead for meeting human needs and regulating environmental problems" (32). Indeed, human needs, particularly in agriculture and medicine, provide strong reasons to seek to preserve biodiversity. As the biologist, Edward O. Wilson, reminds us,

> Organisms are superb chemists. In a sense they are collectively better than all the world's chemists at synthesizing, organic molecules of

practical use. Through millions of generations each kind of plant, animal, and microorganism has experimented with chemical substances to meet its special needs…The special case of chemicals in which the species became a wizard is precisely determined by the niche it occupies.

(Wilson 1992: 285)

Human usage of plant species in agriculture is remarkably undeveloped. Some 30,000 species of plants may be eaten in whole or in part by humans. Of these less than a third have been collected or grown as food. And a mere 20 species provide 90% of human food. Three, wheat, maize, and rice, provide more than half of the food (Wilson 1992: 287–288). In the case of medicines, the under use is even more dramatic. Although 40% of all medicines are derived from organisms, and 20% from plants alone, only 3% of all known flowering plants have been examined for medicinal properties (Wilson 1992: 285). Our ignorance regarding the possible benefits of natural species—including species that are vanishing—is staggering.

Our witlessness about the utility of organisms to us is exceeded by our inability to even estimate within an order of magnitude the number of species that exist on the planet. A large number of new species are discovered each year. This is not due to their emergence, but to growth in human knowledge. Estimates of the number of currently existing species range from 10 to 100 million (Wilson 1992: 132). And, when it comes to recording extinctions, only those species known to have existed can be counted. It seems safe to assume that in addition to known extinctions many more species, never known to have existed, die off. Considering only rainforest biodiversity Wilson is able to estimate that the natural background rate of species extinction is about one species per one million per year, and human activity has increased this between 1,000-fold and 10,000-fold (Wilson 1992: 280). He conjectures that, "we are in the midst of one of the great extinction spasms of geological history" (Wilson 1992: 132).

The extent of biodiversity destruction is staggering, and the potential loss of utility to humans is enormous. That raises important practical problems. One is whether biodiversity loss can be priced. If we are seeking to use resources efficiently, how much should we spend to preserve the potential benefits of biodiversity? The aim of the Ecosystem Services approach to conservation is to answer questions like these, if not for biodiversity in general then with respect to particular localized ecosystems and perhaps individual species. Ignorance, however, prevents answering that question in regards to total planetary biodiversity in a precise book-keeping way. We can't establish the economic value of species not known to exist. Hence, we can't measure the loss of economic value attributable to overall annual species extinction. But even if we had catalogued all existing species, we would still need to consider their relations, such as predation and mutuality. For when a species goes extinct it has an impact, for better or worse, on other species. The loss of one species causes disruptions that could impose other costs. And most important for any cost accounting, we would need to know the full use-value of every species to us. Ignorance regarding the existence of species, how they interact with one another, and their full usefulness renders any attempt at book-keeping deeply suspect.

These problems of measuring value on a planetary scale ramify across ecosystem and species. In the case of a particular ecosystem, depending on how thoroughly it has been studied, there is to a greater or lesser extent uncertainty about the number of species it contains. And even for the known species we often possess limited knowledge regarding both their interactions with other species and their utility to humans. Hence, even when it comes to pricing the services of particular ecosystems and species, limitations of knowledge present major problems. It seems safe to say, that given limits on knowledge, any book-keeping exercise will underestimate, probably massively. As long as there are opportunity costs incurred by environmental protection and restoration, there will be a demand to price the service of the natural item preserved or restored. But there is little reason to assume that the estimated price is accurate.

The encyclical could not keep faith with its own tradition if it considered only loss of economic value when reflecting on ecological destruction. At various points in the first creation story in Genesis 1, the Creator pauses to behold the creation and then judges it good (Genesis 1: 4,10, 12, 18, 21, and 25). It would be utterly implausible to interpret those judgments in terms of economic benefits. So it is not surprising the encyclical says that "[it] is not enough, however, to think of different species merely as potential 'resources' to be exploited, while overlooking the fact that they have value in themselves" (33).

The second way that the encyclical considers the loss of value that occurs in ecological destruction is in term of loss of intrinsic value. The cry of the earth is not simply a grief stricken human response to mounting losses in some accounting ledger. It's not a painful lament for an economic setback. The locution "value in themselves" in Paragraph 33 refers to the value of a species that is not dependent on the species serving some others purpose, either in the ecosystem or for humans. If species also have intrinsic value, then extinction is a loss regardless of whatever diminution to human well-being occurs or whatever harm to ecosystems comes to pass. Insofar as we have reason to regret the loss value, then extinction is regrettable to some extent regardless of whether it diminishes human well-being or ecosystem functioning.

The use of the term "species" rather than "organism" in Paragraph 33 also suggests that the relevant value is not reducible to the value of individuals. When the last organism of a species dies, there is a loss that is other than whatever loss occurs from the loss of the organism itself. This claim is of course consistent with also valuing the organism itself. The encyclical seems also to take the view that individual organisms are valuable, for it refers to the intrinsic value of "lesser beings" (118). This is not an unfamiliar combination of views. A music lover can enjoy a genre of music, and enjoy individual songs or compositions within the genre. We may even admire a particular piece of literature, despite the fact that we generally dislike the genre. The point here is that valuing the class is distinct from valuing its members. But since the class exists only insofar as the members exist, we have an additional reason to value members of an endangered valuable class. Alan Carter offers an illuminating comparison. We care about species as we care about artistic genres; species extinction is analogous to the loss of an entire genre of valuable art (Carter 2010).

The encyclical takes species then as valuable instrumentally, for human purposes, but also intrinsically. We value many things both instrumentally and intrinsically. Education can be valued as a means to pursuing a rewarding career and it can be valued for its own sake. Because instrumental value derives its importance from what it promotes, and instrumental disvalue derives its disvalue from what it threatens, the weight of the value or disvalue is a function of that which is promoted or threatened. In the context of species preservation, it is especially important to note that something's intrinsic value is not necessarily weightier than its instrumental disvalue. So, even if a species of bacteria has intrinsic value, the threat that it poses to the health of other organisms might be significant enough to merit eradicating it. Hence, we might not have reason to regret a species extinction all-things-considered.

The encyclical's affirmation of the intrinsic value of species and organisms entails a non-anthropocentric view of the value of nature. Organisms and species are valuable apart from their utility to humans. The encyclical often expresses non-anthropocentrism in theistic terms. It appeals, for example, to experiences of value in nature as experiences of God in nature.

> [T]he mystic experiences the intimate connection between God and all beings, and thus feels that 'all things are God.' Standing awestruck before a mountain, he or she cannot separate this experience from God, and perceives that the interior awe being lived has to be entrusted to the Lord.
>
> (234)

In the spirit of the ecumenical pursuit of the concerns of environmentalism that the encyclical values, it should be pointed out that non-anthropocentrism need not rely on theism. Non-anthropocentrism is the view that valuable items need not serve some human purpose in order to be valuable. One way to non-anthropocentric natural value might be via theism. The mystic interprets the awe of a mountain as being awe before God. But those who don't experience God need not deny the awe. There may also be awe in the face of the grandeur of the mountain. Likewise, experiences such as the wonder and intrigue of seeing a single-celled organism under the microscope or the breathtaking delight of viewing the Grand Canyon may be aesthetic experiences of just those things, not of a deity in them. They may be experiences of valuing the object intrinsically, not for its propensity to serve human or other aims (Moellendorf 2014: 69–70, 2017). Our experiences of valuing natural items, then, evince the possibility of the theist and the atheist agreeing that intrinsic value is found in nature.

The pleasing properties we perceive when experiencing natural items is the basis of our valuing them intrinsically. But we also value these things because they are not entirely artefactual, even when they are profoundly affected by us through accident or good management. Their origin and constitution also matter to us (Moellendorf 2017). The mystic who sees God in the mountain might believe that the origin of natural value derives from an original act of divine creation; other people might be agnostic about that derivation. In order to value natural items for their non-artefactual character, there is no need to have a belief about the origin of the universe. If the ultimate origin of all that exists is mysterious to us, that does not in any way diminish its value.

There is no reason to think that the theist has the upper hand in providing support for the intrinsic value of nature. Settling the origin of nature one way or another settles nothing at all about its intrinsic value. Claims about nature's origin—whether they involve a deity or not—simply don't determine its value. The claim that the maker of the universe is to be found in the mountain gives us a reason to value the mountain only if we have a reason to value the places in which the maker resides. In order for a claim that we ought to value something to follow from other claims, these other claims must also include claims about what we should value. Ronald Dworkin makes the point nicely:

> There is no direct bridge from any story about the creation of the firmament, of the heavens and earth, or the animals of the sea and the land, of the delights of heaven, or the fires of hell, of the parting of any sea or the raising of dead, to the enduring value of friendship and family or the importance of charity or the sublimity of a sunset or the appropriateness of awe in the face of the universe....
>
> (Dworkin 2013: 25)

Ultimately, any argument that we should value nature can appeal only to arguments from within our normative concerns, not to empirical claims of its provenance.

We can't step outside of our normative concerns to attempt to justify one or all of them. When it comes to natural value, there will always be a logical normative gap between facts about an item's properties, whether intrinsic or relational, and our valuing of those properties. To take a familiar example within environmental ethics, the fact that an organism has a good of its own entails nothing about how we should act vis-à-vis it (Moellendorf

2014: 46). A claim about how we ought to value natural entities will have to be made from within a normative account; it can't be drawn from claims about their origin or their properties. If the mystic values the mountain because God is in it, then she must value God since the value of the mountain does not follow just from the claim that God is in it. An atheist appreciator of the mountain may simply value it for the pleasing properties she perceives.

The encyclical identifies "an excessive anthropocentrism" (116) as a fundamental cause of environmental problems. Indeed, this excess, according to the encyclical, is the source of a great many social problems:

> Neglecting to monitor the harm done to nature and the environmental impact of our decisions is only the most striking sign of a disregard for the message contained in the structures of nature itself. When we fail to acknowledge as part of reality the worth of a poor person, a human embryo, a person with disabilities – to offer just a few examples – it becomes difficult to hear the cry of nature itself; everything is connected. Once the human being declares independence from reality and behaves with absolute dominion, the very foundations of our life begin to crumble, for 'instead of carrying out his role as a cooperator with God in the work of creation, man sets himself up in place of God and thus ends up provoking a rebellion on the part of nature.'
>
> (117)

This is a confusing and deeply controversial set of claims without clear warrant. As I argued earlier, nothing follows about the weight of the valuable item from the claim that it is intrinsically valuable. Even if we should value something intrinsically, we may still have a reason in light of its instrumental disvalue to destroy it. In a world in which trade-offs must be made, even if we accept that an organism is intrinsically valuable, nothing follows all-things-considered about whether that organism should be preserved. Medical science surely depends upon, among other things, exercising a measure of dominion over nature. Through advances in medical science, we are capable of extending and improving human life far beyond what were once thought of as natural limits. We surely have not merited a rebellion by nature by seeking to exterminate or at least subdue deadly viruses and bacteria.

Appealing to non-anthropocentrism does not solve the problem of how to make trade-offs amongst what is valuable. On the contrary, the existence of a plurality of intrinsically valuable items, in addition to humans, raises the prospect of multiple conflicts. There is no short cut to employing careful moral reasoning about the relative weight of that which we value, when we cannot and should not preserve and care for everything that is valuable.

The passage above also errs in suggesting that "the structures of nature itself" can provide normative guidance for human relations. Tennyson observed that nature is "red in tooth and claw" (Tennyson 1849). And John Stuart Mill developed the point for purposes of moral argument:

> People who pride themselves on being able to read the Creator's purposes in his works ought to have seen in the animal kingdom grounds for inferences to conclusions that they hate. If there are any marks at all of special design in creation, one of the things most obviously designed is that a large proportion of all animals should spend their lives tormenting and devouring other animals. They have been well equipped with the instruments needed for that purpose; their strongest instincts push them towards it; and many of them seem to have been so constructed as to be incapable of supporting themselves by any other food.
>
> (Mill 1904)

Any appeal to the normative lessons to be found in "the structures of nature" will either have to overlook the immense suffering to be found in nature or endorse cruel forms of human interaction. Since neither option is tenable, such appeals are better left unmade.

The cry of the earth is a powerful way to think about ecological destruction. There is much to mourn. So many opportunities for human improvement lost, and so many items of wonder, awe, and delight destroyed. But deriding anthropocentrism is more a trope than a solution for the problems of practical deliberation. Certainly, no broad-based agreement can be derived from sectarian religious beliefs. To its credit, the encyclical seeks to go beyond that. Admirably, it seeks ecumenical dialogue. At some points, the encyclical engages, albeit incompletely, in a more promising kind of reasoning about values, such as in drawing a distinction between valuing things intrinsically and valuing them for human purposes. This is where practical deliberation might make progress independent of a sectarian basis. Valuing nature is distinct, however, from seeking normative guidance for human conduct in the structures of nature. No normative guidance can be found in the direction that the encyclical points, namely to nature itself.

The cry of humanity

The second cry recognized in the encyclical is the cry of humanity suffering under grinding poverty. Poverty is an assault on human dignity. The eradication of poverty is a morally mandatory aim of states and the global community. The encyclical admirably proclaims that environmentalism must be guided by a pro-poor agenda. It declares that, "a true ecological approach *always* becomes a social approach; it must integrate questions of justice in debates on the environment" (49). The encyclical continues by invoking the idea of an ecological debt that the global rich owe the global poor:

> A true 'ecological debt' exists, particularly between the global north and south, connected to commercial imbalances with effects on the

environment, and the disproportionate use of natural resources by certain countries over long periods of time...There is a pressing need to calculate the use of environmental space throughout the world for depositing gas residues which have been accumulating for two centuries and have created a situation which currently affects all the countries of the world.

(51)

Attempts to base climate diplomacy on precise metrics of allotted environmental space would likely be a diplomatic nightmare. Any metric would be hugely controversial and invite controversy and resistance. However, a less precise, but no less categorical, requirement that climate policy should safeguard the Right to Sustainable Development of developing and least developed countries is reasonable. And the reasons derive from the importance of energy in achieving poverty eradicating human development and from the capacity of industrialized countries to assume responsibility for a transition to a sustainable global economy without harming the well-being of their citizens.

Hundreds of millions of deaths due to the disease, malnutrition, and physical assaults that are associated with poverty are preventable. Recently, human development strategies in several East Asian countries have made significant progress in eradicating poverty. That progress is partially measurable by improvements in a state's Human Development Index (HDI), compiled by the United Nations Human Development Programme (UNDP). The HDI ranks states on a scale of 0–1. According to the UNDP, the HDI is "a summary measure of average achievement in key dimensions of human development: a long and healthy life, being knowledgeable and having a decent standard of living" (UNDP 2019. More precisely, the HDI of a country is the geometric mean of the following three measures: life expectancy at birth, per capita national income, and the combination of the mean years of schooling for adults and the expected years of schooling for children just starting school. The HDI groups countries into four quartiles, very high human development (0.800 and above), high human development (0.700–0.799), medium human development (0.550–0.699), and low human development (below 0.550) (UNDP 2018).

The Nobel Prize winning economist, Amartya Sen, argues for taking "development as a process of expanding the real freedoms that people enjoy" (Sen 1999: 36). The items measured by the HDI, according to this view, are constituents of human freedom. So, when a country makes progress with respect to the indices of education, income, and health, the citizens are substantively freer. Insofar as real freedom consists, not only in the absence of constraints on action but also the power to act, Sen's view that real freedom is enhanced by human development is highly plausible, but nonetheless incomplete. There may be value to health, income, and education apart from being constituents of freedom. For example, health is instrumentally valuable in the pursuit of valuable ends and meaningful projects. But it also seems valuable for its own sake. A person in confinement with very limited freedom and sharply restricted aims still has reason to value her health. Education is instrumentally valuable in pursuit of ends and projects. The knowledge that education yields serves to promote other values. But knowledge is also valuable for its own sake, regardless of the use to which it is put. By contrast, apart from being a constituent of human freedom, income is limited to instrumental value. Still a great deal of what we have reason to value in modern societies is traded for money. An increase in income for most people permits them to have more of what they value. In sum, the value of human development consists not only in the expansion of human freedom but also in the independently valuable increases in health, educational outcomes, and personal income.

The experience of the last several decades makes it clear that poverty reducing national development strategies involve huge increases in energy consumption. In 1990, China's Human Development level was low. China had an HDI of 0.499. By 2015, China's HDI had risen to the high category and was 0.738 (UNDP 2015). The developmental progress that occurred involved an eight-fold increase in per capita electricity consumption from 0.51 MWh/person to 4.05 MWh/person (IEA China). A similar story can be told for most other countries that have made significant Human Development gains. In 1991, Thailand's HDI was 0.574; by 2015, it had risen to 0.740, a less dramatic rise than China's but still impressive (UNDP 2015). Fueling the HDI improvement was an over three-fold increase in electricity consumption from 0.71 MWh/person to 2.62 MWh/person (IEA Thailand). More broadly, the International Energy Association (IEA 2012) has developed an Energy Development Index (EDI) composed of the following four measures: the percentage of the population with access to electricity and per capita residential consumption, the percentage of modern fuels (excluding electricity in residential fuel consumption, per capita public sector electricity consumption, and the percentage of economic activities in the total final consumption. Each factor is scored on a 0–1 scale, and the EDI is the arithmetic mean of all four (IEA 2012). That scale is devised for ease of comparison with the HDI. And, comparison reveals a strong correlation between HDI value and EDI value (IEA 2012, 547).The evidence is strong that massive increases in energy consumption accompany the promotion of human development and the eradication of poverty.

Human development uses electricity, and the main means by which electricity is generated is through the burning of fossil fuels. Nearly 40% of all electricity currently produced in the world comes by way of burning coal, around 15% by natural gas, and about 5% by oil. It's not surprising then that countries making significant human development gains in the last several decades have also seen a significant increase in fossil fuel consumption and CO_2 emissions. China's per capita CO_2 emissions rose from 1.83 tons in 1990 to 6.59 tons in 2015 (IEA). In Thailand over that same time period emissions rose from 1.43 tons per person to 3.64 (IEA). For countries seeking to make poverty eradicating developmental gains, the use of fossil fuels has been especially attractive.

The experience of the end of the twentieth century and the beginning of the twenty-first century suggests that the pursuit of intelligent national development strategies can make significant human development gains. That experience also makes clear that human development uses massive amounts of energy. Schools, hospitals, and industrial employment all require energy. Human development requires not only intelligent national development strategies but also an international context in which there is reliable access to inexpensive forms of energy.

One plausible interpretation of the "ecological debt" that the encyclical speaks of has to do with the importance of the international context for access to inexpensive forms of energy. The idea is that responsibility for achieving the pressing aim of transitioning to a zero carbon global economy in a matter of decades should be assigned primarily to highly developed countries. They are moral debtors and developing and least developed countries are the moral creditors regarding climate change policy (Moellendorf 2011, 2014). This idea is partially captured in Article 3, Paragraph 4 of the United Nations Framework Convention on Climate Change.

> The Parties have a right to, and should, promote sustainable development. Policies and measures to protect the climate system against human-induced change should be appropriate for the specific conditions of each Party and should be integrated with national development programs, taking into account that economic development is essential for adopting measures to address climate change.

The Right to Sustainable Development can be understood as a claim that developing and least developed countries have on highly developed ones to construct or maintain an international institutional and policy arrangement in which developing and least developed states do not have their prospect for pursuing policies of human development diminished.

In the context of climate change mitigation, such a claim is particularly important. Any successful mitigation policy will require rapid transition to global net zero emissions, by mid-century if warming is to be limited to 1.5°C, and only a couple of decades later to limit warming to 2°C. To effect such a transition, an increase in the cost of fossil fuels in comparison to renewable energy must occur. The energy market is more and more taking care of that as the price of renewable energy falls. Still, in many cases, policy measures will be required to increase the comparative costs of fossil fuels. These will include ending subsidies for and putting a price on fossil fuels. Doing so risks driving up the absolute costs of energy, thereby slowing human development. So, a mitigation regime that respects the Right to Sustainable Development will protect the human development prospects of developing and least developed countries by maintaining access to inexpensive forms of energy. This can include a slower schedule for the phase out of fossil fuels, allowing time for renewable energy technology to mature. But it may also need to include subsidizing the purchase of renewable energy and the development of renewable energy generation facilities in developing and least developed countries because these countries must also transition away from the use of fossil fuels.

The Right to Sustainable Development can be plausibly interpreted as an account of the moral creditors in the context of climate change policy. If developing and least developed countries are the creditors, the debtors are most highly developed countries. Their debt derives from their special capacities to pursue accelerated emissions reductions, to develop and employ carbon dioxide removal technologies, and to subsidize the purchase and development of renewable energy in developing and least developed countries. What is special about their capacity to pursue these aims is that they can do so without diminishing the well-being of their citizenry. Hence, the account of the moral debtors that fits with the understanding of the creditors, as expressed in the above interpretation of the Right to Sustainable Development, is based on the capacity of highly developed countries to assume primary responsibility for climate change without damaging the morally mandatory project of eradicating global poverty.

The account of the rights of developing and least developed countries and the responsibility of highly developed countries that I am defending seems consistent with the claims of the encyclical:

> We must continue to be aware that, regarding climate change, there are *differentiated responsibilities*. As the United States bishops have said, greater attention must be given to 'the needs of the poor, the weak and the vulnerable, in a debate often dominated by more powerful interests'. We need to strengthen the conviction that we are one single human family. There are no frontiers or barriers, political or social, behind which we can hide, still less is there room for the globalization of indifference.
>
> (52)

Taking seriously the Right to Sustainable Development as a constraint on international climate change policy, and holding highly developed states as primarily responsible as a result of the constraint, is one way that climate policy can recognize that "we are one single human family."

Climate change is a problem of global scope, and addressing it appropriately requires international cooperation. Fairness in cooperative burden sharing requires that parties not be made to sacrifice something of fundamental moral importance in order that other parties can be relieved of sacrificing something comparatively far less important. Involuntary poverty is an assault on human dignity and is something that everyone has reason to avoid (Moellendorf 2014). And, the exacerbation of severe poverty is one of the most fundamental threats posed to humans by climate change. Insofar as everyone has reason to avoid such poverty, reasonable agreement that policy should seek to avoid it is possible (Moellendorf 2014). A policy to address climate change that would prevent states from pursuing poverty eradicating human development would be unreasonable. That is one reason to take seriously the Right to Sustainable Development (Moellendorf 2011, 2014). And it is in light of that right that the encyclical's claim that "a true ecological approach *always* becomes a social approach" seems correct.

Prospects for reconciliation

The encyclical seems to suggest the possibility of a kind of reconciliation between humanity and nature.

> Men and women have constantly intervened in nature, but for a long time this meant being in tune with and respecting the possibilities offered by the things themselves. It was a matter of receiving what nature itself allowed, as if from its own hand. Now, by contrast, we are the ones to lay our hands on things, attempting to extract everything possible from them while frequently ignoring or forgetting the reality in front of us. Human beings and material objects no longer extend a friendly hand to one another; the relationship has become confrontational.
>
> (106)

This passage seems to advocate an alternative to a "confrontational" relationship to nature that involves "being in tune" with it and "receiving what nature itself allows." Still, the passage also seems to allow that such harmony with nature is fully consistent with intervening in it.

The encyclical's suggestion for reconciliation is too vague to offer any practical guidance. The view seems to allow interventions in the natural order of things. It explicitly refuses to categorically reject genetically modified crops, seeking instead a case-by-case evaluation (133). And surely modern medicine is not ruled out. But when do our practices stop being a matter of receiving what nature allows and begin to be confrontational? Is eradicating a virus a matter of merely receiving what nature allows or is it being confrontational? If eradication is not confrontational, then it's unclear what would be. But if eradication of a virus is confrontational and nonetheless allowed, then the distinguishing criterion of permissible from impermissible intervention cannot be whether the intervention is confrontational. Hence, there is no clear and plausible criterion for living in tune with nature suggested in the passage.

Humans survive and thrive by transforming nature into habitable environments. And a criterion of being in tune with nature is incapable of guiding our transformative work. Human development proceeds only by massively transforming the natural environment. Humans are certainly not the only species that transform nature into habitable environments, but we have the capacity to do it much more extensively than other species, and making development progress seems to require us to do so. Wilson, with the insight that only a biologist can have, offers a vivid account of how drastic the impact of human development is on the planet:

> Human demographic success has brought the world to the crisis of biodiversity. Human beings—mammals of the 50 kilogram weight class and members of a group, the primates, otherwise noted for scarcity— have become a hundred times more numerous than any other land animal of comparative size in the history of life. By every conceivable measure, humanity is ecologically abnormal. Our species appropriates between 20 and 40 percent of the solar energy captured in organic material by land plants. There is no way that we can draw upon the resources of the planet to such a degree without drastically reducing the state of most other species.
>
> (Wilson 1992: 272)

If this picture of things is basically accurate, then living in tune with nature is simply not a plausible normative criterion for judging human development efforts.

If there is to be some kind of re-calibrating of our thinking about human development efforts in light of damage to the natural environment, it should not be based on a norm of living in tune with nature. A more plausible idea would be to proceed as if the intrinsic value of nature mattered, as surely it does. This is not to suggest any precise limits or constraints to development. One thing seems clear: we should not think that the only way to value the loss of biodiversity that occurs is in terms of a loss in the services that ecosystems provide humans.

Compare valuing nature to valuing art. If we were to wonder whether it makes sense to stop maintaining masterpieces of art we would certainly not think that question is answered by the amount of revenue that can be gained from maintaining them. There may be circumstances in which people might have to make such decisions simply on financial grounds, but surely these circumstances are regrettable. And the circumstances are regrettable because in deciding on that basis we are not fully considering the value of the art allowed to deteriorate. If a masterpiece of art has intrinsic value, then any valuation of it solely in terms of the artwork's promotion of human well-being is a mis-valuation of it. For the intrinsic value that it has is precisely its value apart from the promotion of other valuable matters.

There is also no reason to suppose that the intrinsic value of natural items or systems can be given an accurate monetary value (Moellendorf 2017). Money is the common denominator of items that have use value to human beings. But a comparison of the intrinsic value of natural items or systems with use values to humans along the metric of money seems to miss the point of valuing nature intrinsically. Karl Marx made this point rather more pointedly: "The view of nature that has obtained under the dominion of private property and money is the actual despising and degrading of nature" (Marx 1977: 60). Even if the reality of limited budgets forces us to decide how much we are willing to spend to preserve an intrinsically valuable item, our willingness-to-spend is not necessarily the metric according to which the value of the item is measured. Our willingness-to-spend is influenced by factors that have nothing to do with the properties of the item. It is influenced by how much money is available, by the opportunity costs of spending, and so on. None of these considerations speak to valuable properties of the item.

Suppose that human development required destroying masterpieces of art. We would have reasons to regret the loss of value involved and we would seek ways to minimize it. Certain guidelines, such as the following, would seem reasonable: Seek development projects that are least costly in artistic terms; seek projects that preserve genres of art as much as possible; seek to maintain variety; seek not to cause destruction that has widespread knock on effects. We cannot capture well relationships of mutuality and predation by analogy to art, but some pieces might lose much of their significance as pieces of art if other pieces which they reference or cite are destroyed. Urgency may force us in some circumstances to make development decisions neglecting all of the above considerations and thinking only about financial costs, but certainly that would be regrettable and ordinarily not in keeping with valuing the masterpieces intrinsically.

The analogy offered above does not suppose that we have moral duties to the works of art. Rather, it supposes that care and maintenance are appropriate responses to the intrinsic aesthetic value of masterpieces. Likewise with nature, we need not suppose we owe anything to species for us to have good reasons in light of their intrinsic value to preserve them. And if in fact we do not owe anything to species, human development necessary to eradicate poverty may continue without conflicting moral duties, as long as it is appropriately constrained. Just as we would fail to value great works of art appropriately if we were to destroy them without following guidelines similar to the ones I mentioned, so would our destruction of natural items constitute a failure to respond appropriately to their value if we did not follow analogous guidelines. We have good reasons deriving from the treasure of intrinsic value in nature to seek means of development that are least damaging.

One objection to the position I am defending might be developed along the following lines. If we could take the perspective of the global planner of human development, she would always have a reason based in the moral duty to eradicate poverty to direct funding toward development, even at the regrettable cost of not securing funding to preserve natural value and indeed of permitting projects that destroy such value. Proceeding in this way would eventually destroy all natural value. Hence, the view that I am defending offers no secure defense of the conservation of nature. Indeed, it seems to turn a deaf ear to the cry of nature.

The objection, I think, fails for two main reasons. First, not all human development is morally mandatory. Once the blight of poverty is eradicated, I doubt that there is such a weighty reason to continue to pursue human development. The specter of a case for development without end seems illusory. Second, practically we cannot adopt the perspective suggested above, and the fact that we are not in that position can affect our reasons to act. The practical question will always be limited in scope. Should we proceed with this particular development project or some one of several other possible projects? There won't be a global accounting, but only an accounting based on some limited set of possible projects. And when choosing from that set, the evidence of prospective loss of intrinsic value can play a role in addressing the question of which to choose. Within a budget applied only to a limited set of choices, there may be good reason to make the more expensive choice that preserves natural value because the money that would be saved by pursuing the less expensive choice would not be deployed to pursue some other development projects in any case. My first response assumes the terms of the objection and argues that the conclusion does not in any case follow. My second response denies that for practical purposes we find ourselves in a circumstance relevantly similar to one envisaged by the objection. Taken together, I think that these responses undercut the force of the objection.

Concluding remarks

Laudato Si' is offered in the spirit of dialogue. Pope Francis admirably makes an appeal for "a new dialogue about how we are shaping the future of our planet" (14). My chapter is offered in the same spirit. But my response is quite limited, and there are many interesting points of discussion that I simply could not address. For example, I say nothing at all about the document's rejection of a "culture of relativism" (123), or its condemnation of "the technological paradigm" (108). Nor do I address any of the controversies in the text that are relevant to Christian theology. The encyclical is a rich and complex document. No single response can do it justice. Mine is one of many pieces in this volume that attempts to engage with the encyclical, and each of these responses, being modest in length, will select just a small number of passages to which to respond. No response can presume to judge the encyclical in its entirety. By engaging with the chapters of this volume, the reader may, however, develop a broader understanding of the encyclical than any one of these chapters offers.

I praise the encyclical for maintaining that environmental problems must be addressed as social problems, and in particular must be considered in relationship to the urgent moral demand to eradicate poverty. But in asserting that both the earth and humanity are crying out under the weight of environmental problems, the encyclical does not reduce the value of nature to its value for human beings. The document asserts the intrinsic value of natural items and systems. I argue that there are good reasons to agree. But the encyclical is more optimistic about reconciliation between the projects of poverty eradication and living in tune with nature than I think we should be. Human development is destructive of natural value, yet eradicating poverty requires that we pursue development. Taking seriously the intrinsic value of natural items and systems requires us to think carefully about how to proceed. Without presuming to offer detailed practical advice, I suggest that thinking about the kinds of trade-offs that might be made in preserving masterpieces of art provides some guidance in that regard.

References

Carter, Alan. "Biodiversity and All that Jazz." *Philosophy and Phenomenological Research* 80 (2010): 58–75.

Dworkin, Ronald D. *Religion without God* (Cambridge, MA: Harvard University Press, 2013).

IEA. International Energy Agency. "World Energy Outlook." 2012. www.iea.org/publications/freepublications/publication/WEO2012_free.pdf

IEA China. International Energy Agency. China Indicators. www.iea.org/statistics/statisticssearch/report/?country=CHINA&product=indicators&year=2015

IEA Thailand. International Energy Agency. Thailand Indicators. www.iea.org/statistics/statisticssearch/report/?country=THAILAND&product=indicators&year=2015

Marx, Karl. "*On the Jewish Question*." In David McLellan, ed. *Karl Marx: Selected Writings* (Oxford: Oxford University Press, 1977): 39–62.

Mill, John Stuart. "On Nature." In *Nature, The Utility of Religion, and Theism* (London: The Rationalist Press Association, 1904). www.marxists.org/reference/archive/mill-john-stuart/1874/nature.htm.

Moellendorf, Darrel. "The Right to Sustainable Development." *The Monist* 94 (2011): 433–452.

Moellendorf, Darrel. *The Moral Challenge of Dangerous Climate Change: Values, Poverty, and Policy* (Cambridge: Cambridge University Press, 2014).

Moellendorf, Darrel. "Progress, Destruction, and the Anthropocene." *Social Philosophy and Policy* 34 (2017): 66–88.

Sen, Amartya. *Development as Freedom.* (New York: Alfred Knopf, 1999).

Tennyson, Alfred. "In Memoriam A.H.H." 1849. www.online-literature.com/tennyson/718/

UNDP. United Nations Development Programme, Human Development Data (1990–2015). 2015. http://hdr.undp.org/en/data

UNDP. Human Development Indicators and Indices 2018 Statistical Update: Reader's Guide. 2018. http://hdr.undp.org/en/content/human-development-indicators-and-indices-2018-statistical-update-readers-guide

UNDP. Human Development Index. 2019. http://hdr.undp.org/en/content/human-development-index-hdi

Wilson, Edward O. *The Diversity of Life* (Cambridge, MA: Harvard University Press, 1992).

5 *Laudato Si'* and population

Herman Daly[1]

Introduction

As a Christian of Protestant persuasion, I first viewed Pope Francis as a breath of fresh air in the stuffy Vatican, but little more. After reading *Laudato Si'*, I dare to hope that what I considered merely "fresh air" could actually be the wind of Pentecost filling the Church anew with the Spirit. At a minimum, he has given us a more truthful, informed, and courageous analysis of the environmental and moral crisis than have our secular political leaders. For that reason, I am reluctant to find any fault with this inspiring and generous document. Nevertheless, in the spirit of invited frank dialogue, I think consistency with its basic themes of creation care and justice requires that more attention be given to population growth and its consequences.

Actually, the question of population is conspicuous by its near absence. In an earlier offhand remark, however, Francis said that Catholics don't need to breed "like rabbits," and pointed to the Church's doctrine of responsible parenthood. Perhaps he will follow up on that in a future encyclical. In any case, most lay Catholics in the United States have for some time stopped listening to Popes on contraception. The main references to population in *Laudato Si'* characterized birth control and immigration control as largely excuses for neglecting distributive justice in combating poverty (50). Granted that not all motives are totally pure, might it not also be true that birth control and immigration control are nevertheless necessary policies in the service of justice and creation care? I think that they are.

John T. Noonan, Jr.'s classic book, *Contraception* (Noonan 1986), sorts out the history of Church doctrine on this issue. Noonan demonstrates the lack of a biblical basis for opposition to contraception, as well as the origins of relevant Church doctrine in secular Roman law, which was absorbed into canon law. The ancient Roman meaning of "proletariat" was "the lowest class, poor and exempt from taxes, and useful to the republic mainly for the procreation of children." Clearly, contraception was not indicated for them, although tolerated for patricians. This literal meaning of proletariat as the "prolific" class was lost when Marx redefined the word to mean "non owners of the means of production." But the Roman-Malthusian connection with overpopulation and proliferation of cheap labor has remained real in modern times, even if sometimes denied and always minimized by Marxists as well as Catholics (Daly 1971).

Creation care and justice

The big ideas of the encyclical are creation care and justice, and the failure of our technocratic growth economy to provide either. That is a lot for one document. I understand the wisdom of not trying to do too much at once, of leaving population for later. But it is now later, and time to include population in the larger context of stewardship and "integral ecology" addressed by *Laudato Si'*.

Francis's voice is of course not the first to come from Christians in defense of creation. In addition to his ancient namesake from Assisi, Francis also recognized Ecumenical Patriarch Bartholomew of the Eastern Orthodox Church, who has for two decades now been organizing conferences and speaking out in defense of rivers and oceans, including the Black Sea. The Orthodox Church lost a generation of believers to atheistic communism, but is gaining back many young people attracted to the theology of creation and the actions it inspires. Protestants do not have a single voice, but many theologians, including Jurgen Moltmann and process theologian John B. Cobb, Jr., have long emphasized care of creation and related it to justice. Also some biologists, such as Calvin DeWitt, have a long history of urging stewardship both on their fellow Christians and biologists (See, e.g., DeWitt 2016; also Cafaro 2015). This theology of creation should not be confused with the evolution-denying, anti-science views of some Christian biblical literalists (confusingly called "creationists" rather than "literalists").

Mankind's duty to care for creation, through which humans have evolved to reflect at least the faint image of their Creator, conflicts headlong with the current dominant idolatry of growthism. The idea of duty to care for creation also conflicts with the materialist determinism of neo-Darwinist fundamentalists who see "creation" as the random result of multiplying infinitesimal probabilities by an infinite number of trials. The policy implication of such stochastic determinism is that purposeful policy is illusory, both practically and morally. Creation care is also incompatible with the big lie that sharing the earth's limited resources is unnecessary because economic growth will make us all rich. Francis calls this magical thinking. He skates fairly close to the idea of steady-state economics, of qualitative development without quantitative growth in physical scale of the economy, although this concept is not specifically elaborated. Consider his paragraph 193:

> In any event, if in some cases sustainable development were to involve new forms of growth, then in other cases, given the insatiable and irresponsible growth produced over many decades, we need also to think of containing growth by setting some reasonable limits and even retracing our steps before it is too late. We know how unsustainable is the

behaviour of those who constantly consume and destroy, while others are not yet able to live in a way worthy of their human dignity. That is why the time has come to accept decreased growth in some parts of the world, in order to provide resources for other places to experience healthy growth.

In the last sentence, "decreased growth" seems an inexact English translation from the Spanish "decrecimiento," or the Italian "decrescita" (likely the original languages of the document), which should be translated as "negative growth," or "degrowth," which is, of course, much stronger than "decreased growth." Growth of the human footprint that displaces other parts of God's creation is measured by total resource use (the metabolic entropic flow from depletion to pollution), which of course is the product of per capita resource use times population. Creation care, limiting the human footprint, requires serious attention to both factors. It is incomplete without consideration of population growth, both by natural increase and by net immigration.

The spatial boundaries across which we measure migration, and within which we measure natural increase (or decrease) are principally nation-states. For some purposes, it is the natural increase in the globe as a whole that is most relevant, and we can neglect migration, both international and "inter-planetary," even though the latter (e.g., terraforming Mars), while non-existent, is hailed by some as the future solution to overpopulation. Since populations have spatial boundaries (as well as temporal boundaries to be considered later), it is useful at the outset to digress a bit on the critical concept of boundaries. This is all the more necessary when population is viewed in the overall context of globalization, since "populations" of consumer goods and capital equipment also are born and die within nations, and while "alive" migrate (are traded) across national boundaries.

On borders and boundaries in economic life

John Lennon asked us to imagine a world without boundaries, singing wistfully "imagine there's no countries," and we all know what he meant—a world of human solidarity, peace, and cooperation. Conflicts and war usually involve disputes over borders. So why not just get rid of these troublesome boundaries? Let's have globalization—deregulated trade, capital mobility, and migration—only let's bless them each with the adjective "free" rather than "deregulated." Neoclassical economists assure us that this will lead to peace and prosperity among rational utility-maximizing individuals, minimally governed by a benevolent World Democracy, dedicated to the post-modern values of secularist materialism, eloquently communicated in Esperanto. This vision has its serious appeal to many, but not so much to me, as the reader will by now have guessed. I will try to present the anomalies of this cosmopolitan globalism, arguing that it is really individualism writ large—corporate feudalism in a global commons. Economic and political boundaries are necessary to achieve both national community and a global federation of national communities living in peace and ecological sustainability. Boundaries are also presupposed by the Catholic social doctrine of subsidiarity, advocated in *Laudato Si'*.

Boundaries are both biologically and logically necessary. Skin and membranes are organic boundaries. Within-skin versus outside-skin is a basic boundary condition for life. The skin boundary must be permeable, but not too permeable. If nothing enters or exits the organism, it will soon die. If everything enters and exits, then the organism is already dead and decaying. Life requires boundaries that are neither completely closed nor completely open. A nation's borders are in many ways very different from the skin of an organism, yet neither permits complete closure nor complete openness. Both must be qualitatively and quantitatively selective in what they admit and expel, if their separate existence is to continue rather than be dissolved entropically into its environment.

Logically, boundaries imply both inclusion and exclusion. A world without boundaries includes everything and is often therefore thought to be warm and friendly. But "everything" must include the cold and the unfriendly as well, or it is not everything. Also, without boundaries, B can be both A and non-A, which makes definition, contradiction, and analytical reasoning impossible. So both life and logical thinking require boundaries. While "a world without boundaries" may be a poetic expression of a desired unity, and while it is possible to reason dialectically with overlapping boundaries, it is a major delusion to think that boundaries are not necessary.

It is understandable, yet ironic, that the most fundamental and dramatic boundary of all—that separating the earth from outer space—made clear in the iconic photo of the earth from the moon—seems to have led to a reaction against the very concept of boundaries on our spherical planet, since it is so obviously one whole and unified thing. Yet that beautiful and powerful vision of overall unity hides a world of diversity and difference. And we live on the earth, within that complex living diversity, not on the dead moon with no need for life-defining boundaries.

Natural increase in population

If I can manage to live for a few more years, world population will have quadrupled during my lifetime (from two to eight billion). I doubt that any previous birth cohort has experienced a fourfold increase, or that any future one will either. Birth rates are now below replacement levels in some countries, but remain high in others. The world still adds over 70 million new people each year. Malthus blamed poverty on excessive population; Marx blamed it on exploitation via monopoly ownership of the means of production. Both were right, at least in part (Daly 1971). The policy advocated by modern economists, however, is neither to limit population nor even to end exploitation of labor but rather to buy diminished class conflict by exploiting nature more (economic growth) and labor less. In large part, fossil fuel slaves have replaced wage slaves. And technological advance has enabled the growing scale of exploitation of nature, while to a lesser degree diminishing its intensity. Modernization has now begun to reduce the birth rate, after first having caused the death rate to plummet bringing on the post-World War II population explosion.

Taking the above as a more or less correct picture of where we are now, what should be our policy for the future regarding population growth? And how should it fit with the rest of *Laudato Si*'?

Broadly speaking, the options are: laissez faire (trust providence, or the demographic transition,); or enact policies (either voluntary or coercive) to reduce the birth rate. Both have been done. For example, post-World War II Japan lowered its birth rate by voluntary means, although social pressure to limit births was very strong. It was nevertheless from the bottom up, not top down. The Chinese, after Mao, enacted the top down coercive one-child policy, which significantly reduced the birth rate, although recently they have eased restrictions. Neither Japan nor China has permitted much immigration. My only point here is that policies can, and have, reduced the population growth rate. Also in some countries the demographic transition has led to an "automatic" or "providential" reduction in births without an explicit policy on population.

The historical and traditionally Catholic view is to trust providence, trust God to decide the number of children one is blessed to have. As mentioned earlier, Catholic doctrine also advocates responsible parenthood, which recognizes the need to limit births, but objects to use of the most effective methods of contraception on the grounds of their "artificiality." The traditional position was reaffirmed in Pope Paul VI's *Humanae Vitae,* which was and remains controversial.

I experienced this controversy, and associated reality, while teaching economics in Northeast Brazil in 1968, the year of that encyclical. At that time, population growth in this poorest region of Brazil was very high. Lower class completed fertility was around eight, and upper class was around four, a large differential fertility by class (Daly 1970). The upper class had access to contraceptives and relevant education, the lower class largely did not. Demographic pressure and frequent droughts resulted in considerable outmigration to the rest of Brazil. Both the overall growth rate and the class differential have declined greatly since 1968, and contraceptives are now available on open display in supermarkets, unlike 1968.

There was at the time a heated debate in Northeast Brazil about birth control as a part of development policy. Opposition came from a curious alliance of traditional Catholics, the Oligarchy, Marxists, and Nationalists. The Oligarchy was interested in cheap labor and renewing its supply, the Marxists wanted a revolution ("one more hungry child today is one more guerilla fighter tomorrow" was a slogan), and the Nationalists simply believed that more Brazilians were needed to strengthen Brazil, and to settle and develop the Amazon before foreigners could occupy it. The advocacy of birth control (voluntary family planning) as a social policy for Brazil came from the Brazilian organization *Bemestar Familiar,* as well as some international aid agencies.

Although the traditional Catholic position was made clear in *Humanae Vitae*, the rank and file parish priests of Northeast Brazil varied in their counsel to parishioners. For example, a priest of my acquaintance told me that the overwhelming problem that his parishioners confided to him in confession was their desire and attempt to limit births. For the poor who already had four children, more were an unwelcome burden both on parents, especially the mother, and existing children. This priest definitely counseled responsible parenthood and did not make a big deal out of using condoms. I hoped then that one day he would be Pope, but 50 years later, that has not happened. And one understands why—such a reversal would be seen as a betrayal to millions of older faithful and obedient Catholics, even if a doctrinal correction and liberation for millions of younger ones.

Populations of things relative to people

The population problem should be considered from the point of view of *all* populations—populations of both us humans and our things (cars, houses, livestock, crops, cell phones, etc.)—in short, populations of all "dissipative structures" engendered, bred, or built by humans. Both human bodies and artifacts wear out and die. The populations of all organs that support human life, and the enjoyment thereof, require a metabolic throughput to counteract entropy and remain in an organized quasi-steady-state. All of these organs are capital equipment that support our lives. Endosomatic (within skin) capital—heart, lungs, kidneys—supports our lives quite directly. Exosomatic (outside skin) capital supports our lives indirectly, and consists both of natural capital (e.g., photosynthesizing plants, structures comprising the hydrologic cycle), and manmade capital (e.g., farms, factories, electric grids).

In a physical sense, the final product of the economic activity of converting nature into ourselves and our stuff, and then using up or wearing out what we have made, is waste.[2] Ultimately, that is our "ecological footprint." What keeps this from being an idiotic activity—depleting and polluting, grinding up the world into waste—is the fact that all these populations of dissipative structures have the common purpose of supporting the maintenance and enjoyment of life. As John Ruskin said, "there is no wealth but life," an insight fully in accord with *Laudato Si'*.

Ownership of endosomatic organs is equally distributed among individuals (absent slavery) while the ownership of exosomatic organs is not, a fact giving rise to social conflict. Control of these external organs may be democratic or dictatorial. Our lungs are of little value without the complementary natural capital of green plants and atmospheric stocks of oxygen. Owning one's own kidneys is not enough to support one's life if one does not have access to water from rivers, lakes, or rain, either because of scarcity or monopoly ownership of the complementary exosomatic organ. Therefore, all life-supporting organs, including natural capital, form a unity with a common function, regardless of whether they are located within the boundary of human skin or outside that boundary. This resonates with Francis's Chapter 4 on "integral ecology."

Our standard of living is traditionally measured by the ratio of manmade capital to human beings—that is, the ratio of one kind of dissipative structure to another kind. Human bodies are made and maintained overwhelmingly from renewable resources, while capital equipment relies heavily on nonrenewable resources as well. The rate of evolutionary change of endosomatic organs is exceedingly slow; the rate of change of exosomatic organs has become very rapid. In fact the collective evolution of the human species is now overwhelmingly centered on exosomatic organs. We fly in airplanes and rockets, not with wings of our own. This exosomatic evolution is goal-directed, not random. Its driving purpose has become "economic growth," and that growth has been achieved largely by the depletion of the earth's resources and pollution of its spaces.

Although human evolution is now decidedly purpose-driven, we continue to be enthralled by neo-Darwinist aversion to teleology and devotion to random processes. Economic growth, by promising more for everyone, becomes the *de facto* purpose, the social glue that keeps things from falling apart. But what happens when growth becomes uneconomic, when it begins to increase environmental and social costs faster than production benefits? How do we know that this is not already the case? Studies suggest that it is.[3] If one asks such questions, as Pope Francis is doing, one is usually told to talk about something else, like space colonies on Mars, or unlimited energy from cold fusion, or geo-engineering, or the wonders of globalization, and to remember that all these glorious purposes require growth, in order to provide still more growth in the future. Growth is the *summum bonum*—end of discussion! *Laudato Si'* exposes the idolatry of this vision.

In the light of these considerations, let us reconsider the idea of demographic transition. By definition, this is the transition from a human population maintained by high birth rates equal to high death rates, to one maintained by low birth rates equal to low death rates, and consequently from a population with low average lifetimes to one with high average lifetimes. Statistically, such transitions have often been observed as standard of living increases. Many studies have attempted to explain this correlation, and much hope has been invested in it as an automatic cure for overpopulation. "Development is the best contraceptive" is a related slogan, partly based in fact, and partly in wishful thinking.

There are a couple of thoughts I'd like to add to the discussion of demographic transition. The first and most obvious one is that populations of artifacts can undergo an analogous transition from high rates of production and depreciation to low ones. The lower rates will maintain a constant population of longer-lived, more durable artifacts. Our economy has a gross domestic product (GDP)-oriented focus on maximizing production flows (birth rates of artifacts) that keeps us in the pre-transition mode, giving rise to low product lifetimes, planned obsolescence, and high resource throughput, with consequent environmental destruction. The transition from a high maintenance throughput to a low one applies to both human and artifact populations independently. From an environmental perspective, lower throughput per unit of stock (longer human and product lifetimes) is desirable in both cases, at least up to some distant limit.

The second thought I would like to add is a question: does the human demographic transition, when induced by a rising standard of living,[4] as usually assumed, increase or decrease the total load of all dissipative structures on the environment? Specifically, if Indian fertility is to fall to the Swedish level, must Indian per capita possession of artifacts (standard of living) rise to the Swedish level? If so, would this not likely increase the total load (ecological footprint) of all dissipative structures on the Indian environment, perhaps beyond capacity to sustain the required throughput?

The point of this speculation is to suggest that "solving" the population problem by relying on the demographic transition to lower birth rates could impose a larger burden on the environment, rather than the smaller burden hoped for.[5] Of course, indirect reduction in fertility by automatic correlation with rising standard of living is politically easy, while direct fertility reduction (by voluntary family planning) is politically more difficult. But what is politically easy may be environmentally ineffective.

Population's temporal boundaries and new creation

It might help fit population into *Laudato Si'* to proclaim loudly at the outset that more people (and other creatures) are better than fewer—but only if they are not all alive at the same time! Sustainability means longevity for creation—more people, in the company of other creatures, enjoying a sufficient level of consumption for a good life over more generations—not more simultaneously living high-consuming people elbowing each other, and God's other creatures,[6] off the planet. Nor does it mean a perpetual sequence of generations. Nothing is forever in the present creation—both science and Christianity agree on that, and perhaps other religions do as well. Christianity hopes for a New Creation free from death, sin, and decay. Science is not in the business of hope, although scientism preaches technological Gnosticism—escape from this world through the acquisition of esoteric knowledge leading to the "Singularity." I share the Christian hope, but also accept the scientific description of the present creation and its subjugation to entropy and finitude. As creatures of the present creation we must do the best we can with what we have for however long it lasts, even while we hope for the New Creation as an eschatological faith. (See 100; see also Polkinghorne 2003; Moltmann 2012; Bauckham 2015.)

If our ethical understanding of the value of longevity ("sustainability") is to maximize cumulative lives ever to be lived, subject to a per capita consumption level sufficient for a good life, then we must limit the load we place on the Earth at any one time to avoid degrading the regenerative and absorptive capacities of nature. Fewer people, and lower per capita resource consumption, facilitated by more equitable distribution today, mean more, and more abundant lives for a longer, but not infinite, future. There is no point in maximizing the cumulative number of lives lived in misery, so the qualification "sufficient for a good life" is important, and requires deep rethinking of economics, a shift of focus from consumerist growthism to an ethic of sufficiency, which is explicitly called for by Francis.

Given that the whole present creation is still going to end sometime, why make extraordinary efforts to prolong it, especially if, as the modern intelligentsia assures us, the universe and all life are just random events, as well as temporary? And unless random events can have a conscious idea of what a good life is, then we cannot say how much per capita consumption is sufficient for a good life. Nevertheless, many good people, regardless of their materialist determinism, gratefully and dutifully work hard to preserve creation, even though it is not clear what could elicit their gratitude, energy, and sense of duty. And strangely some theists evidently feel no sense of duty or gratitude even though they would presumably know where to direct it if they felt it.[7] But for some of us gratitude and duty are directed to the Creator and the promise of a transformed New Creation. Like the present creation, the New Creation will be a miracle. It is anticipatory, responding to the lure of objective value from the future. It gives hope in the face of entropy, evil, and finitude, but does not solve our ethical problem of how to share the limited life support capacity of the present creation among the presently living, future generations, and other species. These considerations seem to me to be in accord with the spirit of *Laudato Si'*, although not explicitly addressed.

Belief that the end of the world will occur soon, with lots of life-support capacity left unused ("wasted"), is a tenet of some fundamentalist Christians who consequently consider themselves exempt from the responsibility of creation stewardship. Fortunately, this view seems to be waning, and does not accord at all with Francis's views.

Most scientists will not be happy with talk about miracles and hope in the New Creation. Yet when faced with the ultimate heat death of the universe, and the meaninglessness implicit (and increasingly explicit) in their materialist cosmology, some scientists seem to flinch, and look for optimism somewhere within their materialism. They invent the hypothesis of infinitely many (unobservable) universes in which life may outlive our universe. They were led to this extraordinary idea in order to escape the implications of the anthropic principle—which argues that for life to have come about by chance in our single universe would require far too many just-so coincidences. To preserve the idea of chance as plausible cause, and thereby escape any notion of Creator, they argue that although these coincidences are indeed overwhelmingly improbable in a single universe, they would surely happen if there were infinitely many universes. And of course our universe is obviously the one in which the improbable events all happened. If you don't believe that Shakespeare wrote Hamlet, you can claim that infinitely many monkeys pecking away at infinitely many typewriters had to hit upon it someday.

Such a metaphysics of chance precludes explanation of some basic facts: first, that there is something rather than nothing; second, the just-right physical "coincidences" set forth in the anthropic principle; third, the "spontaneous generation" of first life from inanimate matter before evolution can get started; fourth, the creation of an incredible amount of specified information in the genome of all the irreducibly complex living creatures that grew from the relatively simple information in the first living thing (random change destroys rather than creates information); fifth, the emergence of self-consciousness and rational thought itself (if my thoughts are ultimately the product of random change, why believe any of them, including this one?); and sixth, the innate human perception of right and wrong, of good and bad, which would be meaningless in a purely material world. Explaining these facts "by chance" strains credulity even more than "by miracle."

If purpose is causative, if creation is not merely random, if our reason is capable of understanding its order, and if we can distinguish good from evil—all premises of *Laudato Si'*—then policy, including population policy, seems both a possibility and a duty.

Migration of populations

Global population growth is of course entirely due to natural increase, and migration would hardly be the problem that it is today if the quadrupling of human numbers within one recent lifetime had not brought us from a relatively empty to a relatively full world. However, in the United States, Western Europe, and Canada, recent population growth is mainly due to net immigration, and higher average fertility of immigrants. Curiously, migration used to be the politically safe subject in demographic policy, while natality (birth control) was the most controversial area. That order now seems reversed, though both areas of policy remain important. So it is hard to evade the increasingly difficult and divisive issue of immigration in discussing population policy.

Francis says little about migration, although he explicitly calls for migration control in paragraph 175. While it is clear that he would favor a generous immigration policy, especially for refugees, it is also clear that he rejects open borders. Furthermore, in paragraph 177, he says "individual states can no longer ignore their responsibility for planning, coordination, oversight, and enforcement within their respective borders." Without effective borders responsibility for what happens within them would disappear. Indeed, why would any nation undertake to limit its natural increase if the benefits of such limitation could be canceled by unlimited immigration? Or if the costs of its own population growth could be exported by unlimited emigration? Open borders would stimulate natural increase in the global population. With open borders, the consequences of each nation's reproductive behavior would, via migration, be externalized to the world as a whole, rather than internalized to itself where it would cause a change in behavior—the individualistic tragedy of the open access commons writ large.

There are three fundamental philosophical divergences that contribute to political disagreements regarding border control. Without claiming to have a solution, I would at least like to stop avoiding the issue and try to face its underlying problems in an effort to understand why immigration policy is so contentious.

First, there are differing visions of world community.[8] Some people think that a world without borders is the key to universal peace. Others think that it is the short road to post-national corporate feudalism in a global commons. Count me as sympathetic to the latter view, but with the stipulation that the road to true global community is through the UN model of a federation of loosely interdependent trading nations. The alternative to be avoided is the World Trade Organization (WTO) model of tightly integrated national economies into a single global economy, by free trade, free capital mobility, and free migration, dissolving national communities rather than federating them into a global "community of communities." In the WTO model of global economic integration, local autonomy at the national and sub-national level is replaced either by the centralized control of a world government or by unregulated corporate fiefdoms. Neither alternative is appealing nor consistent with subsidiarity. But that is how I see things. Others will rightly remind me of the dangers of nationalism, and the catastrophe of two world wars and threats of another, and will argue that anything that weakens the nation-state is probably a good idea. Even though I am skeptical of globalism, it is very clear that a federated international "community of communities" requires significant relaxation of national sovereignty in the specific areas of arms control and climate change. These have so far proved a more than sufficient challenge to our limited capacity for international cooperation, and require our focused effort.

A second philosophical divide is the ethical divergence between deontologists and consequentialists, illustrated some years ago in Garrett Hardin's agonizing parable of "lifeboat ethics" (Hardin 1974; see also Hardin 1971). It demonstrates a social trap. Shipwrecked passengers on an already full lifeboat face the dilemma of what to do about other survivors still in the water trying to board. Helping everyone board will overload and sink the lifeboat—no one is favored but everyone drowns (complete justice, but complete disaster, says the consequentialist). Keeping some out is unjust—survival of some at the sacrifice of others, and therefore absolutely wrong (says the deontologist). Once we are in the trap, there is no acceptable way out—a classic tragedy. The lesson of the parable is that we must by all means avoid the trap in the first place—provide more lifeboats on the ship, take fewer passengers on each cruise, and go more slowly through safer passages. That is what a steady-state economy seeks to do. The drowning of people on overloaded boats in the Mediterranean witnessed on the TV news every day underlines the tragic prescience of Hardin's parable.

The difficulty with deontology is that in its devotion to absolute rules of rightness, it is sometimes blind to foreseeable evil consequences. The difficulty with consequentialism is that it can be wrong in its prediction of consequences, especially if they are complex or far in the future. It can also be blind to the absolute nature of certain moral prohibitions.[9]

A third philosophical divide is the conception of people either as isolated individuals, or as persons-in-community. Are we independently defined atomistic individuals related to each other only externally? Or is our personal identity itself constituted by internal relations in community? For the individualist (most economists), external relations, largely mediated by the market, are basic. Consequently, labor mobility and free migration, along with free trade and free capital mobility, are favored policies. But these policies abstract from relations in community, provided by families, places, nations, traditions, religious communities, language, culture—relations that largely define our identity as persons. The focus of immigration policy is usually on costs and benefits to migrants as individuals. But there are also social costs and benefits to migration. The social benefit of cultural diversity is real, but its cost in terms of disunity is also real. Two other social costs are often underestimated—the cost of migration to the receiving community of absorbing the new members (both economically and culturally) and the cost to the sending community of losing mainly its younger and more capable members. For individualism, the costs and benefits to the individual migrant dominate the social costs and benefits. The person-in-community view opposes excessive individualism, but courts the opposite danger of shading into an identity politics that argues not from universal principles, but from the particular history of a specific group with which one personally identifies or sympathizes.

While deep philosophical disagreement on these three issues underlies much of the political fight over migration, there is still basic agreement that the rich have a duty to help the poor, and that includes poor migrants. The question remains, how best to do it—to try to help them repair their failing country of origin, or to abandon the failing country and help them immigrate into a more successful country? Those left behind in the failing country (too old, or too ill, or too needed by others to be able to leave) merit help as well as those capable of migrating. And when the young and capable flee, it is harder to rebuild a failing country. Also, the poor, homeless, or unemployed in the receiving country, who will have to compete for jobs and social services with the new immigrants, should not so easily be written off by cosmopolitan elites as "nativists" or "racists" when they object to mass immigration, any more than all Muslim immigrants should be written off as probable terrorists.

Ultimately, we all must all play the hand that we are dealt by fate, and at least initially bloom where we were planted. We do not choose our parents, our generation, or our genetic inheritance any more than we chose our original nationality. However, we can modify nationality by migration. That, however, does not make migration the solution to the fundamental unfairness of the world. Individual or small-scale migration is not a problem. Mass migration is a different matter. It may be inevitable in a bloody revolution. But like a revolution, or a natural disaster, it reshuffles the entire deck, altering the hands previously dealt, by changing risks, wages, property values, and prices. Every relative price change in land, labor, and capital caused by mass migration entails both winners and losers throughout the whole population. Whether that will make the world more just, or simply more uncertain, with a new set of arbitrarily determined winners and losers, is a question with no clear answer.

The Marshall Plan and Care packages after World War II, along with refugee resettlement, and the future possibility of limiting our ecological footprint to provide space for others, offer a better model for generosity than open border mass migration. That at least is my judgment, and I think it is consistent with *Laudato Si'*, although not explicitly considered therein.

All peoples need to think honestly and clearly about these difficult questions. A first step toward clear and honest thinking is to insist on distinguishing legal from illegal immigrants, and economic migrants from refugees. Lumping them all together as "immigrants" and then referring to any policy of border control or selectivity as "nativism" or "bigotry" is unhelpful, unfair, and unrealistic. A second step is to better distinguish winners and losers resulting from past mass immigration, and to share the costs and benefits more equitably between them.

A third, and most important step, is to realize that the growth economy in the United States and other countries, protected by militarism, is contributing to wars over remaining resources and ecological space, and will increase the numbers of people displaced by war and by ecological destruction. The growth strategy of the "bigger pie"—more things for more people—will just lead to a larger ecological and social disaster. In the empty world of two billion people into which I was born, along with Pope Francis, one could share the growth optimism of most economists. But in today's full world of over seven billion, it is time to stop whistling in the dark. GDP growth (so-called economic growth) can no longer substitute for living within, and equitably sharing, the limited carrying capacity of creation. This is in the spirit of *Laudato Si'*. And erasing national borders, while it has some appeal, unfortunately leads to the tragedy of open access commons, which is a bad way to share—an issue not explicitly recognized in the encyclical.

Further political conflicts in immigration policy

Some will think that I am attacking a straw man, because, they will say, no sensible person really advocates open borders. They simply advocate, it will be said, "more generous levels of immigration, and a reasonable amnesty for existing illegal immigrants." I agree that in the United States some form of conditional amnesty is indeed necessary as the lesser evil, given the impasse created by past non-enforcement of our immigration laws. Deporting 12 million long-settled residents is too drastic and would create more injustices than it would rectify. But unless we enforce immigration laws in the future, there will soon be need for another amnesty (the first, often forgotten, was in 1986), and then another — a *de facto* open-borders policy. Nevertheless, the policy of open borders should be fairly discussed (and voted on in a national referendum?), not only because some people explicitly advocate it but also because many others implicitly accept it by virtue of their unwillingness to face the alternative.

Pope Francis diplomatically avoided specific consideration of the immigration policies of different countries. However, a serious discussion of open borders should recognize that every country in the world has a policy of limiting immigration. Emigration is often considered a human right, but immigration requires the permission of the receiving country. Some countries allow many legal immigrants (e.g., the United States, Canada). Others allow few (e.g., Japan, China). Would open borders be good for Japan, or Germany, or Greece, or for an independent Catalonia, if that should come about? Do any political parties in member countries advocate open borders for the European Union with respect to the rest of the world? Should the areas of the Amazon reserved for indigenous people be open to free immigration? Should Bhutan, bordered by the world's two most populous countries and trying to preserve its culture and ecosystems, declare a policy of open borders? Should national parks and wildlife reserves be opened in the name of free immigration?

There are also arguments about the emigration side of open borders — even if emigration is a human right, is it unconditional? Might "brain-drain" emigrants have some obligation to contribute something to the community that educated and invested in them, before they emigrate to greener pastures?

Immigrants are people, and they deserve to be well treated; immigration is a policy, and it deserves reasoned discussion in the public interest. It seems that neither expectation is fulfilled, perhaps partly because the world has moved from largely empty to quite full in only one lifetime, and because some politicians and journalists pejoratively label anyone opposing a policy of open borders as "anti-immigrant."

It is undeniable, as frequently repeated, that historically the United States is a country of immigrants. The near genocide of Native Americans is treated in popular US culture as an unfortunate collateral effect of celebrated European immigration. And the cheap-labor legacy of slavery (involuntary immigration) has not yet disappeared. Whether that immigration history dictates that in the future the United States should welcome large numbers of immigrants is another very different question, and is now much debated, especially the de facto cheap-labor policy of implicitly "welcoming" illegal immigrants. Working-class resentment against elitist cheap-labor policies, including automation, off-shoring, lax enforcement of our immigration laws, as well as wage-lowering H-1B visas for skilled workers, contributed strongly to the angry, divisive, and unfortunate results of the 2016 presidential election.

In a relatively empty world, with an empty continent (neglecting again the Native Americans) free immigration was reasonable. But we now live in a full world, much of which is at war and so ecologically ravaged by uneconomic growth that it cannot support its existing population, much less further growth. Should the United States continue to welcome the poor and displaced of the world as generously inscribed on the Statue of Liberty? All of the poor of the world, or only some? How many? Which ones? Do the poor and unemployed citizens in our own country have a say in those decisions, or only the employing class? How can these decisions be made democratically? As suggested earlier, would not a new Marshall Plan plus Care packages along with refugee resettlement, as after World War II, help more people while hurting fewer than would the mass migration implicit in open-borders globalization? Should we not at least discuss this alternative?

Many Americans, including me, think that the heirs of conquest and slavery deserve priority in the US job market over new immigrants, especially illegal immigrants. Likewise for the many Americans of all races living in poverty. Some other Americans, unfortunately, seem to feel that if we can't have slaves, then the next best thing is abundant cheap labor, guaranteed by lax enforcement of our immigration laws, off-shoring of jobs, and automation.

We have in the United States a strong cheap-labor lobby that uses immigration (especially illegal immigration) to force down wages and break labor unions, as well as weaken labor safety standards. This is less the fault of the immigrants than of our own elite employing class and pandering politicians. The immigration issue in the United States is largely an internal class battle between labor and capital, with immigrants as pawns in the conflict. Class division is more basic than the racial and ethnic divide in current US immigration politics, although the latter is certainly not absent. Mass immigration is not the only cheap-labor policy. There is also especially off-shoring of jobs (mistakenly labeled free trade). And there is automation. Automation is in effect a cheap-labor policy because it renders labor redundant. But it also lightens the burden of labor and increases the potential for leisure. Nevertheless, until we have a principle of distribution beyond income-through-jobs (e.g., a universal basic income), the role of automation and Artificial Intelligence will be to continue to cheapen labor and increase income inequality. An older cheap-labor policy, considered earlier, was restricted availability of birth control to the working class. The stated aim was often to protect the morals of the public by, for example, prohibiting the sending of birth control information through the US Mail. It was mainly the working class who lacked contraceptive information. The remaining laws to this effect (the Comstock Laws in Massachusetts and Connecticut) were only repealed in the 1960s and 1970s. Today birth control information is available, but employers can (for religious reasons) opt out of covering contraceptives in employee health plans. Instead of trying to exonerate one factor by blaming the others, we should recognize that all are cheap-labor policies that serve upper class interests, even if sometimes clouded by other motivations. They cannot be considered part of any "preferential option for the poor" preached in Catholic social doctrine, including *Laudato Si'*.

The United States is also a country of law, as well as a country of immigrants. Illegal immigration falls outside the rule of law, and renders moot all related policy deliberations about balancing interests for the common good. It is hardly democratic to refuse to enforce democratically enacted immigration laws, even though the laws could be improved, and even though difficult individual cases arise, as with any law. Humane provisions for difficult cases must be worked out: for example, children brought here illegally by their parents 20 years ago should not be deported to what is for them a foreign country for something beyond their control. We have judges to deal with difficult cases, as well as statutes of limitation regarding the time period within which certain laws must be enforced, and this principle could be applied to immigration laws. The DREAM (Development, Relief and Education for Alien Minors) Act and DACA (Deferred Action for Childhood Arrivals) are movements in this direction. However, complete amnesty for illegal immigrants would further the larger trend toward impunity, and it is unfair to, and resented by, many legal immigrants who have obeyed our immigration laws. One could, with complete reason and consistency, vote to increase our legal immigration quota, and at the same time favor stricter enforcement of our laws against illegal immigration.

Surely our immigration laws could be improved. Indeed, the 1995 US Commission on Immigration Reform, chaired by the late Texas Congresswoman and civil rights champion, Barbara Jordan, made a good start, but was ignored for reasons already suggested. Her commission called for lower legal immigration quotas, stricter family reunification criteria, and enhanced border control, as well as stricter sanctions against employers of illegal immigrants. The last embraced the caveat that ethnic profiling would likely result without a secure national identification system, since employers are not able to adjudicate false documents. A secure identification system would of course make it easier to identify illegal immigrants and is often opposed by open-borders advocates and libertarians. The present Congress should build on the good work of the Jordan Commission, but they seem to have forgotten it. However, the recent Cotton-Purdue bill revives it in part—but has little chance of rational discussion, much less improvement, given the polarized, personalized, and politically toxic atmosphere currently surrounding immigration policy.

In developed countries, immigration boosters are especially interested in opening borders to young workers to help cover social security shortfalls resulting from the older age structure caused by slower natural population growth. The cheap-labor lobby is joined by the cheap-retirement lobby. Apparently, the immigrants are expected to die or go home as soon as they reach retirement age and would start receiving rather than paying into social security. Also, while working they are expected to boost fertility and population growth sufficiently to postpone the necessity of raising the retirement age or lowering benefits. Population growth as a social security policy is expected, indeed required, to continue indefinitely in Ponzi scheme fashion.

Conclusion

Laudato Si' clearly identifies the driving cause of the global environmental crisis as a growthist economic system out of control, careless of both the destruction of nature and the unmet needs of the poor. Francis asks us to rethink our fundamental priorities in search of a truer understanding of the purpose of economic life:

> For new models of progress to arise, there is a need to change models of global development; this will entail a responsible reflection on the meaning of the economy and its goals with an eye to correcting its malfunctions and misapplications. It is not enough to balance, in the medium term, the protection of nature with financial gain, or the preservation of the environment with progress. Halfway measures simply delay the inevitable disaster. Put simply, it is a matter of redefining our notion of progress....
>
> (194)

It is easier to pretend that there is no conflict between growth and care of creation—that unlimited "economic" growth can support an ever-growing and ever-migrating population of people and their products, as long as prices are correct. The idea of a steady-state, sustainable, economy goes out the window, and the idolatry of growthism is reaffirmed as the "win-win" option that it might have been in the empty world of the past, but cannot be in the full world of the present.[10] If the United States, or any country, could just set an example of how to live justly and sustainably within its ecological limits (i.e., take *Laudato Si'* seriously), that would be a splendid contribution to the care of creation and peace on Earth. Given such a good national example, migration to and from the exemplary country could help spread its good policies, as could simple observation of its customs and laws.

Notes

1 Emeritus Professor, School of Public Policy, University of Maryland. The author is grateful to Professor Robert McKim for helpful suggestions.

2 See Nicholas Georgescu-Roegen 1971. "Waste" is too neutral a term. In fact annual production of goods that accumulate into a stock of wealth requires the joint production of "bads" that accumulate into a stock of "illth." The negative terms are absent from the indexes of economics textbooks, and unsubtracted in national accounts.

3 Index of Sustainable Economic Welfare, Genuine Progress Indicator, Global Footprint, See also H. Daly, "Economics for a Full World," www.greattransition. org/publication/economics-for-a-full-world. More recently the Lancet medical journal (NYT, October 19, 2017) finds that the financial costs from pollution are some $4.6 trillion annually, about 6.2% of the global economy. If annual growth in Gross World Product is around 2.2%, and cost due to pollution is 6.2%, then with reasonable accounting we would have a net financial decline of some 4% annually. If that financial decline represents welfare loss, and it surely does since we are talking about reduced health and life expectancy, then the benefits of production growth are being more than canceled out by the costs of the pollution generated by that growth. In other words, so-called "economic" growth has become uneconomic at the present margin. So far that seems to have escaped the notice of most economists!

4 An earlier writer (Carver 1924: 34) defined standard of living as "the number of desires that take precedence in the individual choice over the effective desire for offspring," thus anticipating the basic idea of the demographic transition.

5 This is an empirical question. Is fertility being reduced to make room mainly for cars and refrigerators, or for parks and leisure?

6 Both Pope Francis and his namesake express a love for God's non-human creatures. Although "you are worth more than many sparrows" (Matt. 10:31), it follows that a sparrow's worth cannot be zero, and further, "Are not five sparrows sold for two cents? Yet not one of them is forgotten before God" (Luke 12:6). Maximizing cumulative numbers over time applies to populations of all living creatures, including sparrows, but does not tell us how much of the ecosphere's carrying capacity should be reserved for non-human creatures. Naturalist E. O. Wilson has recently suggested one half as a somewhat arbitrary preliminary answer. One suspects that Francis's answer would be "more than at present." However, one also surely expects that Francis takes seriously the statement that a human is worth more than many sparrows. How many sparrows he wisely declines to speculate. Francis would buy more ecological space for sparrows by reducing luxury consumption by humans, not by limiting human numbers. One can agree on that as a first step (*pace* demographic transition advocates), but eventually growth in cumulative numbers of even frugal humans means fewer cumulative sparrows, and vice versa. Environmentalists often value other species instrumentally according to their ecological services to mankind. In addition, there is the intrinsic value of other species, also affirmed by Francis (see paragraphs 140 and 90), as sentient creatures of God who presumably both suffer and enjoy their own lives to varying degrees. Intrinsic value is usually neglected by ecologists, but emphasized by humane societies. Humane societies lean toward deontology; ecologists toward consequentialism.

7 Indeed, some Evangelical Christians in the current Trump administration are a clear and present danger to creation.

8 For a helpful discussion, see Amstutz 2015.

9 While the main lesson of the parable remains to avoid the trap, the ethical question of what to do if you are actually in the trap also remains. For the strict

consequentialist, the answer seems to be just save as many lives as you can with the limited resources available. This is similar to the medical practice of triage—devote your scarce resources to those you are able to help, don't waste time either on those who will recover without your help, or on those who are hopeless cases. The overall principle is clear, and usually favors helping first those who are nearest, and whose situation you best understand. As the airlines say, "put on your own oxygen mask first before helping others." Some deontologists will consider this nationalistic or nativist, if their rule of right action is that everyone anywhere counts equally, and that any priorities are unjust. Regarding triage, the deontologist might reach the same practical conclusion as the consequentialist if his rule of right action is to "maximize total lives saved with limited resources." But if his rule is more absolute, for example, "never deny aid to any individual who needs it," then we have an unresolvable conflict—an implicit denial that resources are limited. Deontologists argue that the end does not justify the means. Consequentialists ask, if the end doesn't justify the means then what does? Absolute commandments, presumably. The Catholic Church's prohibition of artificial contraception seems deontological; its advocacy of responsible parenthood seems consequentialist. Francis does not resolve this venerable philosophical problem in *Laudato Si'*, and I certainly cannot. As an economist I lean in practice toward consequentialism, but recognize that for truly absolute values deontology should prevail. At a more general level, I believe that the economist's absolutist end of GDP growth is often considered a deontological commandment that trumps the consequential collateral damage of the ecological ruin of creation.

10 H. Daly, *From Uneconomic Growth to a Steady-State Economy*, Edward Elgar Publishing, 2014.

References

Amstutz, M. R. 2015. "Two Theories of Immigration". *First Things*, December.

Bauckham, R. 2015. *The Bible in the Contemporary World*. Grand Rapids, MI: Wm. B. Eerdmans Publishers.

Cafaro, P. 2015. "Conservation Biologists Have a Powerful New Ally". *Biological Conservation*, 191, 839–841.

Carver, T. N. 1924. *The Economy of Human Energy*. New York: MacMillan.

Daly, H. 1970. "The Population Question in Northeast Brazil: Its Economic and Ideological Dimensions". *Economic Development and Cultural Change*, July, 18 (4), 536–574.

Daly, H. 1971. "A Marxian-Malthusian View of Poverty and Development". *Population Studies*, (London School of Economics), March, 25 (1), 25–37.

DeWitt, C. 2016. "Earth Stewardship and *Laudato Si*". *The Quarterly Review of Biology*, September, 91 (3), 271–284.

Georgescu-Roegen, N. 1971. *The Entropy Law and the Economic Process*. Cambridge, MA: Harvard University Press.

Hardin, G. 1971. "Nobody Ever Dies of Overpopulation". *Science*, 12 February, 171 (3971), 527.

Hardin, G. 1974. "Commentary: Living on a Lifeboat". *BioScience*, 24 (10), 561–568.

Moltmann, J. 2012. *Ethics of Hope*. Minneapolis, MN: Fortress Press.

Noonan, J. T. Jr. 1986. *Contraception: A History of its Treatment by the Catholic Theologians and Canonists*. Cambridge, MA: Belknap Press.

Polkinghorne, J. 2003. *The God of Hope and the End of the World*. New Haven, CT: Yale University Press.

6 Rethinking our treatment of animals in light of *Laudato Si'*

David L. Clough

The encyclical *Laudato Si'* builds on and extends previous Roman Catholic church teaching on animals to affirm their value as beloved creatures of God and reject anthropocentric claims that they were created merely to provide for human needs. It draws on the Franciscan tradition to affirm other animals as our sisters and brothers, and notes that these relationships have implications for our treatment of animals. The encyclical fails to connect concern for other-than-human animals with critiques of industrial animal agriculture, however, which is an odd omission given its consideration of other practical issues such as the genetic manipulation of plant and animals, its express concern for biodiversity, and its call for an ecological conversion in the context of climate change. In this chapter, I begin by surveying the valuable framework the encyclical sets up for understanding the place of animals in Christian theology and ethics. I then describe how we are using animals for food today. Finally, I make the case that the encyclical's framework demands obvious and urgent changes in the way we make use of other animals for food.

What does the encyclical say about animals?

The most striking aspect of the understanding of animals in *Laudato Si'* is its deep grounding in a Franciscan account of our affective relationships with fellow creatures. This suggests that the Pope's decision to take the name "Francis" represented a profound theological commitment. The encyclical opens by recalling that St Francis of Assisi refers to the earth as mother and sister (1). A few paragraphs later, it recalls in more detail the way Francis would burst into praise after contemplating "the sun, moon, or the smallest of animals" communing with all creation. For Francis, "each and every creature was a sister united to him by bonds of affection," and for that reason "he felt called to care for all that exists" (11). This emphasis on affection and relationship is an ongoing theme in the encyclical: all creatures belong to God, which grounds the conviction that

> as part of the universe, called into being by one Father, all of us are linked by unseen bonds and together form a kind of universal family, a sublime communion which fills us with a sacred, affectionate and humble respect.

(89)

This communion is fully inclusive: "When our hearts are authentically open to universal communion, this sense of fraternity excludes nothing and no one" (92). Scriptural mandates about care for donkeys, oxen, mother birds and their young, and sabbath rest for domesticated animals show that biblical laws "dwell on relationships, not only among individuals but also with other living beings" (68). The bonds of affection joining humans with other creatures are rooted in their relationship with God: "Each organism, as a creature of God, is good and admirable in itself" (140). This extends even to the humblest of creatures:

> Every creature is thus the object of the Father's tenderness, who gives it its place in the world. Even the fleeting life of the least of beings is the object of his love, and in its few seconds of existence, God enfolds it with his affection.
>
> (77)

The encyclical does not flinch from the negative affections our relationship with other creatures provokes:

> This sister now cries out to us because of the harm we have inflicted on her by our irresponsible use and abuse of the goods with which God has endowed her. We have come to see ourselves as her lords and masters, entitled to plunder her at will. The violence present in our hearts, wounded by sin, is also reflected in the symptoms of sickness evident in the soil, in the water, in the air and in all forms of life. This is why the earth herself, burdened and laid waste, is among the most abandoned and maltreated of our poor; she 'groans in travail' (Rom 8:22). We have forgotten that we ourselves are dust of the earth (cf. Gen 2:7); our very bodies are made up of her elements, we breathe her air and we receive life and refreshment from her waters.
>
> (2)

This is a profound appreciation that the bonds of affection that unite us with other creatures cause us pain when we recognize that those we love are suffering at our hands. It is this relationship of love with all fellow creatures that shows us the wrongness of relating to nature as "masters, consumers, ruthless exploiters, [who are] unable to set limits on their immediate needs" and the need instead to take on the radical poverty of Francis, which was "a refusal to turn reality into an object simply to be used and controlled" (11).

The stern critique of "tyrannical anthropocentrism" in the encyclical is a second and closely related theme. It repeatedly affirms the need to reinterpret the Christian theological tradition in the context of the environmental crisis in which we find ourselves:

> Although it is true that we Christians have at times incorrectly interpreted the Scriptures, nowadays we must forcefully reject the notion

that our being created in God's image and given dominion over the earth justifies absolute domination over other creatures. The biblical texts are to be read in their context, with an appropriate hermeneutic, recognizing that they tell us to "till and keep" the garden of the world (cf. Gen 2:15).

(67)

A similar point is made later as part of the case that it is modern anthropocentrism alongside the technocratic paradigm that are the roots of the ecological crisis (Chapter 3, 101–136):

An inadequate presentation of Christian anthropology gave rise to a wrong understanding of the relationship between human beings and the world. Often, what was handed on was a Promethean vision of mastery over the world, which gave the impression that the protection of nature was something that only the faint-hearted cared about. Instead, our "dominion" over the universe should be understood more properly in the sense of responsible stewardship.

(116)

Modern anthropocentrism is a contradiction of recognition of creaturely bonds of affection: "Clearly, the Bible has no place for a tyrannical anthropocentrism unconcerned for other creatures" (68). The encyclical notes that the Roman Catholic Catechism "clearly and forcefully criticizes a distorted anthropocentrism" in stating that "[each] creature possesses its own particular goodness and perfection...Each of the various creatures, willed in its own being, reflects in its own way a ray of God's infinite wisdom and goodness." The encyclical also quotes the Catechism's recognition of the ethical implication of this teaching to "respect the particular goodness of every creature" and "avoid any disordered use of things" (69, quoting the Catechism of the Catholic Church, 339).

It is notable that the anthropocentrism the encyclical criticizes is of variously qualified kinds—"modern," "tyrannical," "distorted," "excessive," "misguided"—rather than anthropocentrism as such. Acceptable forms of anthropocentrism are not spelled out or defended, but the encyclical does seek to avoid its language about a universal communion between all creatures being interpreted as erasing differences in value between humans and other creatures: "This is not to put all living beings on the same level nor to deprive human beings of their unique worth and the tremendous responsibility it entails" (90). The encyclical also affirms the importance of keeping a concern for human well-being connected to concerns for other creatures:

A sense of deep communion with the rest of nature cannot be real if our hearts lack tenderness, compassion and concern for our fellow human beings. It is clearly inconsistent to combat trafficking in endangered species while remaining completely indifferent to human trafficking, unconcerned about the poor, or undertaking to destroy another human being deemed unwanted. This compromises the very meaning of our struggle for the sake of the environment.

(91)

The reference to unwanted humans connects Roman Catholic opposition to abortion to concern for animals, which is in accordance with the new consistent pro-life ethic argued for by a growing number of theologians (e.g., Camosy, 2013). The encyclical's linking of concern for vulnerable humans and animals is defensive at this point: questioning the validity of concern for animals that does not also oppose abortion. Like many Christian ethicists, I recognize that feminist concerns about the control of women's bodies need to be weighed heavily in considering the ethics of abortion. In most cases of the exploitation of animals, there is no parallel countervailing consideration. For that reason, I disagree with the position of the encyclical that approving abortion in any circumstances makes concern for animals inconsistent. The wider point, however, that concern for human well-being, the well-being of other animals, and the well-being of the environment as a whole need to be held together is welcome and important.

A third key theme in the treatment of animals in the encyclical is the affirmation of their place in the work of God in Jesus Christ and in Christian doctrines of redemption. The encyclical affirms that "the destiny of all creation is bound up with the mystery of Christ"; that the Johannine formula that "the Word became flesh" indicates that "one person of the trinity entered into the created cosmos, throwing in his lot with it, even to the cross"; and that therefore "particularly through the incarnation, the mystery of Christ is at work in a hidden manner in the natural world as a whole, without thereby impinging on its autonomy" (99). God's solidarity with creatures in the incarnation is closely connected to the inclusion of all creatures in God's redemptive purposes:

> The ultimate purpose of other creatures is not to be found in us. Rather, all creatures are moving forward with us and through us towards a common point of arrival, which is God, in that transcendent fullness where the risen Christ embraces and illumines all things. Human beings, endowed with intelligence and love, and drawn by the fullness of Christ, are called to lead all creatures back to their Creator.

(83)

To the best of my knowledge, this strong affirmation of the place of all creatures in God's redemptive purposes goes beyond previous papal teaching. In December 2014, the New York Times and other newspapers around the world reported that during a papal audience the Pope had told a distraught young boy whose dog had recently died that "[one] day, we will see our animals again in the eternity of Christ. Paradise is open to all of God's creatures." (Gladstone 2014) In fact, the story turned out to be an error and was subsequently corrected, but only a few months later, *Laudato Si'* affirmed a theology of redemption with a place for dogs alongside God's other creatures. There is no suggestion in the encyclical that the redemption of creatures other than the human is effected merely through the redemption of humans, or merely as species representatives rather than individuals, as some Christian accounts of redemption suggest. Instead, "all creatures" are being led with us "back to their Creator," suggesting that our bonds of affection with other-than-human creatures celebrated in the encyclical will be part of the new creation and children weeping over the loss of their companion animals can be reassured.

Laudato Si' can be recognized, therefore, as a striking new moment in church teaching not only in relation to the interconnections between human and environmental well-being but also in relation to animals. Its celebration of a Franciscan recognition of our affective bonds of kinship with fellow creatures, its rejection of presentations of Christianity legitimizing human domination over other animals, and its affirmation of the place of animals in God's work of redemption through Christ are each significant points of reference for considering the ethics of our treatment of animals. In the next section, I make the case that these commitments in the encyclical have obvious and urgent implications for changing the use Christians make of other animals for food.

How are we using other animals for food?

Humans make use of other animals in all kinds of ways. In Volume II of *On Animals*, treating theological ethics, I describe and evaluate the ways we make use of animals for clothing and textiles, for labor, for research experimentation, for sport and entertainment, as pets and companions, and the impacts of human activity on wild animals. The longest chapter in the book by some margin, however, is the one devoted to the use we make of other animals for food. This is because the number of animals used for this purpose is several orders of magnitude greater than those used for other purposes—between six and eight trillion per year on my estimates—because of the impoverished lives imposed on the vast majority of farmed animals and because of the wider impacts of human behavior on wild animals as well as humans and the environment. One illuminating perspective on the scope of our use of other animals for food comes from biomass estimates by Vaclav Smil (2011). By 1900, the combined biomass of all domesticated animals had grown to exceed the biomass of wild land mammals by 3.5 times. That was the result of a combination of big increases in livestock numbers, and big decreases in wild land animals, significantly driven by the need to make space for all those livestock: we displaced wild animals in order to make space for raising domesticated animals for food. In the following 100 years, a near quadrupling in the biomass of domesticated animals was a major factor in the halving of wild land mammal biomass so that by 2000, the biomass of domesticated animals was 24 times greater than that of all wild land mammals. Domesticated chickens alone are nearly three times the biomass of all wild birds. And in the same 100 years, we reduced numbers of fish in the oceans by 90% (Bar-On et al., 2018; Lotze & Worm, 2009). Raising livestock in these numbers is a major contributor to an anthropogenic mass extinction event comparable with those found in the geological record. If we continue on this trajectory, there will be virtually no wild animals to be concerned about. If we combine this with the realization of the cruelly impoverished lives we inflict on farmed animals, the vast majority of which are raised in unnatural and crowded industrial environments, we can see that our use of other animals for food is an obvious priority for our attention on grounds of scale, intensity, and impact.

Once we have seen that the human use of other animals for food has a priority claim on our attention, the next step is to examine our practice and its impacts. In the context of the encyclical's concern for thinking in a connected way about animal creatures, human welfare, and the environment, the remainder of this section will provide a survey of what we are doing in relation to these three categories.

Approximately 98%–99% of all animals killed for food are fish. About half of these are wild-caught, and half raised in intensive farms. Both are problematic: wild-caught fish suffer significantly in the capture process and over-fishing in many contexts has led to the literal decimation of populations, as well as the destruction of non-target species and sea beds. Farmed fish live in crowded and monotonous environments that subject them to increased risk of disease. Fish farming also contributes to the depletion of wild fish stocks because on average farmed fish are fed twice as much wild-caught fish. Chickens are the most numerously farmed animal, with 66 billion killed for meat in 2014 and a further eight billion used for eggs (Clough, 2019). The vast majority of these birds are raised in industrial broiler sheds or battery cages. Modern broiler chickens have had their bodies and physiology entirely reconfigured so they eat rapidly and reach slaughter weight in as little as 35 days. They are raised in huge warehouses with artificial day and night manipulated to optimize their growth, automated feeding and water, and human interaction reduced to carrying out the dead once or twice a day. As their bodies grow beyond the capacity of the legs to bear their weight they suffer significant pain, before being roughly crated for the journey to slaughter, where automated stunning techniques often fail to ensure they are unconscious before their throats are cut. Male chicks of laying strains of hens are useless to the industry, so are killed at a day old by being gassed, dropped live into a grinder, or just left to die in refuse sacks. Most laying hens live in small crowded battery cages for their 18 month laying life, before being slaughtered. Most ducks are raised for meat in similar intensive conditions, together with other poultry.

Pigs are the mammals most commonly killed for meat, with 1.5 billion slaughtered in 2014. The majority of these animals are also raised in industrial sheds with no opportunity for their preferred behaviors, such as rooting in the earth, and in environments so monotonous that their tails have to be docked to avoid them being chewed off by their fellow inmates. Rabbits are the next most numerous farmed animal, with nearly a billion killed in 2014, most of whom are raised in small cages. Sheep and goats are more commonly raised extensively outdoors, but intensive systems are growing in popularity for dairy production, and many sheep are now subjected to live export involving long journeys by road or on the decks of ships before facing uncertain welfare at slaughter. Intensive dairy facilities for cows are even more common. These cows never go outside or graze grass, are forcibly artificially inseminated, have their calves taken from them at birth, and are killed for beef when their milk productivity falls after three or four lactations on average. Beef cattle often do have access to the outdoors, but are now commonly fed grain rather than grass for at least part of their lives in bare feedlots to fatten them for slaughter.

The most direct human impacts of these novel ways of raising and killing animals are on the humans who work in the industry. They are subjected to high risks of physical and mental injury while working on fast-moving production lines with mechanized knives for low pay. Those who do these unattractive and dangerous jobs in most contexts are disproportionately women, members of ethnic minorities, and migrants. Raising animals as we are doing currently is also a problem for global food and water supplies: 78% of agricultural land is now devoted to animal agriculture and over a third of global cereal output is now fed to livestock, 92% of which is wasted in comparison to the nutrition that would be derived if humans consumed the grain directly. Producing one kg of beef requires 10–20 times the water required by producing the same calories from plant-based sources.

Industrial methods of raising animals are also raising threats from zoonotic diseases such as swine and bird flu that are likely to cause major human pandemics with high mortality rates. The antibiotics that must be fed to intensively farmed animals to control infections in their crowded environments are contributing to the growth of antibiotic-resistant bacterial strains that present a major challenge to the efficacy of basic modern medicine: 80% of antibiotics in the United States are fed to farmed animals. Finally, the current overconsumption of animal products in many developed nations is also causing dietary health problems, with increasing incidence of coronary heart disease, cancer, type 2 diabetes, and stroke.

Current patterns of raising farmed animals are also problematic for the environment. Farmed livestock are a major and growing contributor to greenhouse gas emissions, representing 14.5% of global emissions according to a 2013 United Nations estimate (Gerber et al., 2013). The intensive farming of animals also causes local environmental problems. Animal manure releases ammonia and discharge from the lagoons of excrement created by large pig farms and cattle feedlots often escapes into local water supplies causing pollution and bacterial poisoning.

On the basis of this short survey, it is readily apparent that the new patterns of raising animals intensively on an unprecedentedly large scale are causing very serious problems for farmed and wild animals, for human welfare, and for the environment. In the next and final section of this chapter, I consider the implications of viewing our current patterns of raising farmed animals through the lens of the encyclical's account of a Christian understanding of animals.

What are the implications of the encyclical for our use of animals for food?

In the first section of this chapter, I outlined three key features of *Laudato Si*'s discussion of animals: the celebration of our affective bonds of kinship with fellow creatures, the rejection of Christian teaching legitimizing human domination over other animals, and the affirmation of the place of animals in God's work of redemption. In the second section, I argued that the raising of animals for food was an obvious priority for attention, and then surveyed the ways in which modern industrial agriculture impacts on farmed and wild animals, humans, and the environment. In this final section, I argue that the encyclical's understanding of animals indicates the need for urgent changes in the rearing and consumption of animals that are left unaddressed by the encyclical.

The fundamental ethical question raised by the encyclical's discussion of animals is how we should we treat our kin, the sister and brother animal creatures *Laudato Si'* affirms as the object of God's loving care and who are moving with us to redemption in Christ. Given the multiplicity of our engagements with fellow animal creatures, the full answer to that question will be extensive and nuanced, but it is possible to identify some obvious and far-reaching conclusions on the basis of the major features of the use of animals for food surveyed above. Loving care for fellow animal creatures should mean a commitment to enabling their flourishing where we can, and certainly not subjecting them unnecessarily to impoverished lives and suffering. Industrialized animal agriculture very obviously fails to enable the flourishing of farmed animals, and very obviously subjects them unnecessarily to impoverished lives and suffering, as well as being a major contributor to the current mass extinction of wild animals. Raising other animals for food in this way cannot be justified in relation to human welfare because, as noted above, it is contrary to human interests as well: it exacerbates human food and water security by wasting a large proportion of global grain production and by using land and water resources inefficiently, subjects workers to high risks of physical and mental injury, and causes direct problems for human health. Sometimes, the exploitation of other animals for food has been justified on the basis of the need to feed a growing human population, but it is now clear for reasons noted above that raising and consuming animals as we are doing currently is an obstacle to such efforts. Modern animal agriculture is also damaging for the environment, contributing significantly to climate change and pollution. If *Laudato Si'* is right that Christians must reject the tyrannical anthropocentrism that ignores our affective bonds with sister and brother animals and recognizes that we need to attend to them alongside concern for human neighbors and the environment, Christians have obvious reason to resist the operations of industrialized animal agriculture.

Making the case that industrialized animal agriculture is both a very serious problem for humans, other animals, and the environment and at odds with the Christian vision of human relationships with fellow creatures outlined in *Laudato Si'* makes the encyclical's omission of any discussion of problems in our use of other animals for food notable. This is one of the most obvious examples of a practice exhibiting the unrestricted anthropocentrism and the lack of solidarity with our mother and sister earth and our sister and brother animal creatures that the encyclical rejects. Industrialized animal agriculture most clearly falls under the "irresponsible use and abuse of the goods with which God has endowed" the earth; most clearly contributes to "the symptoms of sickness evident in the soil, in the water, in the air and in all forms of life"; and most clearly leads to the groaning of creation (2). On the basis of the analysis of the encyclical, Christians have a clear imperative to reconsider their complicity with a practice that is damaging to fellow animal creatures, to human welfare, and the environment.

Unlike many other complex issues confronting us, the actions Christians should take on the basis of *Laudato Si'* in relation to the animals we use for food are clear: we need to (1) reduce consumption of animal products and (2) move to higher welfare sourcing for the remaining products.

Reducing consumption is the crucial first step for a wide range of reasons. It would allow improvements in farmed animal welfare that are impossible at current levels of production; reduce the land used for animal agriculture and therefore protect habitat for wild animals; improve human food and water security; reduce risks from zoonotic diseases and antibiotic resistance; and improve human dietary health. Individuals can contribute to reducing consumption in a variety of ways: such as eating animal products at fewer meals, or adopting a vegetarian or vegan diet. Corporately, Christians can act to reduce consumption by reconsidering the food served in churches or the food policies of other institutions informed by Christian values.

Moving to higher welfare sourcing of any animal products we continue to consume is a key second step. This will contribute to ensuring that farmed animals enjoy lives with more opportunity to flourish in the modes of life particular to them, which is fundamental to recognizing them, as the encyclical does, to be sister and brother creatures of the God Christians worship. This requires attention to the lives and deaths of the animals that are behind the products we consume. Labelling of products can help with such decisions by identifying for consumers products derived from animals that have been raised on pasture, allowed to range freely, and reared according to organic certification schemes, but even better is to get to know and support local farmers seeking to provide good lives for the animals in their care. Such products will be more expensive than the products of industrial animal agriculture because it is the cruel industrial systems that make them cheap, but in association with reducing overall consumption of animal products, eating less and better animal products need not be more expensive.

In the first section of this chapter, I made the case that *Laudato Si'* is an important new statement of a Christian understanding of our relationship with fellow animal creatures. It celebrates a Franciscan recognition of our affective bonds of kinship with fellow creatures, it rejects Christian teaching legitimizing human domination over other animals, and it affirms the place of animals in God's work of redemption in Jesus Christ. In the second section of the chapter, I set out the ways we are using animals for food currently, and the dire impacts of our practice for animals, humans, and the environment. In the third section, I argued that while the encyclical does not examine the implications of its theological account of animal creatures for modern industrial animal agriculture, this novel practice is a conspicuous example of the tyrannical anthropocentrism criticized by the encyclical and of the damage to our sister and brother creatures it condemns. As a result, Christians convinced by the encyclical to listen to the cries of the earth and her creatures have strong reasons urgently to rethink their practice by reducing their consumption of animal creatures and moving to higher welfare sources for animal products they continue to consume. In making such changes, Christians may participate in the ecological conversion for which the encyclical calls, and live into its vision of humans alongside other creatures as "a kind of universal family, a sublime communion which fills us with a sacred, affectionate and humble respect" (89).

References

Bar-On, Y. M., R. Phillips, and R. Milo. 2018. 'The Biomass Distribution on Earth'. *Proceedings of the National Academy of Sciences*, USA, 115 (25), 6506–6511.

Camosy, C. 2013. *For the Love of Animals: Christian Ethics, Consistent Action*. Cincinnati, OH: Franciscan Media.

Clough, D. 2019. *On Animals: Vol. II. Theological Ethics*. London: T&T Clark/Bloomsbury.

Gerber, P. J., H. Steinfeld, B. Henderson, A. Mottet, C. Opio, J. Dijkman, A. Falcucci, and G. Tempio. 2013. *Tackling Climate Change through Livestock: A Global Assessment of Emissions and Mitigation Opportunities*. Rome: Food and Agriculture Organization of the United Nations.

Gladstone, R. 2014. "Dogs in Heaven? Pope Francis Leaves Pearly Gates Open". *New York Times*, 11 December.

Lotze, H. K., and B. Worm. 2019. "Historical Baselines for Large Marine Animals". *Trends in Ecology and Evolution*. 24(5), 254–262.

Smil, V. 2011. "Harvesting the Biosphere: The Human Impact". *Population and Development Review*. 37(4), 613–636.

7 "We were nowhere. We've got somewhere." Does *Laudato Si'* go far enough, and is the Church on board for the climate journey?

Paddy Woodworth

…without serious reflection and education at an individual and community level Laudato Si' will be ineffective, because what is called for here will involve massive changes.

(McDonagh 2017: 26)

…the most one can expect is superficial rhetoric, sporadic acts of philanthropy and perfunctory expressions of concern for the environment.

(*Laudato Si'* 54)

Laudato Si' offers much of value to all who share concerns about the multiple environmental crises threatening our world. So I'm painfully aware that it may seem ungracious for any environmentalist, and especially for an agnostic brought up in a different faith tradition to the Pope's, to offer a critique that highlights its shortcomings. And it seems all the more ungracious after listening to the patently authentic passion and gratitude with which Catholic environmentalists talk about this encyclical. They say it has opened doors to eco-strategies within the Church, doors they had long found firmly closed. They also say that it has given the Church a front-row seat at national and international environmental policy-making, where it had hitherto often been conspicuous by its absence or by its silence.

There is a purely pragmatic reason, too, not to sound critical notes: they may be exploited by the enemies of environmentalism. At a moment when some of the most powerful figures in world politics are aggressively rejecting the counsel of scientists regarding climate change and biodiversity loss, it may appear irresponsible to give anything less than an unqualified welcome to this very remarkable document.

It comes, after all, from the leader of a vast and influential global human community, and it gives a ringing and comprehensive endorsement to cutting edge climate and environmental science. It unequivocally accepts the scale and urgency of both the climate change and biodiversity loss crises. It recognizes the evidence that these phenomena are largely the result of human activity and are driven by our current economic and social models. It repeatedly suggests that radical changes are required in these models, and in our individual lifestyles, to cope with these crises.

In the words of the veteran Catholic environmental campaigner, Fr Sean McDonagh: "In this short document Pope Francis has moved the Catholic Church from the periphery of global engagement with ecology to the very heart of the debate" (Pope Francis and McDonagh 2016: xiii).

It comes at a moment, too, when so many Christians in the resurgent "evangelical" movement, especially in Latin America and the United States, are overtly anti-science, and often endorse reckless consumption because of their belief that the acquisition of wealth is a sign of God's grace. They preach that humanity has an unqualified right to exploit planetary resources, regardless of ecological limits. So it is certainly good to hear a Pope accepting the suite of environmental analyses that perhaps find most comprehensive expression in the Earth Charter,[1] a document cited prominently in his text (207), and going on to challenge, at least at a theoretical level, the ideology of consumerism and unlimited "growth" that drives our political economies.

Moreover, environmentalists of all faiths, and of none, will recognize and share the encyclical's palpable sense of distress about the state of our world: "God has joined us so closely to the world around us that we can feel the desertification of the soil almost as a physical ailment, and the extinction of a species as a painful disfigurement" (90). This is an echo, surely, of Aldo Leopold's troubling insight that "One of the penalties of an ecological education is that one lives alone in a world of wounds" (Leopold 1993: 165).

It is also very welcome that the Pope consistently highlights the links between the issues of environmental degradation, social injustice, and personal well-being. He asserts correctly that each of these problems can be solved only if the others are attended to at the same time. The encyclical is thoroughly imbued with this key insight, far too often missed by many environmentalists: "the bond... between concern for nature, justice for the poor, commitment to society, and interior peace" is "inseparable" (10). If President Macron had read these passages in the encyclical, he might not have so insensitively sparked off a popular uprising in 2018 with a measure designed to mitigate climate change. The *gilets jaunes* protests are a response to a carbon tax that hits the French working poor much harder than it hits the fossil fuel corporations. This mis-step feeds the very powerful disinformation machines of those corporations, which propagate the notion that climate change activists are a comfortable elite, happy to destroy working-class jobs.

In addition, environmentalists must welcome Pope Francis's repeated insistence that all creatures exist in connection with each other, the core point of Chapter 4, "Integral Ecology." This reflects the central principle of the science of ecology.

The encyclical also contains passages of great beauty, clearly emanating from a deep compassion for all human beings, an awe at the wonder of the natural world, and a recognition of our personal links to particular places. One does not have to share the Pope's religious faith in order to appreciate his deep reverence and love for what he calls "Creation" and what an agnostic like myself calls "Nature":

> Soil, water, mountains: everything is, as it were, a caress of God. The history of our friendship with God is always linked to particular places which take on an intensely personal meaning; we all remember places, and revisiting those memories does us much good. Anyone who has grown up in the hills or used to sit by the spring to drink, or played outdoors in the neighbourhood square; going back to these places is a chance to recover something of their true selves.
>
> (84)

What's not to like, then, in this remarkable document, if you are concerned about the environment, social justice, and human happiness? Quite a lot, in my view.

And I think it is appropriate to say this here, despite the reservations I have expressed above. After all, Pope Francis appeals directly for "a new dialogue about how we are shaping the future of our planet" (12), and also addresses this appeal not just to the faithful, but to "all people of goodwill" (62). So I believe it shows both the encyclical and its author the respect they deserve if I set out what I see as its deficiencies. In summary, my biggest concern lies in the Pope's failure to issue sufficiently clear calls to specific actions, when he addresses the resolution of the crises he describes so well. Above all, I want to point out that the encyclical fails to mandate the Church itself to take actions within its own very substantial secular organization and material resources, and lead by example. And this relates to my final question: to what extent has this encyclical had any significant effect among the Catholic faithful worldwide, and within Catholic institutions?

In addition, I will raise some other questions that have troubled me on reading *Laudato Si'* and I will start with these because I believe they may be, at least in some cases, relevant to the failure to include strong calls to action. But I must add immediately that, having now researched and written this chapter, I am much more keenly aware of how much inertia, hostility, and sheer incomprehension the Pope has had to overcome, both within institutional Catholicism and among the much of the laity worldwide, to carry his arguments as far he has. And I am also much more aware of how the encyclical has undoubtedly empowered those Catholics who were already environmentally conscious and active, to canvass support for campaigns to mitigate climate change and protect biodiversity within the Church, and in some cases to leverage big shifts in policy from their hierarchies. So in raising these questions, I would like to reiterate that I am in no way diminishing the positive qualities briefly mentioned above, and so ably celebrated in other chapters in this book. But I would still ask why the Pope did not express much more clearly how these qualities can be made manifest in the real world, by all of us, but especially by the institution he leads and by its members.

I will divide what I see as the encyclical's shortcomings into several categories. Some problems derive from the Pope's analysis of Judeo-Christian concepts of the human relationship with nature and the evolution of industrial capitalism. These relate in particular to issues such as patriarchy, and whether we humans enjoy some God-given "dominion" over the natural world, and to attempts to build an ethic of "sustainability" out of the Biblical narrative. Other problems derive from a religious vision that imposes a romantic or idealistic interpretation of phenomena in the natural world, with which philosophers and artists have had increasingly difficult encounters in recent centuries.

I have neither the competence nor the space to deal with the above questions in any detail, but I think it is important to flag them, as they may have some bearing on the points that follow.

And I will highlight one major environmental issue—and in fairness, there is probably only one, which is remarkable in itself—on which most environmentalists will explicitly and radically disagree with the encyclical. The Pope rejects, and indeed caricatures, the contention that population growth is a significant factor in environmental degradation (50).

Next, I will briefly address the omission of certain environmental strategies and concepts that I believe would have reinforced the Pope's arguments: natural capital accounting and ecological restoration. Then I will look at the issue of the absence of clear calls to specific action, and the disjunction between radical rhetoric and vague aspirational phrases. It is precisely because the Pope occasionally makes boldly radical points on social and economic issues that I find his lack of follow-through disappointing.

I will relate his reluctance to make such calls to his tendency to treat social forces as abstractions, and to portray our societies as dominated by a disembodied "technocratic paradigm," not by concrete human beings and social classes driven by unbridled appetites for wealth and power. In a word, I think what drives our societies is a capitalist paradigm, whose essentials are hardly subject to question since the Reagan/Thatcher revolution, imposed on the rest of us by the social classes who benefit from it.

In this context, I will ask why, as the head of a hierarchical structure with vast educational, social, and economic resources, the Pope has failed to instruct the Church to systematically implement environmentally friendly policies, such as divestment, and to energetically disseminate the encyclical's environmental insights at all levels throughout the Church's vast educational systems.

Finally, I will consider to what extent the encyclical has had an impact among the faithful to date, and in the wider world, and how this impact might be augmented in the immediate future. I will do this in conversation with Fr Sean McDonagh, a priest with a long history of environmental and social activism who had significant input into the scientific text of the encyclical, and with Catherine Brennan, a nun who has been exceptionally active in promoting the encyclical's message in Ireland.

Is there really a sustainability narrative in the Bible?
Did a patriarchal God grant humanity dominion, or stewardship, over nature?

> We are not God. The earth was here before us and it has been given to us. This allows us to respond to the charge that Judeo-Christian thinking, on the basis of the Genesis account which grants man "dominion" over the earth (cf. Gen 1:28), has encouraged the unbridled exploitation of nature by painting him as domineering and destructive by nature
>
> (67)

Christian environmentalists naturally seek narratives underpinning their commitment to sustainable living in their own sacred texts. Pope Francis is no exception. But he hits a familiar stumbling block, because right at the beginning of the Bible story, as most translations have it, including the one used here in the encyclical, God gives Adam "dominion" over nature and the services it provides us with. And this, as the Pope says above, has led many commentators to see the biblical account of creation as a key historical and cultural source of the human behavior that has led to the environmental crisis. To this day, this passage is used by some Catholics, and many "evangelical" Protestants, to justify their unsustainable exploitation of nature. For environmentalists, their interpretation of the Bible makes them part of the problem, not part of the solution.

Before the encyclical considers this problem directly, Pope Francis argues for a cure to what he recognizes, with admirable clarity, as our diseased culture of untrammeled exploitation of nature, and the consumerism that propels it (27, 34, 203). But the cure he proposes will, to many of us, also appear, however unintentionally, to be a cause of the disease. The proper way, he writes,

> to restore men and women to their rightful place, putting an end to their claim to absolute dominion over the earth, is to speak once more of the figure of a Father who creates and who alone owns the world.
>
> (6)

It would be both naïve and arrogant to imagine that the Pope would abandon the central Christian doctrine of a single, omnipotent, and patriarchal creator God. And yet, it is hard to see how the concept, as expressed here, of God as the sole owner of the planet is other than a projection of our own desire for exclusive proprietorial rights on nature.[2] One cannot but hear echoes of the farmer or factory owner who declares: "I built up this business, I can do what I like with it."

Of course, Pope Francis's intention is quite the opposite because he clearly believes our God-given role on the Earth is to live sustainably, in harmony with all its creatures and ecosystems (115).

However, the biblical evidence he quotes to underpin this belief seems at best tenuous to any observer not reading the text through the lens of his faith. The Judeo-Christian God did not leave very clear instructions about the human role in this regard, and such injunctions as he did leave tend, on most readings, in the other direction. And indeed, as we've seen above, the Pope concedes that Christians have often read them as justifying unbridled exploitation of natural resources. But his claim that this is a distortion is surely based more on his own assertions than on the texts themselves.

> The biblical texts are to be read in their context, with an appropriate hermeneutic, recognizing that they tell us to "till and keep" the garden of the world (cf. Gen 2:15). "Tilling" refers to cultivating, ploughing or working, while "keeping" means caring, protecting, overseeing, and preserving. This implies a relationship of mutual responsibility between human beings and nature. Each community can take from the bounty of the earth whatever it needs for subsistence, but it also has the duty to protect the earth and to ensure its fruitfulness for coming generations.
> (67)

To make the case for this environmentally benign reading, he cites a verse from Deuteronomy that has become a staple of efforts to extract an environmentally friendly narrative of sustainability from the Bible: the requirement to leave the mother bird alive when taking eggs or young from the nest (68). This is sensible environmental advice to be sure, though it would have been better to suggest leaving some of the eggs or young as well. But it is a very isolated text in the vast Old Testament narrative; a very fragile structure on which to build sustainability into biblical teaching. Compared to the prolific ecological wisdom inscribed in some—though by no means all—Native American and other "indigenous" lore, Judeo-Christianity has, at the very best, an impoverished environmental component in its foundational texts.

Coming to the New Testament, the encyclical curiously chooses a quotation about Jesus which is most obviously read as an endorsement of dominion though, again, Pope Francis clearly intends it to be read as the opposite:

> Jesus lived in full harmony with creation, and others were amazed: "What sort of man is this, that even the winds and the sea obey him?".
> (98)

God the Son is here, like God the Father earlier, portrayed as a supreme commander, a metaphor that conjures up mastery, and not "full harmony."

The charge that the Bible is a source of our environmental woes clearly troubles the Pope a lot; he returns to it again and again:

> An inadequate presentation of Christian anthropology gave rise to a wrong understanding of the relationship between human beings and the world. Often, what was handed on was a Promethean vision of mastery over the world, which gave the impression that the protection of nature was something that only the faint-hearted cared about. Instead, our "dominion" over the universe should be understood more properly in the sense of responsible stewardship.
>
> (116)

The difficulty is that, as far as I can gather from biblical scholars, and from the Pope's own repeated use of the word,[3] "dominion" is the best way to translate the word used in the scriptures. Had that word been "stewardship," it would indeed be easier to square with contemporary environmental thinking about sustainability. And curiously, the Pope himself only uses this very helpful concept of stewardship on one other occasion in the encyclical (236).

The encyclical is on surer ground interpreting other sayings of Jesus, which do lend themselves more easily to favorable ecological interpretation. Jesus used the "lilies of the field" and the "birds of the air" as exemplars for accepting and taking pleasure in our natural condition, and contrasts their beauty, acquired without acquisitive labor, to the vain glories of human consumption, exemplified by the court of King Solomon. This could be read as a very radical environmentalism, a critique of the shift by Homo sapiens from hunter-gatherer societies to economies built on agricultural and then industrial labor. This reflects an existential anxiety about our specifically human, as opposed to simply biological, nature. This anxiety may even inform the story of the Fall itself.[4] The Pope does not take his interpretation that far, but he does use these sayings as teachings that help us "to overcome that unhealthy anxiety which makes us superficial, aggressive and compulsive consumers" (226).

Despite the encyclical's passionate espousal of social justice, and its repeated critiques of consumerism, the Pope does not avail of the saying of John the Baptist which is one of the sharpest critiques of the acquisitiveness and selfishness underlying both historical inequalities of wealth and the consumerism that exacerbates those inequalities today: "He that hath two coats, let him impart to him that hath none; and he that hath meat, let him do likewise."[5,6]

A naively romantic vision of nature?

There is another aspect of the encyclical that must surely present difficulties both to scientists and to lay people who have grappled with a painful paradox inherent in our love for nature. While ecology shows us that all creatures do indeed live in relationship to one another, this relationship is by no means always benign. In our world, the lion does not lie down with the lamb; it tears its throat out.

The canon of nature-writing in English has grappled with this issue for a long time. William Wordsworth is a formative poet for many English-speaking people, as we try to articulate our first innocent love for our local "wild places." He was not entirely blind to this difficulty about Nature's apparently essential complicity with pain and suffering. But he did not focus much on it. One of his successors as a grand old man of English poetry, Alfred Tennyson, saw it all too clearly. He prefigured the emotional impact of Darwinism in some powerful stanzas of "In Memoriam" (1849), calling into question not only nature's benevolence but also the motivation of its Creator. He highlights the contradiction between the apparent brutality of the struggle for survival and the vision of a harmonious universe espoused by the conventional Christian

> Who trusted God was love indeed
> And love Creation's final law –
> Tho' Nature, red in tooth and claw
> With ravine, shriek'd against his creed –

In the next century, Aldous Huxley would write a gently scathing essay, "Wordsworth in the Tropics." He argued, long before anyone dreamed up the term "Anthropocene" that the great romantic poet's Europe is so "well gardened" that it is "remade in his [Man's] own image." Had Wordsworth traveled to southern latitudes, Huxley wrote, he would have had to confront a less domesticated nature that, while often still very beautiful, could be very threatening, even "inhumanly evil."[7]

Some contemporary writers have linked these concerns directly to the theological question known as theodicy, exploring whether we can reconcile the concept of an omnipotent and utterly good Creator with a natural world that encompasses many grim realities. Annie Dillard went deeper than most in her extraordinary memoir/reflection, *Pilgrim at Tinker's Creek*, and similar sharp anxieties mark the work of poets as different as Seamus Heaney and Mary Oliver.

It seems strange that this issue about the nature of nature is not even acknowledged in what is undoubtedly the Vatican's most significant statement about the natural world and our relationship to it. Instead, for Pope Francis, as for the saint whose name he has chosen, every aspect of nature seems to be an entirely unproblematic expression of God's goodness. Each species gives "glory to God by their very existence" (33). He approvingly quotes from the Catholic Catechism: "Each creature possesses its own particular goodness and perfection... Each of the various creatures, willed in its own being, reflects in its own way a ray of God's infinite wisdom and goodness" (69). These quotations are not isolated examples—similar views are expressed in several other sections of the encyclical (83, 85, 120, 149, 221). It's tempting to ask how a caterpillar might respond to this benign vision of nature, as its internal organs are slowly consumed from the inside by the larva of a parasitic wasp, as slow and horrifying and agonizing a death as a science fiction writer might dream up. And if it is asking too much to expect empathy with a caterpillar, what about a human infant whose existence is similarly terminated by a plague bacillus?

One must welcome the Pope's obvious awareness of, and awe in the face of, the extraordinary biodiversity produced by evolution, and the significance of every species in that vast web. And what he is doing in these passages is, often explicitly, an attempt to counteract the dangerous dualism that has dominated much Catholic (and Protestant) theology: the teaching that only the spirit is good, and that the world and the flesh are synonymous with the Devil. Nevertheless, it is very doubtful whether his universally benign reading of nature will be convincing to contemporary readers. His arguments might be more compelling to such readers if he had at least acknowledged the presence, if you'll forgive the phrase, of the snake in the garden. The skeptic might say that, by ignoring these aspects of the world he has risked presenting nature as blandly as a Patience Strong greeting card.

The elephant in the room of the new Vatican environmentalism: "Demographic growth" or overpopulation?

The questions raised above are contextual. Obviously it is none of my business to question Catholic theology or scriptural interpretation as such. But where that theology and interpretation impact our relationship with nature, then I think it is legitimate to at least raise flags about them, because they may contribute, however inadvertently, to underpinning cultural attitudes that do not promote effective action on climate change or biodiversity.

The way the Pope deals with the population question is in a different category. It is the one point on which those environmentalists who do not accept traditional Catholic teaching on birth control are likely to disagree radically and absolutely with the encyclical. While much more unites us than divides us, it would be doing no favors to anyone to ignore this disagreement over what the Pope calls "demographic growth" and what I would call overpopulation.

In a single paragraph (50), the Pope rules out consideration of our rapidly increasing human population as a significant contributor to the environmental crisis. Given that the United Nations predicts that the world's human population will increase from eight billion in 2023 to ten billion in 2056, and that this increase of two billion is equivalent to the entire world population 90 years ago, this papal dismissal of the population factor seems an utterly unfounded value judgment. And it sits very uneasily with his own repeated acknowledgment that the environment has been damaged and degraded to an unprecedented degree over this very period. If, as the encyclical repeatedly recognizes, humans are the cause of the current climate and biodiversity crises, it seems only reasonable to seek to limit—voluntarily, of course—human populations as part of our response.

The Pope introduces this topic with a misleading statement: "Instead of resolving the problems of the poor and thinking of how the world can be different, some can only propose a reduction in the birth rate" (50). With respect, the vast majority of environmentalists see these issues not as mutually exclusive alternatives, but as questions that need our simultaneous attention. Yes, we must lift the poor out of poverty, and yes, we must think differently about—and drastically reduce—our own consumption of the world's resources. But we must surely also promote birth control to limit, and ultimately reverse, population growth. Unfortunately, the Catholic Church's outright rejection of "artificial" contraception in a previous encyclical, *Humanae Vitae*, appears to make it impossible for Pope Francis to embrace this viewpoint.

Instead, he falls back on a view expressed by his predecessor, John Paul II, that "demographic growth is fully compatible with an integral and shared development" (50). He sets up a false opposition by claiming that any focus on population reduction is an

> attempt to legitimize the present model of distribution, where a minority believes that it has the right to consume in a way which can never be universalized, since the planet could not even contain the waste products of such consumption.
>
> (50)

Once again, I would stress that a critique of contemporary wealth distribution, and the dominant model of consumerism, is an integral part of almost every environmentalist's position. Failure to recognize that current patterns of population growth are also a major cause of damage to our common home is to ignore a very big elephant in the room.

Pope Francis continues his very brief foray into this complex territory by implying that eliminating our current (and undoubtedly scandalous) levels of food waste could alleviate poverty regardless, apparently, of how many children the world produces. This paragraph shows a lamentable lack of awareness of the impact of overpopulation, not least on women and girls. Beyond a vague statement that *"attention needs to be paid* to imbalances in population density, on both national and global levels" (italics mine), he simply does not recognize the problems caused by unlimited population growth. This vagueness, sadly, is all too typical of the diffidence of other prescriptions in the encyclical that I will be looking at below.

All the evidence suggests that the education of women, coupled with the availability of affordable birth control, is the gateway to better lives for all, and a much healthier environment. Undoubtedly, many Catholics are ahead of the Pope here, and have long abandoned, implicitly or explicitly, the teaching of *Humanae Vitae*. Still, in an encyclical that is so in tune with contemporary environmental thinking on so many issues, it is troubling to find this dogma against birth control repeated here.

What is included in the encyclical, for good or ill, is obviously significant. But so is what is excluded. In my next section, I will look at two areas where recent—and not-so-recent—advances in environmental thought and practice appear to have been ignored.

Missing in the encyclical 1

Natural capital accounting: a conceptual tool revealing all the links between economic policies and environmental impacts

Pope Francis repeatedly asserts that our dominant economic and social models have a very negative impact on biodiversity, and are driving us towards a climate catastrophe. He is sharply critical of the "deified market", and the "economic powers" which

> justify the current global system where priority tends to be given to speculation and the pursuit of financial gain, which fail to take the context into account, let alone the effects on human dignity and the natural environment.
>
> (56)

But the encyclical does not explore, much less embrace, recent advances in thinking about why our societies fail to "take the context into account," why our leading policy-makers mostly appear blind to the environmental consequences of economic policies. This blindness is often manifested in a "silo" mentality in different departments of the same government administration, or different sections of the same business corporation. There is a major conflict, if I may give an example from my own home place, between the aspirations of the Irish Department of Communications, Climate Action and Environment to reduce greenhouse gas emissions in line with our obligations under the Paris Treaty, and the policy of the Department of Agriculture to substantially increase beef and dairy production, which is rapidly increasing those very emissions.

While this conflict undoubtedly has roots in political short-termism—there are many more votes in cash for farmers now than there are in preventing climate problems 20 years down the road—it also reflects the fact that we currently lack an economic metric that captures the costs and benefits of the whole range of the ecological consequences of our economic policy. Or, as Pavan Suhkdev, the Study Leader on an invaluable report on The Economics of Ecosystems and Biodiversity (TEEB)[8] put it: "the witchcraft of the markets has made nature invisible."[9] Conventional accounting methods and neo-classical economics simply do not capture more than a fraction of our real relationship with our world.

Since the full TEEB report was published in 2011, natural capital accounting has been increasingly adopted around the world as a methodology for enabling societies to make better decisions about actions that impact our environment. The methodology is still in its adolescence, and is often contested in details, but it is increasingly accepted as a vital tool to assist us in reducing the often unintended consequences of our policies.

Conventional accounting will often reveal only a single beneficial resource value in a particular landscape, and will therefore inadvertently hide many of the costs of extracting that resource.

To account for a forest, for example, solely as timber, is to miss many other benefits a woodland provides. It fails to account for the cost of losing numerous services when the forest is clear-felled. These services include: air purification, water filtration, flood mitigation (saving costs of damage to local homes/businesses/farms), pollination (benefitting local agriculture), income indirectly derived from recreation (if the woodland attracts tourists to the area), and carbon sequestration (especially important in the struggle to slow down climate change).

Other benefits, very important but sometimes less easily quantifiable in financial terms because they may in fact be infinite, are also missed by considering the woodlands' value solely as timber: health benefits, physical and mental, to local communities who use the woodland for exercise and recreation; aesthetic values; and habitat for biodiversity, as an intrinsic good in itself.

To a degree, natural capital accounting is the logical, fully ecologically informed extension, of the "polluter pays" principle that has long been widely accepted to prevent damage to air, soil, and water. Applying it to climate change is controversial (because it would hurt multiple vested interests very severely), but self-evidently fair; more importantly still, it would inhibit the adoption of environmentally damaging policies from the outset. To go back to the example of expanding the Irish beef and dairy herds, if farmers had to pay for climate damage in proportion to the methane their cattle emitted, they would be nudged very rapidly into seeking less environmentally damaging ways of profiting from food production.

There are a number of points in the encyclical where this type of analysis could have significantly enhanced the arguments the Pope is making (36, 184, 190, 195), and in particular here:

> The economy accepts every advance in technology with a view to profit, without concern for its potentially negative impact on human beings. Finance overwhelms the real economy. The lessons of the global financial crisis have not been assimilated, and we are learning all too slowly the lessons of environmental deterioration. Some circles maintain that

current economics and technology will solve all environmental problems, and argue, in popular and non-technical terms, that the problems of global hunger and poverty will be resolved simply by market growth. (109)

There is, in my view, no more effective way of making "the real economy" visible to policy-makers and the general public than natural capital accounting. It is not a magic bullet, and does not in itself address the core problems of societies dominated by social classes wedded to inequality and unregulated capitalism. But it does make the unsustainable nature of their economic project much more visible, and in great detail. Natural capital accounting ought to be factored into ongoing efforts, theoretical and practical, to realize the aspirations for sustainability expressed in *Laudato Si'*.

Missing in the encyclical 2

Ecological restoration—an innovative and hopeful conservation strategy, echoing Christian ideas of eternal renewal

It would be absurd to expect the Pope to have included in the encyclical the full gamut of options for mitigating climate change and conserving biodiversity.

However, I think it is worth making a brief case for the inclusion of the strategy of ecological restoration, which has rapidly advanced, in science and in the field, since it was first conceptualized in the American Midwest in the 1980s.

Like most of us, I suspect, I grew up thinking we could take two approaches to the ecosystems that make up the natural world: we could "develop" them for our own purposes, thus inevitably changing them, likely degrading them and often destroying them; or we could "preserve" them, clearing them of people, building a fence and excluding everyone except tourists and scientists.

Then I was invited on a weekend of "prairie restoration" on the International Writing Program at the University of Iowa in 2003, by the program director, poet Christopher Merrill, and the great American novelist and natural history writer, Peter Mathiessen. I have to admit I was initially very puzzled by the phrase "ecological restoration." To me, restoration was something you did to a damaged painting, a house, a guitar, a car. The idea that you could even attempt to restore something with as many moving and interconnected parts as an ecosystem seemed counter-intuitive, not to say hubristic. How could we possibly resolve such a complex equation when we didn't even know the names, let alone the functions, of many of the elements that made it up?

But then, as I visited prairies that had been completely replaced by monocultural corn production, yet were now flourishing with almost their full component of characteristic plants, and many of their characteristic insects, birds, and mammals, I became fascinated by the promise of this concept.

I traveled six continents over ten years researching the theory and practice of restoration in very different ecological and social contexts, eventually producing the first book to look at the strategy in a worldwide context.[10]

I learned three things: ecological restoration is a young science and an imperfect art in the field, but restorationists are making enormous progress; climate change and other global manifestations of human environmental impacts make restoration more difficult every year; restoration is also becoming an invaluable tool for mitigating climate change, sequestering greenhouse gases, and restoring biodiversity, and is now embraced as such by most of the world's major conservation organizations and many governments, and not a few corporations.[11]

I think it is a pity that this rapidly developing field is not recognized in the encyclical, apart from a single passing reference (58). And I think this particularly disappointing because restoration surely has an underlying message that resonates very happily with the Christian gospel of resurrection, renewal, and redemption. I hope what I write next will not be regarded as blasphemous, and certainly it is not so intended. But if Christianity teaches that no individual, no matter how depraved, is beyond salvation, at least on this side of death, then restoration teaches us that no ecosystem, no matter how degraded, is beyond pretty full recovery at least on this side of the extinction of its key component species. At a moment when it is very easy for environmentalists to fall into utter despair at the relentless tide of loss that our surveys register, isn't this good news, and worth celebrating?

A persistent failing: the blurring of calls to action

I now come to what I feel to be a persistent flaw in the encyclical. I was initially, and very happily, surprised by the Pope's very sharp and accurate critique of the social and ideological factors that are degrading our planet (consumerism, throwaway culture, deification of market forces, valuing private profits over the common good, paradigm of infinite growth, privatization of water, protection of banking interests, and so on). And I was impressed by his firm reiteration of the ethical necessity of raising the poor out of poverty while curbing and reversing environmental damage.

What disappointed me was how tentative, and even timid and insipid, the solutions he suggested were. Perhaps I need to give some context here:

Coming to the encyclical from outside the Catholic Church, I no doubt carry baggage that I am not aware of, and the reader must be the judge of that. But I can certainly freely confess to one pre-conception, that I believe can be validated by history. I understand the Church to be not only a hierarchical, but an authoritarian, organisation. And this authority is vested in the figure and person of the Pope in a manner that is not open to dispute by the faithful. When he is speaking ex cathedra, whatever he enunciates is beyond the possibility of error. It's true that this happens much less frequently than many, inside and outside the Church, may imagine – the doctrine of papal infallibility has only been formally invoked once since it was first promulgated officially in 1870. But it has certainly created an impression, which appears to be more or less accurate, depending on a pope's character, of enormous magisterial power concentrated in the papacy.

This impression has been confirmed in recent times by the impact of the aforementioned *Humanae Vitae* encyclical (1968), in which Pope Paul VI articulated the doctrine that artificial contraception was sinful. While this was not an ex cathedra pronouncement in technical terms, most Catholics at the time accepted it, however reluctantly, as unquestionable. Intimate behavior in countless marriages was dictated by this teaching. This is surely about as high an indicator of the power of a physically remote authority as one can imagine. There were immense consequences for the emotional lives of Catholic couples, for the economic welfare of Catholic families, and for the size of the human population.

So I hope it's reasonable for an outsider to come to an encyclical like *Laudato Si'* expecting the Pope to instruct his flock pretty specifically how they should behave in relation to the issues he is raising. Especially when those issues are exceptionally important and urgent for the future of the human race, and of the natural world as we have known it for millennia. So it was a surprise to find that a tone of diffidence dominates almost every sentence in the document where the Pope is saying that his flock, or the world in general, need to change their behavior. Where one might have expected to find an unambiguous edict to end some bad practice or correct some major misframing of economic imperatives, one finds an almost timid request.

Typical phrases at these moments include: "efforts need to be made" (47), "attention needs to be paid" (50), "they need to acknowledge" (172), "agreements are urgently needed" (173), and "society must put pressure on governments" (179).

And while the Pope obviously cannot issue instructions to governments, or to society in general, I was under the impression that he could indeed issue instructions, or at the very least strong moral imperatives, to the vast planetary network of institutional and physical structures under the control of his Church: banks, seminaries, universities, schools, hospitals, with their attendant buildings and land holdings, and so on. An explicit instruction to all financial institutions linked to the Church to divest from fossil fuels would have sent a powerful signal, and led by example. Instead, he only expresses broad aspirations to the world in general, such as the statement that "fossil fuel technology needs to be progressively replaced without delay" (165). Indeed, the word "divestment" is not mentioned in the encyclical. One of the few acts of social resistance that he explicitly endorses is consumer boycotting of "certain products" (206). Note that even here he not only avoids specifying what products should be boycotted, he does not declare that the Church will use its very considerable purchasing power to exercise this instrument. In terms of environmental education, the Church clearly has the real-world power, through its seminaries and schools to exercise enormous influence, but Pope Francis can only offer us his "hope" that it will do so (214). Is it any wonder that the response of the Church on the ground to the encyclical has been, with some honorable exceptions discussed below, so very tepid? The contrast with the Church's energetic and militant closing of ranks in policing the rejection of contraception called for by *Humanae Vitae* is stark, and sad.

I am very aware that there is an irony in a writer who is critical of authoritarianism urging the Pope to be more forceful and more insistent in his prescriptions for behavior. And I believe that, in general terms, it is very much to Pope Francis's credit that he has presented such a graciously humble image of his person and his office to the world. In a period when demagogues are on the rise, he is indeed a breath of fresh air.

Given the urgency of the issues we are discussing, however, one might have hoped at least for much more direct guidance, at least to his own flock, on exactly how their faith requires them to behave in relation to the environment.

It appears to me that two factors inhibit the Pope from being much more clearly prescriptive.

The first is his insistence that what he calls the "technocratic paradigm" conditions our economic and political behavior, a topic that dominates much of Chapter 3, with many other references. I would argue that the actions and policies of technocrats are in fact conditioned by the demands made by those who hold economic and political power, and it is this power structure that needs to be changed. But it is easier to heap blame on an abstraction like the "technocratic paradigm" than to directly confront the greed of the interest groups responsible for the production of human poverty and ecological degradation.

The second factor is related. The Catholic Church has almost always—the defeated and flawed Liberation Theology movement being the big exception—sided with conservative forces in society, and against radical change in power structures. This pope is different, and yet remains the same. He fully recognizes the urgent need for radical change at all levels if we are to avoid environmental catastrophe. And he recognizes that a relatively small elite controls most of the levers of power. It seems rational to think that the only way this will change is by the mobilization of the powerless against these elites, but the Pope mentions "social unrest" as a threat, rather than a necessary (though undoubtedly risky) game-changer (204). This is made quite explicit in the prayers that conclude the encyclical. They do not call on the poor to take action. Instead, they call on the rich and powerful to change their hearts (246). Good luck, as they say, with that.

It seems likely that this Pope made the only call he could, given the conservative nature of the Church, and his own, much more attractive, genuine humility. But one of the regrettable consequences, probably facilitated by his diffidence, is the very slow response of the faithful, at local, national, and international levels, to the encyclical. Indeed, in many cases, one cannot talk of response, there has hardly been awareness that it has been promulgated.

I want to conclude, however, on a more optimistic note, by recounting my conversations with two people who have made enormous efforts to promote the encyclical's best ideas, and whose own experience shows why those Catholics who had already embraced environmental awareness and activism have generally welcomed *Laudato Si'* so warmly.

Only connect: an Irish missionary becomes a champion of eco-theology on the other side of the world

Fr Sean McDonagh grew up loving the natural world he experienced in his rural Irish childhood, but initially he saw no link between this love, and his love for his Catholic faith. He would have to travel to the other side of the world, to minister as a missionary to the T'boli people in the rapidly vanishing forests of the southern Philippines in the 1980s, to see that these two loves are intimately connected. This insight, interwoven equally closely with a passion for global social justice, has driven his prolific activism and writing for several decades. But it is only with the publication of *Laudato Si'* that he feels that this vision has entered the Catholic mainstream.

Now in his 70s, he lives between the Colomban Missionaries' massive headquarters at Dalgan Park, Ireland, where he has developed a nature reserve alongside the River Boyne, and his late mother's home in Tipperary, where he fills in for over-stretched local parish priests in a rapidly declining institutional Church. Despite some recent illness, he is a bundle of vibrant intellectual curiosity, radiating passionate commitment to faith and nature. He lights up the cavernous, gloomy, and often empty corridors of Dalgan Park with irrepressible good humor. He is an optimist in spite of his keen awareness that the global environmental storm is only in its early stages, and despite the dark things he has already seen in his career, at home and abroad.

"The logging I saw in the Philippines in the 1970s was devastating," he says. "The topsoil was disappearing, the drinking water was contaminated."[12] The scale of biological and topographical change he witnessed there made it easy for him to understand, decades later, the concept of the Anthropocene, the idea that human activity is creating a new geological era on our planet.

He found that the Filipino Catholic Church was supportive of the T'boli's fight for social justice, but was myopic about the destruction of their environment. By 1988, however, the national Conference of Bishops had published the world's first Catholic pastoral letter with an environmental theme, "What is happening to our beautiful land?" It was drafted by McDonagh. But it took a long time for his insistence that ecology, social justice, and theology were inextricably entwined to gain traction in the Vatican. In his 1990 book, hopefully if prematurely entitled *The Greening of the Church*, he raised the very sensitive issue of overpopulation. In a chapter called "Are there too many mouths to feed?," he dared to point out that *Humanae Vitae* had failed to take account of the ecological concept of "carrying capacity," which shows that there are limits to the population any ecosystem can support. "That didn't go down so well in Rome," he says dryly.

At home in Ireland, he often met blank incomprehension from his colleagues. An editor at *The Furrow*, a highly regarded Catholic religious journal, asked whether he might have intended an article he submitted, "The Pain of the Earth," for an agricultural publication. McDonagh persisted, though, and *The Furrow* published it. Even those he might have expected to be his natural allies were unresponsive. Trócaire, an Irish Catholic aid agency, was ahead of its time in linking poverty relief to social justice. But it was a bridge too far for the organization when McDonagh applied for a grant for re-afforestation. "What's that got to do with the Gospel?" an executive asked him.

As he became increasingly involved in the international environmental movement, attending conferences like the 1992 Earth Summit in Rio de Janeiro, he was struck by the fact that "you'd hardly ever see a Catholic there." He found that the Protestant denominations grouped in the World Council of Churches "were way ahead of us in this field." He goes further, and sees mainstream Protestants as having a relationship to nature in their rituals of worship, such as their harvest festivals, for example, that Catholics have largely lost.

I couldn't help but wonder if the Catholic Church was really so entirely deaf to the reverberations of the environmental movement. Surely, I asked him, the leftist Theology of Liberation movement in the Church in the 1970s and 1980s had embraced environmental agendas?

"No," he says quietly but firmly. "A Latin American liberation theologian, who now thinks very differently, assured me in this period that ecological theology was the preserve of the middle classes." This did not impress McDonagh: his T'boli parishioners, who were fully aware that their suffering was caused by environmental degradation, and sought guidance on this issue from their priests, were hardly a privileged elite.

It was only in the 1990s, he says, that he noted some shifts, as Brazilian bishops began to respond to the loss of the Amazon rainforest. But until the papacy of Francis, he still found that efforts to connect theology, ecology, and social justice were marginalized within the Church. "I think I was regarded as a problem," he says. But the biggest obstacle was not hostile opposition but an utter lack of understanding of the issues: "Huge apathy, ignorance, especially clerical ignorance."

His voice must have been heard in high places, however, because in October 2014 he got a call from Cardinal Peter Turkson, who had been entrusted by the newly elected Pope Francis to oversee the drafting of an encyclical on the very issues closest to McDonagh's heart. And over the next three months, he says, he drafted most of the material on climate change and biodiversity in *Laudato Si'*, drawing on assistance from colleagues all over the world, including two eminent Irish scientists and thinkers, the geologist and botanist John Feehan, and the climatologist John Sweeney. He did not see the document again until it was published, though he learned at one point that there were efforts to remove the biodiversity sections.

"I wrote a strong letter," he says, again quietly. Those sections were retained. One of the points he makes repeatedly in interviews and articles since its publication is that this encyclical is not only about climate change, it is also a very strong warning against the sixth great extinction.

Overall, he is "very happy" with the final version, though he would, predictably, prefer it to have gone further in several respects. He was particularly relieved that the science on human-driven climate change was presented so uncompromisingly. "I thought that there might be a 'perhaps' inserted on this issue, but I'm delighted there wasn't."

Translating the encyclical into effective action

McDonagh has a clear vision for how the encyclical should be translated into meaningful and effective action, both within the Church and beyond its doors. It's worth noting here that for McDonagh, "the Church" is not the clerical hierarchy but the "People of God," the definition embraced, however ineffectively, by the Second Vatican Council.

He outlined his ideal plan of action succinctly in his introduction to a collection of essays he edited on *Laudato Si'*.[13] His plan is based on what he calls a "synodal process" of intensive environmental education and social engagement. It would have three phases, starting with every parish, then moving to a national level in every country, and finally evolving to an international scale, over a period of at least three years.

He particularly stresses the importance of education, pointing out he finds even his environmentalism students today are often poorly informed about the causes of climate change. He believes that the Catholic laity and clergy both desperately need better information and that the encyclical offers an efficient vehicle for transmitting it. He is emphatic that the local or parish level of the process (and indeed beyond that) should not be led by priests, but by the laity, in keeping with the "People of God" concept. But he also believes that the clergy should be much, much better informed about the natural world themselves, starting with their intellectual formation as priests. "In seven years of study for the priesthood, not one minute is given to the theology of nature," he says. Yet he believes it could be relatively easily integrated, by linking common concepts between human society and nature. "To learn about community, what better place to study it than sitting under an oak tree?"

He also argues eloquently that, since Catholics center their faith life around ritualized acts of worship, of public and private celebration, reflection and prayer, the form these acts take—the liturgy—should echo the encyclical's embrace of the natural world as a central and ever-present expression of our experience of God's love and goodness. "There is no point in having a new theology without creating a new connection to the natural world in the liturgy," he says.

However, it's arguable that *Laudato Si'* only addresses this issue obliquely. For example, the Pope suggests that the Eucharist itself, properly understood, has always been an expression of the fusion of the material and the spiritual: "the Eucharist is also a source of light and motivation for our concerns for the environment, directing us to be stewards of all creation" (236).

While acknowledging, yet again, that I am a total outsider to such matters, I think it is legitimate to speculate that this environmental aspect of the Eucharist has a pretty invisible profile in the current liturgy, at least to most participants. The Pope also refers to the need to revive the custom of giving thanks to God before and after meals to strengthen "our feeling of gratitude for the gifts of creation" (227). And he does conclude the entire document with two new prayers, but, speaking again as outsider in this field, I have to say that these prayers did not strike me as having the inspiring timbre of great liturgical poetry.

Yet the Catholic Church has, obviously, a most distinguished track record in the creation (and the production) of meaningful collective rituals, an essential aspect of human life that the post-religious world has been painfully poor at elaborating for its own needs. The philosopher Bill Jordan, author of one of the most thoughtful books about ecological restoration, *The Sunflower Forest*, has made interesting observations on how the development of social rituals created by artists might assist in resolving community conflicts around conservation issues, but progress in this area remains very limited.[14]

I suggest to McDonagh that much more could be done to integrate environmental awareness into Catholic acts of worship, and the templates are already there: the heritage of the Church, with its rites of passage like baptism, confirmation, marriage and funerals, surely offers rich opportunities for building much richer environmental elements into its liturgical calendar.

He not only agrees enthusiastically, he adds that "the liturgy needs to be completely rewritten. Totally!" That project obviously presents a huge challenge, but again McDonagh points to small beginnings as indicators of a change in the right direction. Shortly after the encyclical was published, Pope Francis announced that the Catholic Church would celebrate 1 September as the Day of Prayer for Creation, following a lead set by the Orthodox Church in 1989, and embraced by other major European churches in 2001.[15]

The next step, McDonagh says, has been to join with the ecumenical "Season of Creation" movement so that the period from 1 September to

St Francis's feast day, 4 October, may now become a "new season for the Church, like Christmas, Advent, or Lent," with a special focus on nature and environmental issues at Sunday Masses as a starting point. Response in Ireland has been muted so far, but it's expanding: one Sunday was officially devoted to the new season last year, two this year (2019) and, McDonagh hopes, four in 2020.[16]

These advances will not, one would imagine, be enormously contentious within the Church today. But resistance is more likely to arise within the synodal process McDonagh envisages, should it ever take place. The encyclical's calls to undertake radical practical measures to mitigate or reverse climate change and biodiversity loss will have awkward implications for many of us, in many places. McDonagh does not shy away from these painful issues, which will inevitably not only challenge our deeply ingrained consumerist lifestyle but also our cherished cultural and social practices. Indeed, entire livelihoods in key economic sectors of society would be subjected to very uncomfortable scrutiny.

"In Ireland it [the Synodal process] may call into question the morality of our heavy meat diet, not just because of its impact on the local environment but on the planet as well," he has written.

> Our diet must change significantly because it contributes to global warming, and this will only happen through robust debate and dialogue. Naturally, if these changes are to take root, profitable farming alternatives would have to be suggested and supported in order to sustain the farming community in the area.[17]

Anyone even vaguely familiar with Irish culinary culture, and especially with Irish farming, will recognize immediately that such discussions will require exceptionally strong and sensitive modulation. Indeed, Irish government policy, reflecting pressure from the farming lobby, still plans for significantly increased dairy and beef production at least up to 2025, despite the consequences in higher greenhouse gas emissions. Any hint of criticism sparks very angry defensive rhetoric from powerful farming constituencies. And farming communities are often also bastions of Catholic practice in a nation that has increasingly turned its back on the Church. So in raising environmental issues, the Church undoubtedly risks alienating many of its most faithful adherents.

This is only one small and local instance, but it is surely fairly typical of the roadblocks that the synodal process would encounter worldwide. Nevertheless, McDonagh asserts that such a movement, going from local to global to culminate in a major international conference, "would be a huge boost to ecological thinking and action around the world and the Catholic Church could play a vital role in facilitating the whole process."[18]

McDonagh's strategy for implementing *Laudato Si'* is undoubtedly admirable, if dauntingly ambitious. He has been consistently advocating this strategy around the world at conferences and through the media, for almost four years, since the encyclical was launched. But has any progress been made toward formally launching such a synodal process, anywhere? Has the plan even taken off anywhere at a parish level?

"No," he concedes immediately. But then he quickly goes on to stress the progress that has been made—progress that is already very significant, and advancing fast. So he is not despondent. The context for his upbeat assessment is probably to be found in comments he made to me at the outset of our interview, about the complete dearth of environmental awareness in Catholic institutions prior to the encyclical's publication. "We were nowhere. We've got somewhere. We no longer have to argue our position that climate change is happening, because it's so clearly set out in the encyclical. In terms of a single jump, this is extraordinary."

He then points to small initiatives on the ground since the encyclical, which he believes are real advances. For specifics, he suggests I talk to Catherine Brennan SSL. She sits on the national *Laudato Si'* working group with McDonagh, and is a founder member of Eco Congregations Ireland (ECI). This organization set up in 2005 to encourage "churches of all denominations to take an eco approach to worship, lifestyle, property and finance management, community outreach and contact with the developing world."[19] It offers parishes resources for becoming more environmentally aware, and more environmentally friendly in the impacts of their institutions and their personal lives. When they reach a particular standard, they are awarded the status of "eco congregation."

Brennan echoes McDonagh's experience of finding little understanding or support for ecological initiatives within Catholic Church structures in Ireland prior to the encyclical. She has no doubt that *Laudato Si'* has been a turning point. Its publication, she says, "was followed by an air of excitement, gratitude and hope. It gave the imprimatur (I use the word loosely here) to the many in Ireland already involved in the care of God's creation."[20] It has been followed, she continues, by a steady flow of lectures, conferences, and articles.

> Laudato Si' groups have been set up in parishes and are becoming eco congregations. Before publication, we had four [Catholic] parishes with awards...now over a dozen Catholic parishes have full awards, and over 20 are working on the ECI programme.

She says the national *Laudato Si'* working group is playing a key role in "planning practical actions as follow up...and making sure the encyclical has a place in religious education programmes in primary and post primary schools."

Pope Francis visited Ireland for the World Meeting of Families in 2018, an event attended by almost 40,000 people from more than 100 countries. Brennan and her colleagues availed of this opportunity to give the encyclical's message a higher profile. They created an educational "Our Common

Home" garden in a convent opposite the meeting venue, using art, crafts, Celtic traditions, and children's games to spread the word about evolution, biodiversity, water protection, and food, liberally illustrated by quotations from *Laudato Si'*.

Brennan points out that the working group has also collaborated with the National Biodiversity Data Centre and the All-Ireland Pollinator Plan to produce a guide specifically for faith communities, advising on the creation of local pollinator habitats. The guide draws heavily on the encyclical in its opening pages, and encourages readers to use its resources to help their parishes become eco congregations.

It would be very misleading to suggest that the Catholic Church in Ireland has developed a powerful and extensive green grassroots movement as a result of *Laudato Si'*. Less than 50 Catholic parishes are, so far, engaged at any level in the eco congregation movement. There are 1365 parishes in the country as a whole.[21]

In the context of previous inertia, the advances since the encyclical are certainly notable. But in the context of the urgency of the environmental crisis, a vast amount of work remains to be done to turn the Irish Catholic Church into an agent of environmental change in time to make a real difference to our futures.

Divesting from fossil fuels: Irish bishops make significant moves

But one other development must be mentioned as it indicates that the encyclical has had a significant impact at another level within the Church. On the eve of the Pope's visit to Dublin in 2018, the Irish Catholic Bishops' Conference announced that it had decided to "divest its resources from all fossil fuels." It was the second bishops' conference in the world to do so. And the bishops made it clear that:

> In doing so, we are responding directly to Pope Francis' call in his 2015 encyclical letter Laudato Sí (on care for our common home) by moving away from fossil fuels "without delay" (paragraph 165).[22]

Bishop William Crean, who made the announcement, is chairman of Trócaire, the aid agency that had failed to see any link between deforestation and the gospel in the 1980s. Trócaire has now become perhaps the leading institutional advocate of the encyclical's message in Ireland, as Bishop Crean pointed out:

> Trócaire is to the fore in terms of tackling the disruption that climate change is already causing to our living environment. Over the past decade we have seen more intense storms, devastating floods, prolonged droughts and higher temperatures. The impact in terms of human suffering to families is devastating. Climate change is already leading to forced

migration, separation of families and increased pressure on resources. Girls and women are often in the front line of this added burden.

Avoiding further climate change and protecting our common home requires a major change in direction, as Pope Francis outlines in Laudato Sí. In particular, it requires a major shift in our energy and investment policies away from highly polluting fossil fuels toward cleaner renewable energy.

Our announcement, whilst modest in terms of financial resources, is more than just symbolic. It is about joining the growing social movement, led by young people across the world, calling for the realignment of our financial policies to safeguard their future.[23]

The Irish bishops' initiative is all the more remarkable as they had been seen by Irish Catholic environmentalists as almost totally unengaged with environmental issues until this point. (They did produce an environmental pastoral in 2009, but there was, in the words of one well-informed observer, "absolutely no follow up.")

The global response to the encyclical within the Catholic Church: more questions than answers

In researching this chapter, I have sought information from a number of sources, some of them very senior within the Vatican, on the extent to which *Laudato Si'* has impacted on the policy and practice of the secular institutions controlled by the Catholic Church, and on the encyclical's impact on the lives of ordinary Catholics worldwide through responses at the parish level. I did not have the time or resources to pursue these questions extensively, and much more work would need to be done to provide definitive answers. But the responses I did get repeatedly suggested that, again with honorable exceptions, the impact of the Pope's appeal on his own faithful has been mostly been very muted indeed.

A distinguished American scientist and conservation advocate, who is also a member of the Pontifical Academy of Sciences, offered what I found was a fairly typical view from within the Church:

> Anecdotally, the impact in the US has been limited, at least at the overt level, with few sermons or actions based on the Encyclical. On the other hand, about two-thirds of the people in the U.S. now think climate change is a serious problem, of personal importance, and that something needs to be done about it, and that it is much better than it was a few years ago.

He suggested I look at the US Conference of Bishops website for further information.

You need to drill quite far down into that website to find references to the encyclical. It does not feature on the home page, and "environment," even as a general term, does not even figure as a main section of the Bishops' "Issues and Action" page. It seems fair to conclude that this absence indicates that, despite the Pope's exhortations, the US conference is not prioritizing climate and biodiversity among its commitments. That said, "Environment" is one of numerous sub-headings under the "Human Life and Dignity" section, and when you do reach the "Environment" Page, the encyclical is certainly prominently headlined. And this page may also lead you to the US Catholic Climate Declaration, which commits individuals and institutions to supporting the goals of the 2015 Paris Climate Agreement. Seven hundred and ninety US Catholic institutions have signed the declaration, which may sound impressive in a country so subject to skeptical messages about climate change from political, and indeed religious, leaders. But when you begin to break this number down, and find that it includes less than 200 US parishes across the whole country, it is evident that a huge amount of work remains to be done before climate action becomes central to US Catholic life on the ground.

I also contacted the chancellor of the Pontifical Academy of Sciences, Bishop Marcelo Sánchez Sorondo, who frankly told me that

> Unfortunately I regret to inform you that I have no way of measuring the impact of Laudato Si'. Nevertheless, my impression is that the Encyclical obtained greater success in the non-Catholic world in universities, where I have been invited to speak, and is only now garnering the interest of the Catholic world. Personally, I think this is due to the fact that Catholic universities in general do not have faculties of science, so they aren't able to evaluate the problem from a scientific point of view.

This view, that the encyclical has had more traction outside than inside the Church, was reiterated by several other contacts.

A more upbeat analysis is offered by John Sweeney, the leading Irish climatologist, and member of the Irish LS group with Sean McDonagh, Catherine Brennan, and others, who writes (email to author, 6 February 2019):

> the progress has been remarkable, especially outside Ireland. Laudato Si' was underestimated at the time of its launch but has proven to be a significant document with I believe great longevity. Many Catholic parishes outside Ireland have set up LS groups and I have attended both the launch conference and anniversary conferences in Rome where the appeal of the document to a wide spectrum of society was apparent. It is especially an important issue for many young people…
>
> Divestment has now gone beyond the universities, faith groups and government to impinge on other areas in the charitable sector and ethical investment sectors.

Nevertheless, I found it very difficult to quantify, in terms of the Church's total resources and total institutions, just how significant the encyclical has been to date. Several further inquiries to the Vatican referred me on to the Global Catholic Climate Movement, and so I hoped that this movement might offer the kind of global information I was looking for. The movement's spokespersons referred me to links on their website, which do show that there are hundreds of Catholic organizations and institutions worldwide that have responded to *Laudato Si'*, in some cases taking the step of divesting from fossil fuels.[24]

But I still felt that, to assess this information, I needed to be able to place it in the context of the Church's total resources. Obviously, it is a good thing that some Catholic organizations are responding, but the statistical significance of the information is only possible to evaluate if we know how many organizations have not responded. So I sent the GCCM these follow-up questions:

> While I find the [information] on your website... helpful, what I'm finding difficult to grasp is [the] relative significance within the Church as a whole. It's obvious that a significant number of Catholic organisations have supported divestment, and that substantial funds have been divested, but I guess my problem is that I have no way of measuring them against the Church's total membership, or total financial holdings.
>
> In other words, what percentage of Church funds has been divested from fossil fuels, and what percentage of Church funds remains invested in fossil fuels? What percentage of Bishops' Conferences have divested, and how many remain with fossil fuel investments?
>
> Finally, I'm also wondering if anyone has any figures, even an estimate, of the percentage of parishes around the world in which *Laudato Si'* has been actively taught and made a significant impact on the parish life in worship and practical actions?

Despite resending these questions several times, over several weeks, stressing that I was now beyond the deadline for submitting the first draft of this chapter, I received no further response.

The reader must make their own assessment as to whether, in this case, absence of evidence is evidence of absence. But one would imagine that, if *Laudato Si'* were making the kind of impact the encyclical itself makes very clear is both essential and urgent for the future of humanity, then the Church would be trumpeting it from the rooftops.

In a final attempt to find even an approximation to answers to my questions, I wrote to Tomas Buitendijk, a PhD student in Environmental Humanities, who happened to publish a very pertinent *Irish Times* Op Ed article, "It's Time for a Green Lent," just as I was finishing this chapter.[25] He had no more answers than I had, but he did have an analysis that I think is very perceptive, and has the insight that comes from being an active churchgoer:

> It seems to me that *Laudato Si'* has been received in two very different ways. The first is one of growing awareness of and engagement with the changes Pope Francis suggests: this approach is mostly found at the

(higher levels) of church administration, in Catholic green movements (quite a few of which predate the publication of *Laudato Si'*) and certain (urban) parishes. For instance, a number of Bishops' Conferences (including the Irish one) took steps to divest from fossil fuels, and there are parishes who have adopted measures to 'green' their buildings and have started discussing green theology in the community.

The second type of engagement, or rather lack of engagement, is widely evident at the grassroots level. Most parishioners, at least in Ireland, have never heard of *Laudato Si'* and are unlikely to adopt its radical suggestions. The document has not made its way into our homes and we do not seek to effect Pope Francis's recommendations in our daily lives.

The disparity between these two ways of engaging with the recommendations in *Laudato Si'* is at least partially caused by the complex and layered structure of the Catholic Church and by the fact that encyclical documents, being issued by the Pope, originate at the very top of that structure. Previous encyclicals, such as *Humanae Vitae*, were aimed at distributing dogmatic teaching. Since dogma needs only to be accepted or rejected, it reverberates through the church community easily. This is especially the case when it can be captured in a single statement (e.g., "contraception is bad" or "the family is the central unity of society"). As a result, *Humanae Vitae* had a profound impact in the church, all the way down to the level of the individual believer.

But *Laudato Si'* is radically different. It calls for complete societal reform and demands significant sacrifices on the part of many people. Moreover, its recommendations are not easily summarized. How could such a multifaceted and revolutionary message be spread throughout the complex and layered structure of the church? How could it reach the people? This could only be achieved through intense and enduring effort on the part of everyone involved - including individual parishioners. I believe this engagement has been partial at best - more often, it has been completely absent. As a result, the societal change envisioned in *Laudato Si'* has largely failed to materialize.

I am also indebted to another student, Alex Erwin at the University of Illinois, for permission to use his (unpublished) essay "*Laudato Si'*: Has There Been an Impact Among The Christian Community?" He sought information from his (divorced) Catholic parents, who worship in different Illinois parishes, and found that the encyclical had barely been mentioned, if at all, at local Catholic services and events. This is an experience that does seem quite representative anecdotally in the United States and elsewhere, though hard statistics are generally lacking. However, he also noted a paper[26] by Nan Li et al., based on interviews with 1,400 people before and after the encyclical was published. Li found that, where Catholics were aware of the encyclical at all, it did motivate liberal Catholics toward more active concerns about climate. But conservative Catholics, faced with a clash between the moral imperatives expressed in *Laudato Si'*, and the skepticism about climate change articulated by their favored political leaders, actually hardened their own climate skepticism, and lost respect for Pope Francis. Erwin concludes:

> the majority of Catholics are either not aware of the Pope's guidance on the matter, have disputed it, or are actively taking actions that contradict the teachings. To remedy this, I believe Pope Francis needs to call on all bishops and priests to more actively promote the teachings of *Laudato Si'*. There are surely some adult Catholics too rooted in their beliefs to change, so I believe that applying the new teachings surrounding the creation story and climate change to Catholic grade schools would have the greatest long-term impact.

One has to ask, though: does humanity have time to wait that long? A great deal of thought, work, passion, and commitment has created *Laudato Si'*, a document of unique and urgent significance within the teaching of the Catholic Church, and one which has generally had a very warm welcome from the environmentalist community.

However, unless the Church itself can galvanize an internal process to make this teaching central to the daily lives of believers, and to the real-world practices of its own secular institutions then, as an outsider, I must express the fear that, in the words of the encyclical itself, the mainstream Church's commitment to restoring our almost-ruined common home will remain, despite the dynamic efforts of people like Sean McDonagh, Catherine Brennan and many others, mostly at the level of

> … superficial rhetoric, sporadic acts of philanthropy and perfunctory expressions of concern for the environment.
>
> (54)

And then neither the Cry of the Earth, nor the Cry of the Poor, will have been heeded.

Notes

1 Earth Charter, The Hague, 2000; http://earthcharter.org/discover/what-is-the-earth-charter/
2 Christian ecofeminists have extensively and, in my very limited experience of their work convincingly, critiqued the impact of the traditional Christian vision of an exclusively male and patriarchal God on our relationship with the environment (for a survey, see for example 'Ecofeminism: the Challenge to Theology' by Rosemary Radford Ruether: www.unive.it/media/allegato/dep/n20-2012/Ricerche/Riflessione/4_Ruether_Ecofeminism.pdf).
   I do not dwell on this issue here because patriarchy is so embedded in mainstream Catholic teaching, and it would be naïve to expect the Pope to challenge it in this document.

3 The Pope sometimes falls back on the idea of humanity's innately supreme place in nature even when not quoting the Bible, albeit conceiving it as a role to be exercised responsibly rather than a power to be arbitrarily wielded: "The work of *dominating the world* calls for a union of skills and a unity of achievement that can only grow from quite a different attitude" (219) (Italics mine).

4 For a thought-provoking discussion of the idea that the evolution ("Creation"?) of our natural world, far from being a benign and innocent enterprise, is a "universal scandal" since it inevitably obliges animals, including humans, to survive by killing and eating other created beings, see Jordan 2003: 72–73, 137–159. Jordan argues that we need to differentiate 'guilt', which applies to our optional violations of moral codes, to "shame," which we have no choice but to feel before the biological facts of our existence. He argues that this sense of 'shame' can be resolved by innovative cultural and even liturgical "performances" and that ecological restoration projects provide excellent vehicles for this process. I have discussed these ideas further in Woodworth 2013: 404–405.

5 The Gospel According to St, Luke, 3:11, King James version.

6 Since writing this section, I have had the illuminating experience of reading Margaret Daly-Denton's chapter in this book, "Laudato Si' and the Re-interpretation of the Scriptures." Daly-Denton sheds much light on how various strands of ecological hermeneutics approach the Bible, and the distinctive ways in which the approach of Pope Francis and his collaborators fit into this new tradition. I'm delighted to find that some of the points that trouble me in the encyclical's appeal to the Bible, the rather inconsistent struggle with the biblical use of the word "dominion" for example, are explored in a much more erudite fashion in her contribution. However, reading her essay has also clarified for me why, as an agnostic, I have doubts about the project of turning scriptural texts into environmental teachings. And my comments, despite some overlap, are inevitably different from Daly-Denton's in a fundamental way. I concur entirely with her statement that "the application of an ecological hermeneutics to the Bible makes little sense outside the Judaeo-Christian faith communities. Ecological Hermeneutics is practised by and intended for people whose approach to the plight of our planet is shaped by their faith in God…" Since I do not belong to any of these faith communities, and therefore do not have any reason to expect that the Bible might be a source of ecological wisdom or ecological ethics, I am perforce at a considerable distance from members of those faith communities as they attempt to find a coherent sustainability narrative in the Old or New Testament. And I have to state frankly that, from where I stand, such attempts mostly seem very unconvincing. If God did, as it were, dictate the Bible, I can see very little evidence that S/He is an environmentalist. I am, however, delighted that so many Christians are deeply concerned about the state of the Earth, and that *Laudato Si'* is increasing their numbers.

7 https://danassays.wordpress.com/collected-essays-by-aldous-huxley/aldous-huxley-essays-wordsworth-in-the-tropics/

8 www.teebweb.org/

9 Author interview published in *The Irish Times* August 27, 2011: www.irishtimes.com/life-and-style/people/the-capitalist-environmentalist-and-the-price-of-nature-1.608632

10 Woodworth 2013.

11 The Society for Ecological Restoration's Primer on Ecological Restoration is recognized as a key guiding document by, among others, the International Union for the Conservation of Nature, Parks Canada, the TEEB reports, Nature Conservation Foundation India, the Food and Agriculture Organization, the United Nations Environment Programme, and Kew Royal Botanic Gardens. Ecological restoration is also a major plank in the Global Strategy for Plant

Conservation; it features as a leading element in the Aichi Targets (2011–2020) of the Convention on Biological Diversity, including the very ambitious goal of restoring 15% of degraded ecosystems across the world over the next ten years (www.cbd.int/doc/strategic-plan/2011–2020/Aichi-Targets-EN.pdf).

The SER Primer is available for download at https://cdn.ymaws.com/www. ser.org/resource/resmgr/custompages/publications/SER_Primer/ser_primer.pdf

SER's International Standards, which may supersede the Primer, are currently being updated, but the first edition can be seen at https://cdn.ymaws. com/www.ser.org/resource/resmgr/docs/SER_International_Standards.pdf

12 All quotations from McDonagh are from an interview with the author in January 2019, unless otherwise attributed.
13 McDonagh 2017: 27–29.
14 Jordan 2003:189.
15 https://seasonofcreation.org/about/
16 Email to author, 6 February 2019.
17 McDonagh 2017: 28.
18 Ibid., 29.
19 http://ecocongregationireland.com/about
20 These and the following quotations are from notes sent by Catherine Brennan following an interview with the author, February 2019.
21 The Catholic Church in Ireland operates as one organisation in the separate political jurisdictions of the Republic of Ireland and Northern Ireland.
22 www.catholicbishops.ie/2018/08/24/statement-by-bishop-william-crean-announcing-the-decision-of-the-bishops-conference-to-divest-from-fossil-fuels/ accessed 7 February, 2019.
23 Ibid.
24 https://catholicclimatemovement.global/announcements/
25 www.irishtimes.com/opinion/it-s-time-for-a-green-lent-1.3813976
26 Li et al. 2016. 367.

References

Francis, Pope and Sean McDonagh. 2016. *On Care for our Common Home: Laudato Si' with Commentary by Sean McDonagh*. New York: Orbis Books.

Jordan, William R. 2003. *The Sunflower Forest: Ecological Restoration and the New Communion with Nature*. Berkeley: University of California Press.

Leopold, Aldo. 1993. *Round River*. New York: Oxford University Press.

Li, Nan, Joseph Hilgard, Dietram A. Scheufele, Kenneth M. Winneg, and Kathleen Hall Jamieson. 2016. "Cross-pressuring Conservative Catholics? Effects of Pope Francis' Encyclical on the U.S. Public Opinion on Climate Change", *Climatic Change*, 139 (3–4), 367–380. doi:10.1007/s10584-016-1821-z

McDonagh, Sean. 2017. "A Prophetic Challenge for the Twenty-First Century", in *Laudato Si': An Irish Response*, ed. Sean McDonagh. Dublin: Veritas Publications.

Woodworth, Paddy. 2013. *Our Once and Future Planet: Restoring the World in the Climate Change Century*. Chicago: University of Chicago Press.

Part 3

Scriptural, theological and philosophical aspects

8 *Laudato Si'* and the reinterpretation of Scriptures in light of the ecological crisis

Margaret Daly-Denton

As would be expected of any writing in the Christian ethical tradition, Pope Francis's appeal on behalf of our common home draws extensively on the Judeo-Christian Scriptures. His use of the Bible demonstrates how faith convictions can offer believers ample motivation to take better care of Earth (64) by embracing an integral ecology that acknowledges both the social and the environmental dimensions of the present global crisis (139). But the role of the Bible in the encyclical goes far beyond the sixty-or-so formal biblical quotations and the numerous biblical allusions. Francis suggests that "by constantly returning to their sources religions will be better equipped to respond to today's needs" (200). *Laudato Si'* models a particular way of reading the Scriptures: allowing the ecological crisis to be the context in which believers might listen to their sacred texts (67). It thus encourages the development of ecological hermeneutics, an emerging discipline within contemporary biblical studies that has immense potential to provide resources for humanity's response to the "cultural, spiritual and educational challenge" (202) that the plight of our planet presents.

This chapter first reviews the development of an ecological hermeneutics in recent years, some of the problems that its practitioners have encountered and some of the new possibilities that it has opened up for biblical scholars to make their unique contribution to the healing of Earth's ills. It then compares the way certain biblical passages feature in *Laudato Si'* with the way(s) they are read by scholars working at the cutting edge of ecological hermeneutics today, noting both the convergences and the divergences. A brief survey of what I consider to be important initiatives in reading the Scriptures in view of the ecological crisis follows. This records salient moments in my own experience of learning how to read and respond in an earth-conscious mode. It also shows my own perspective as an appreciative but occasionally critical addressee of *Laudato Si'*.

Ecological hermeneutics

The emergence of this new methodology among biblical scholars writing in English can be traced to the pioneering work of the Australian scholar

Norman C. Habel and his Earth Bible Team who produced around the turn of this century a seminal five-volume series of exploratory attempts to read the Bible from an ecological perspective. In these chapters, various authors re-read in the light of the present ecological crisis a part of the Bible, of which they already had a specialized knowledge (Habel 2001a, 2001b; Habel and Balabanski 2002; Habel and Wurst 2000, 2001). As part of the brief to these scholars, the Earth Bible Team, in dialogue with ecologists, devised a set of Guiding Ecojustice Principles. These stressed the intrinsic worth of Earth and all its components as a purposefully designed community of interconnected and mutually dependent beings. Their definition of the role of humankind as responsible custodianship in partnership with the whole earth community was not only a critique of the ethos of mastery but also a riposte to the tendency in the eco-theological discourse of the time to tone down the idea of dominion over the Earth (Gen 1:26) into stewardship, a concept that they regarded as equally anthropocentric. The Ecojustice Principles also alerted readers to "the voice" of Earth as heard in the Judeo-Christian Scriptures, a voice raised both in celebration and in lament and resistance (The Earth Bible Team 2002). From 2004 onwards, scholarly reading of the Bible from an ecological perspective was promoted and animated by a newly constituted Ecological Hermeneutics Seminar at the annual meetings of the Society of Biblical Literature and it is in this ongoing international collaboration that eco-hermeneutical methodologies have continued to be refined and developed (Habel and Trudinger 2008).

One important advance has been the broadening of approaches beyond the initial Guiding Ecojustice Principles. A greater methodological diversity now informs a successor project, "An Earth Bible Commentary," currently appearing as each volume on an individual book of the Bible is completed.[1] For example, the suspicion-identification-retrieval scheme, familiar from feminist critique has been found to work well for ecological hermeneutics, as shown in Anthony Rees's work on Numbers for this Commentary (Rees 2015). In a different vein, Elaine Wainwright has developed for her ecological reading of Matthew's gospel her own adaptation of the socio-rhetorical approach: an eco-rhetorical approach that works in conversation with the writings of major contemporary ecological and eco-feminist theorists (Wainwright 2016). Sigve K. Tonstad's approach to Romans aims to be "respectful of Paul's concern and primary errand," while "restoring to Paul the ecological given-ness that traditional interpretations have ignored or taken away" (Tonstad 2017: x–xi).

Another significant international and inter-religious initiative in mobilizing the religious resources of the world on behalf of the environment was the series of conferences sponsored by Harvard University around the turn of the Millennium and the resulting series of books, "Religions of the World and Ecology," which includes volumes on the Jewish and Christian traditions and the resources for ecology in their shared and distinctive

Scriptures (Hessel and Ruether 2000; Tirosh-Samuelson 2003). The biblical chapters in these two volumes have been a valuable resource for people learning how to read the Bible from an ecological perspective.

A further development of ecological hermeneutics has been the collaborative research project on Uses of the Bible in Environmental Ethics at the University of Exeter. Its participants include not only biblical scholars but also two research scientists turned theologians (one in biochemistry, the other in cell biology). A particularly valuable output from this initiative is a collection of chapters entitled *Ecological Hermeneutics* (Horrell, Hunt, Southgate and Stavrakopoulou 2010). An important contribution to the refining of eco-hermeneutical methodologies has been the Exeter group's critical assessment of various kinds of appeal to the Bible made in contemporary environmental debate. They would put these appeals into three categories: apologetic "recovery" readings where the Bible's "ecofriendliness" is presumed as a given that can be retrieved through "correct" interpretation, readings of resistance that subject the Bible to the critique of external principles (e.g., several of the Earth Bible Team's Guiding Ecojustice Principles), and readings that find in the Bible a basis for the rejection of the ecological agenda (e.g., literalizing readings of apocalyptic writings). Their own preferred approach, an ecological hermeneutics poised between recovery and resistance, is two-pronged. First, our contemporary experience and scientific knowledge of ecological issues can become a hermeneutical lens through which we might look at the biblical writings and see something new. And second, rather than just picking out supposedly eco-friendly verses from the Bible—what the Exeter scholars call "eco-theological mantra texts"—we should try to see how the over-arching understanding of the world as God's creation, that is reflected in various biblical writings and actually underpins much biblical thought, might be activated as a "character-forming" counter-narrative to the myths that capitalist societies have until now been living by (Horrell, Hunt, and Southgate 2010: 11–59).

As ecological hermeneutics has developed internationally, there has been a growing recognition that the Bible is often "an inconvenient text" for ecologists, that it is not consistently eco-sensitive, that it frequently portrays the earth being ravaged, particularly in writings of an apocalyptic tendency (Habel 2009). At times, ecological readings require a certain "going against the grain" of the text. Thus a nuanced reading of Jesus's invitation to learn from the birds of the air and the lilies of the field (Matt 6:28)—a passage often assumed to be "ecological"—or of the story of the Gadarene pigs (Matt 8:28–34) will have to face up to their problematic valuing of the human over the other-than-human (Wainwright 2016: 89, 109–114). It is important to stress that such critique of the biblical writings is not inconsistent with reverence for it as Sacred Scripture. In fact, the application of an ecological hermeneutics to the Bible makes little sense outside the Judeo-Christian faith communities. Ecological Hermeneutics is practiced by and intended for people whose approach to the plight of our planet is shaped by their faith in God, and who, with Ellen Davis, regard environmental irresponsibility as "the undoing of what God has made and sustained" (Davis 2009: 11). It also arises out of a conviction that God's gifts to humankind include "a mind for thinking with" (Sir 17:6). To recognize that the Bible contains many culturally and historically conditioned human apprehensions of God and of God's intentions for human beings is in no way to underestimate its capacity to mediate an encounter with the Divine. Nearly 50 years ago, the Roman Catholic Church decided to omit several psalm verses and even three entire psalms from its Liturgical Psalter because of their imprecatory character (Sacred Congregation for Divine Worship 1971: par. 131). This may well turn out to be a useful precedent.

Finally, it cannot be sufficiently stressed that to read the Scriptures in this way is not to suggest that the writers of the Hebrew Bible, or Jesus or the early Christians had an ecological consciousness. Eco-hermeneutics is an attempt to tap into the ongoing generativity of sacred texts, the meaning that lay thousands of years ahead of them when they were first written, but that jumps off the page when we read them in the twenty first century, standing on our damaged Earth. When suggesting, as part of his appeal "to every person living on this planet" (3), that even people who do not share the Judeo-Christian faith perspective can still respond to it at the aesthetic or philosophical level, Pope Francis would appear to be using David Tracy's idea of the "classic text" that, because it bears a certain excess of meaning and a certain timelessness, can confront and provoke us in our present horizon (Tracy 1981: 101–107). As he puts it, "Religious classics can prove meaningful in every age; they have an enduring power to open new horizons" (199). The ecological horizon is most certainly one of them. Finally, ecological hermeneutics is emphatically not an abandonment of critical biblical scholarship. It depends and builds upon conventional scholarly approaches. Nevertheless, it does something quite different.

The creation narratives in *Laudato Si'*

As would be expected, *Laudato Si'* makes frequent reference to the two creation narratives in Genesis (Gen 1:1–2:3 and Gen 2:4–25). From the first account, Section 38 refers to God creating humankind in the divine image (Gen 1:26) and seeing that everything created was very good (Gen 1:31). From the second account, Section 2 reminds us that we are dust of the earth (Gen 2:7); Sections 67 and 124 urge us not only to till and keep the garden of the world but also to make it fruitful (Gen 2:15); Section 217 states unequivocally that "living our vocation to be protectors of God's handiwork is essential to a life of virtue; it is not an optional or secondary aspect of our Christian experience."

All other references in *Laudato Si'* to the first account concern what has come to be known as the mandate to dominate: to fill the earth and subdue it and to have dominion over every living thing (Gen 1:26–28). Sometimes, the encyclical attempts to resolve the well-known difficulties associated with this presentation of the role of humankind in the world as mastery and conquest by blending it with the more "earth-friendly" second creation narrative. The problems arising from an attempted harmonization of two narratives written from quite different perspectives become apparent, for example, when Section 66 states that [sin] distorted our mandate to "have dominion" over the earth (Gen 1:28) and to "till it and keep it" (Gen 3:17–19). This supposed dual mandate smooths over the manifest inconsistency between the more heavily anthropocentric first narrative and the second, written by an ancient author who portrays God as a gardener (Gen 2:8) and generally shows far more empathy with the earth and concern for its flourishing.

Pope Francis is at pains to point out that exploitation is not a correct interpretation of the biblical idea of "dominion" (67). In fact, he calls for putting an end to the claim on the part of human beings "to absolute dominion over the earth" (75). Instead of a Promethean vision of mastery over the world... human "dominion" over the universe should be understood more properly in the sense of responsible stewardship (116). According to this construal, the human being exercises lordship over everything, but in a correct understanding of this lordship, is a responsible steward (Latin, *conscius administrator*).[2] The first thing to notice here is that the "dominion" that in Genesis was to be exercised over "the fish of the sea and over the birds of the air and over every living thing that moves upon the earth" has become dominion over the entire world and even, possibly, the universe (Latin, *universum*: the whole world, the universe). The claim that the human being is either the earth's or the universe's "conscientious administrator" makes absolutely no sense to people who know that if the story of the emergence of the universe were to be represented by a 24-hour clock, the appearance of human beings happened at a few seconds to midnight!

In some passages, the encyclical is clearly advocating a recovery reading of the dominion issue. The problem is that "we Christians have at times incorrectly interpreted the Scriptures" (67), but an explanation of the text that fits with our contemporary ecological concerns can be retrieved through correct interpretation. From this "recovery" perspective, it is clear that "the Bible has no place for a tyrannical anthropocentrism unconcerned for other creatures" (68).

> If a mistaken understanding of our own principles has at times led us to justify mistreating nature, to exercise tyranny over creation, to engage in war, injustice and acts of violence, we believers should acknowledge that by so doing we were not faithful to the treasures of wisdom which we have been called upon to protect and preserve.
>
> (200)

Such a reading takes human superiority over the more-than-human world for granted, but attempts to soften it. Elsewhere the encyclical explains this superiority "not as a reason for personal glory or irresponsible dominion, but rather as a different capacity which, in its turn, entails a serious responsibility stemming from our faith" (220). Again the "stewardship" solution is proposed.

In a rather perplexing reference to the mandate to dominate, Section 219 calls for the development of "community networks to tackle a task that isolated individuals, no matter how well motivated, cannot achieve." According to a quotation from Romano Guardini's writings, this task is "the work of dominating the world." On closer inspection, however, this turns out to be a case of mistranslation that has occurred only in the English version of the encyclical. There is no reference whatever to "dominating the world" in either Guardini's original German or the Latin text of Section 219. The task (Latin, *opus*: work) being discussed in this paragraph is what Pope Francis calls "ecological conversion." This involves the changing of a utilitarian, consumerist mindset into a social and ecological consciousness. The Letter insists, citing Guardini, that this cannot be achieved by the efforts of individuals, or even by the united efforts of people who think in an individualistic way. A joining-up of strengths and the bringing together of contributions will be needed (Latin, *Necessaria erit virtutum coniunctio et unitas contributionum*) because ecological conversion has to be about the conversion of communities. The fact that such a glaring interpolation in a "mastery" vein could slip through in the Vatican's official translation of the encyclical into English brings up an important point. It is well known that Popes do not actually write every word of their encyclicals themselves. They have an international panel of advisors who are also involved in the translation work. As with the documents of the Second Vatican Council and numerous Vatican documents since then, it is frequently possible to discern different voices of varying persuasions. A good example would be the way the promotion of the vernacular in the Liturgy Constitution of Vatican II is counter-balanced by an insistence that Latin remains the official language of the liturgy (*Sacrosanctum Concilium*, Liturgy Constitution of the Second Vatican Council 1963: par. 36).

It is not too surprising then that the handling of the "dominion" issue in *Laudato Si'* is not entirely consistent. The genre of an encyclical is such that critique of previous church teaching is "out of bounds," so one would hardly expect to find in *Laudato Si'* readings of the Bible from the "resistance" end of the recovery-resistance continuum. In view of this, the statement that "In our time, the Church does not simply state that other creatures are completely subordinated to the good of human beings" (69) is quite striking.

In recent eco-hermeneutical studies, a consensus has emerged that the biblical assertion of human dominion over the other-than-human (Gen 1:26–28) urgently cries out for a reading of resistance. The need for such a reading is especially clear when we read the reiteration of God's mandate addressed to Noah and his sons after the flood.

> Be fruitful and multiply, and fill the earth. The fear and dread of you shall rest on every animal of the earth, and on every bird of the air, on everything that creeps on the ground, and on all the fish of the sea; into

your hand they are delivered. Every moving thing that lives shall be food for you; and just as I gave you the green plants, I give you everything.

This human superiority is celebrated in a well-known psalm passage used frequently in Christian liturgy, although, interestingly, not cited in *Laudato Si'*:

> ... what are human beings that you are mindful of them,
> mortals that you care for them?
> Yet you have made them a little lower than God,
> and crowned them with glory and honor.
> You have given them dominion over the works of your hands;
> you have put all things under their feet,
> all sheep and oxen, and also the beasts of the field,
> the birds of the air, and the fish of the sea,
> whatever passes along the paths of the seas.
>
> (Ps 8:4–8)[3]

Obviously, there is a certain poetic hyperbole here, as well as in the Genesis passages. It is also important to remember that in the ancient Mediterranean world where the worship of various forces of nature was pervasive, such a statement of human dignity was remarkable. However, there is no getting away from the fact that the Hebrew verbs in the Creator's mandate to the newly created human beings are particularly violent. As Habel has shown, *kabash* (translated as "subdue" in Gen 1:28 NRSV) means heavy handed control, subjugation, oppression, and is even associated with sexual assault (Esth 7:8; Neh 5:5). *Rada* (translated as "have dominion" in Gen 1:28 NRSV) is used not only of kings (1 Kgs 4:24) but also of oppressive taskmasters (1 Kgs 5:16) (Habel 2009: 5–6).

For people who find the idea of a "resistance" reading of the "mandate to dominate" unacceptable, the Book of Wisdom, which, as we will see, is cited several times in *Laudato Si'* may perhaps model an alternative approach. The prayer that a reimagined "Solomon" makes there to God the Creator who formed humankind to have dominion over the creation is a plea for the gift of the divine wisdom by which the world was made in the first place (Wis 9:1–4; see Prov 8:22–31).[4] However, if we are to read the Bible intelligently, it is difficult to see an alternative to a resistance reading of the "dominion" passage. And this is where the above-mentioned diversity of readings that co-exist in *Laudato Si'* comes in. Even though the general tendency is to blame the damage that the concept of mastery has caused on incorrect interpretation of Gen 1:26–28, several chinks open up for a more critical reading of Gen 1:26–28. One may well suspect that in such passages Francis's own voice is heard. In his opening diagnosis of the ecological crisis, for example, he refers to our proclivity for seeing ourselves as "lords and masters" of "our Sister, Mother Earth ... entitled to plunder her at will" (1–2). He contrasts St Francis of Assisi's response to the world around him with our attitude: "that of masters, consumers, ruthless exploiters" (11). "We must forcefully reject" this notion of "absolute domination over other creatures," he writes (67). Restoring ourselves to our rightful place in the world means "putting an end to our claim to absolute dominion over the earth" (75; cf. 224) "rejecting every tyrannical and irresponsible domination of human beings over other creatures" (83) "avoiding the dynamic of dominion," (222), recognizing the prevailing "technocratic paradigm" for the ethos of mastery that it is (106; 224).

An ecological mantra text

As mentioned above, Christian eco-theological writings frequently appeal to certain biblical verses that have come to be regarded as "proof" of the Bible's eco-friendliness. One is Jesus's saying, "I have come that they may have life and have it abundantly" (John 10:10, not used in *Laudato Si'*). If by "they" Jesus meant "all creatures," then surely he was an ecologist! Another example is "the cosmic Christ," usually traced back to the portrayal of Christ's role in the all-encompassing scope of the creation as depicted in Col 1:15–20, especially the line, "All things were created through him and for him." Eco-hermeneuts tend to be hesitant about the way such passages are bandied about as "ecological mantra texts." In fact, a close study that attends to their wider context can often yield rich resources for an earth-conscious reading, but the result inclines to be quite different to what a decontextualized snippet of Scripture might have suggested.[5]

The first biblical quotation in the encyclical is a reference to what is probably the most frequently cited ecological mantra text, Paul's description of the creation "groaning in travail" (Rom 8:22, cited in Section 2 and in the concluding "Christian prayer" in Section 246). Francis sets us up to interpret this groaning as the lament of the overburdened, abandoned, and maltreated earth. However, in its original Pauline context, the groaning is not lament. It is the shouting and moaning of a woman experiencing birth pangs. It is audible exertion confident of a positive outcome: a new life. The use in the Vatican's English translation of the archaic noun "travail" obscures somewhat, for a present-day audience, the imagery of parturiency that is so much more evident in the official Latin text *congemiscit et comparturit*. It is the common experience of women who have given birth that labor pains are quite different to other kinds of pain, and, for that reason, women holding a new born in their arms tend not to say, "Never again!" As the female members of the community behind John's gospel knew, "When a woman is in labor, she has pain, because her hour has come. But when her child is born, she no longer remembers the anguish because of the joy of having brought a human being into the world" (John 16:21). So there is a definite positivity about "groaning in labour pains" (NRSV). For Paul, it is of-a-piece with the "eager longing" (Rom 8:19) with which a new birth is awaited.

In the Jewish apocalyptic world-view that was Paul's natural habitat, childbirth was frequently used as a metaphor for the coming of the new aeon, the arrival of what the synoptic evangelists call the kingdom/reign, *basileia* of God, and of what the Fourth Evangelist calls "eternal life," *zoē aiōnios*, the life of the [new] aeon (Isa 13:8; 26:17–18; 1 Thess 5:3; Mark 13:8; Rev 12:1–2). In Paul's view, the resurrection of Jesus had inaugurated this aeon, but his followers still lived in "this present time" (Rom 8:18), awaiting the full establishment of God's reign. In Paul's understanding, this in-between period of "eager longing" (Rom 8:19), hope, and waiting with patience (Rom 8:24–25), is also a time for the often painful, but ultimately productive exertion involved in being part of God's work to restore all that has been distorted and damaged (Rom 8:19–20) and to bring everything into alignment with the original loving design for the creation, God's "plan for peace, beauty and fullness" (1 Cor 15:25–28; Section 53). That is why in Romans, it is not only the creation that groans and we ourselves that groan (Rom 8:23), but the Spirit who utters "groans (NRSV: sighs) too deep for words" (Rom 8:26). This is entirely consonant with the Scriptures that speak of God bringing a new era to birth. "For a long time I have held my peace, I have kept still and restrained myself; now I will cry out like a woman in travail, I will gasp and pant" (Isa 42:14).

In recent years, the way Rom 8:22 is employed in eco-theological dis-course has come under the scrutiny of biblical scholars.[6] More appropriate biblical imagery for "the cry of the earth" (1, 2, 53) can be found in nu-merous prophetic passages where Earth, adversely affected by war, human rapacity and injustice, raises her voice in lament (e.g., Joel 1:10–12; Hos 4:1–3). That being said, *Laudato Si'* does come close to Paul's thought in Romans 8 when discussing God's continuing work of creation. "Many of the things that we think of as evils, dangers or sources of suffering, are, in reality, part of the pains of childbirth which [God] uses to draw us into the act of cooperation with the Creator" (80). Furthermore, the encyclical's evocation of the Pauline groaning of creation is actually effective, but in a someone different way to what is indicated in Section 2. The fact that in Romans 8 Paul mentions not only human beings but also the creation itself is a powerful reminder that the task of restoration is not just about humanity but involves and profoundly affects the more-than-human world. And then there is something wonderfully encouraging about the idea of the Holy Spirit groaning and straining with us to bring a healed and renewed earth into being.

The encyclical's use of deutero-canonical books (the Apocrypha)

One of the great gifts that *Laudato Si'* has brought to the Christian churches is the way it draws on writings that for the last 500 years have not been part of the Bible in traditions stemming from the Reformation. In the present day, with the increasing ecumenical use of the *Revised Common Lectionary* at Sunday worship, passages from these books are now heard at least occasionally, but these works remain undiscovered treasures for many Christians.

Laudato Si' contains five quotations from the Wisdom of Solomon (the Book of Wisdom). Thought to have been written in Egypt, possibly in the city of Alexandria, where there was a large Jewish Diaspora, this composition is nowadays dated to somewhere between 30 BCE and 70 CE. It is attributed, in the pseudepigraphical conventions of the time, to King Solomon. Its value for Christians comes from the fact that it was written in Greek, the language of the New Testament writings, that it dates from around the time of Jesus and the earliest Christian writers, and that it opens a window on Jewish interpretation of the Scriptures at that period. As a literary product of the profoundly Hellenized Judaism that was the matrix of Christianity, it shares many commonalities of thought with the Gospel of John, although whether the Fourth Evangelist actually knew it is not certain.

As Pope Francis has clearly discovered, the Wisdom of Solomon preserves precious Jewish insights about God as the lover of all that lives, about the world as God's creation and revelation, and about the role of humankind within it. Section 94 (quoting from the Paraguayan bishops) cites it to stress the equal dignity of the rich and the poor. "It is God who made both great and small" (Wis 6:7). Speaking of how Francis of Assisi was being faithful to Scripture (as was Paul; see Rom 1:20, cited in Section 12) when he saw nature as a magnificent book through which God speaks to us, the encyclical states, "Through the greatness and beauty of creatures one comes to know by analogy their maker" (Wis 13:5, cited in Section 12. See also Section 85). Explaining how "God's love is the fundamental moving force in all created things," it quotes a prayer from the Book of Wisdom, a poetic response to the divine declaration that everything in the creation is "very good" (Gen 1:31):

> For you love all things that exist,
> and detest none of the things that you have made,
> for you would not have made anything if you had hated it.
> How would anything have endured if you had not willed it?
> Or how would anything not called forth by you have been preserved?
> You spare all things, for they are yours,
> O Lord, you who love the living,
> For your immortal spirit is in all things.
>
>   (Wis 11:24–12:1, partially cited in Section 77)

Elsewhere in the encyclical, a quotation from this passage makes the point that we human beings are not free to claim ownership over the created things of this world (Wis 11:26, cited in Section 89).

When reading in Section 82 about the danger inherent in our idea that "might is right," I thought at first that Pope Francis might be alluding to what the ungodly rulers say in the Wisdom of Solomon, "Let our might be our law of right" (Wis 2:11). However, the inverted commas in the Vatican's translation serve merely to indicate that a popular English saying (that may originally have come from Wis 2:11) has been used to translate *Cogitatio, quae fortioris arbitrium roborat*. It is quite possible though that the Book of Wisdom has shaped Francis's thought to such an extent that it shines through in his text without necessarily being intentionally cited. Section 46 goes on to quote Jesus's critique of "the rulers of the Gentiles" for the oppressive way in which they exercise their power (Matt 20:25–26). This resonates with the continuation of the Wisdom passage. The author is presenting a profile of rulers who—unlike Solomon who prayed that Wisdom would guide his rule (Wis 9:1–18)—think they are entitled to exploit Earth's gifts recklessly for their own pleasure. "Let us enjoy the good things that exist," they say, "and make use of the creation to the full ... everywhere let us leave signs of enjoyment, because this is our portion, and this our lot" (Wis 2:6–9). Whether or not the evocation of this passage that I, as one reader, see in Section 82 was intended or not, this is an example of the way the encyclical works. Its biblical quotations trigger our memory of other related passages, inviting us to discover in the Scriptures that we know well, new meanings that present us with new challenges.

The other deutero-canonical book that *Laudato Si'* draws upon is the Wisdom of Jesus Son of Sirach, usually called "Sirach" for short but also known as Ecclesiasticus. This was written sometime between 200 and 180 BCE. Until the discovery of ancient Hebrew manuscripts in the nineteenth and twentieth centuries, this work was known only in a Greek translation. When explaining that the mandate to care for the garden of the earth in Gen 2:15 involves not only preserving it but also tilling it and making it fruitful, Section 124 quotes Sirach's statement that laborers and craftsmen "maintain the fabric of the world" (Eccles/Sir 38:24). In its original setting, this saying is a somewhat condescending acknowledgment of manual work coming from a scribe who would have led a privileged life with leisure (Sir 38:24) to pore over the Scriptures, penetrating their subtleties and seeing out their hidden meanings (Sir 38:34–39:3). Again, if we were to see Pope Francis's use of Sirach as an invitation to explore this book further, we would find that Sirach acknowledges that farm work was created by the Most High (Sir 7:15). The Greek word translated as "farm work" is *geōrgia*, which means work on/with the land/earth (Greek, *gē*: earth, land; *ergon*: work). So, a farmer or gardener is a *geōrgos* the very word that Jesus uses for his Father (John 15:1; NRSV, "vinegrower").

Another quotation from Sirach, in Section 124 which deals with the need to protect employment, forms part of the encyclical's argument that "developing the created world in a prudent way is the best way of caring for it." As an example of the ways that we can be instrumental in bringing out the potential that God has inscribed in the created world, *LS* 124 instances the medicinal use of plants by quoting The Wisdom of Jesus Son of Sirach: "The Lord created medicines out of the earth, and the sensible will not despise them" (Sir 38:4).

Striking new readings of Scripture

Laudato Si' is full of arresting and challenging new readings of the Scriptures. Section 95, for example, asks, What does "You shall not kill" (Exod 20:13) mean when 20% of the world's population consumes resources at a rate that robs the poor nations and future generations of what they need to survive? Section 70 reads the Cain and Abel story (Gen 4:1–16) as a demonstration of how disregard for a sibling ruins our relationship with others, God and the earth, and how restoration is possible if we recover and respect the rhythms inscribed in nature by the Creator. Sometimes, the appeal to the Bible is so subtle that it is more of an evocation of a biblical motif than an actual quotation. When, for example, Pope Francis writes, "Because of us, thousands of species will no longer give glory to God by their very existence, nor convey their message to us; we have no such right" (33; cf. Section 69), he is clearly echoing a recurrent theme in biblical hymns familiar from the liturgy, such as the *Benedicite* (Dan 3) and numerous psalms, notably Ps 148:3–5, cited in Section 72.

In the final chapter of the encyclical where Pope Francis speaks of the small ways that we can cultivate ecological virtues, he offers quite a novel interpretation of a saying of Jesus, "Do not let your left hand know what your right hand is doing" (Matt 6:3–4). Jesus was talking about almsgiving, but here is Pope Francis applying this to everyday domestic matters: avoiding the use of plastic, separating household refuse, turning off unnecessary lights, not running a tap unnecessarily, to mention just a few of the "simple daily gestures" (230) listed in Section 211. I find this immensely insightful because even in our kitchens we are called to perform hidden deeds of care for the earth: to be responsible about the "detergents and chemical products" (29) that we may otherwise carelessly let down the sink, for example. As Francis says, even in these small matters we are called "quietly to imitate [God's] generosity" (220). I think that, without any disrespect, this application of Matt 6:2–3 to far less significant and less demanding actions than almsgiving might be seen as whimsical. Pope Francis has a good sense of humor, and Jesus's witty saying clearly appeals to it. The fact that this interpretation is a little quirky in no way makes it superficial. And this is so encouraging for the work of ecological hermeneutics. Several times in recent years, I have invited study groups to look at John's story of Jesus feeding 5,000 people (John 6:1–13) from an ecological perspective. Invariably, they have heard Jesus's command to his disciples, "Gather up the fragments left over, so that nothing may be lost" (John 6:12) as an appeal to avoid food waste, to recycle, and to repair whatever damage our consumption has done to the earth. For some biblical scholars, this is to trivialize the saying. Surely, the filling of 12 baskets with the left-over food is a symbolic representation of the overflowing abundance of the "eternal life" that Jesus gives, not a trite instruction to pick up after a picnic! For me, the way Pope Francis responds to the Bible in *Laudato Si'* and, in particular, his occasional whimsicality, gives nothing less than a papal blessing to the many people who listen to this story with an intentionally earth-conscious sensitivity and hear something different: a new [ecological] commandment that challenges "the throwaway culture" (16, 22, 27, 43, 123) and the heedlessness with which the wealthy of the earth "leave behind them so much waste which, if it were the case everywhere, would destroy the planet" (90).

Laudato Si' is a blessing for ecological hermeneutics in two ways. First, it encourages this new approach to the reception of the Bible in our faith communities, and provides excellent examples of how this might be done. Even the instances where the cogency of some of the encyclical's appeals to scripture might be questioned inspire and urge further study so that "principles from the Judeo-Christian tradition ... can render our commitment to the environment more coherent" (14). Second, *Laudato Si'* urges us, not just to eco-sensitive Bible reading, but to practical engagement and advocacy for the sake of the earth. It commonly happens that when Christians become involved in activism for justice, that certain biblical passages suddenly become searingly "living and active" (Heb 4:12). One might think, for example, of the British abolitionists' appeals to the Bible in support of their campaign against slavery. Early eighteenth-century readings of the Bible from the perspective of slavery focused on passages that urged considerate treatment of slaves (e.g., Deut 15:12–17), but as their active involvement in the abolition movement grew, Christians began to see in other passages, especially those based on "The Golden Rule" (Matt 7:12; Gal 5:14; James 2:8), a critique of the whole institution of slavery so that eventually slave holding was regarded as incompatible with Christian faith. Then there is the fascinating story of how, from the 1960s onwards, the quest for social justice in the basic Christian communities of South America led to the reading of the Book of Exodus in a new way. People deprived of their fundamental human right to land and housing recognized their story in that of the landless Israelites journeying through the desert. This challenged an "official" church, accustomed to being allied with the rich and powerful, to make "a preferential option for the poor" and consequently to work out a whole new way of being church. Nowadays, something similar is happening as Christians become more and more engaged in the care of our common home. It is the conviction of one present-day environmental activist, Bill McKibben, that "the deepest religious insights on the relation between God, nature, and humans may not emerge until religious people, acting on the terms indicated by their traditions, join [environmental] movements. The act of engagement will itself spur new thinking, new understanding" (McKibben 2001: 305).

Notes

1 To date, volumes on Genesis 1–11, Luke, Deuteronomy, Job, Numbers, Matthew and Romans have been published by Sheffield Academic Press. Bloomsbury/T & T Clark have now taken over the series and have so far published volumes on John and Ecclesiastes.
2 E contrario hominis, universi quidem domini, conceptio recte retenta, ea est quae ipsum officii conscium vult administratorem.
3 Cited in the NRSV gender-inclusive language version. The original Hebrew has "man" understood generically as a reference to humankind.
4 For a more detailed explanation of this suggestion, see Daly-Denton 2017: 61–63.
5 For John 10:10, see Daly-Denton 2017: 140–141; For Col 1:15–20, see Horrell, Hunt and Southgate 2010: 87–115.
6 For example, Byrne 2010: 83–93; Horrell, Hunt and Southgate 2010: 63–85; Tonstad 2008:141–149 and Tonstad 2017: 238–260.

References

Byrne, Brendan. 2010. "An Ecological Reading of Rom 8:19-22: Possibilities and Hesitations" in Horrell, David G., Cherryl Hunt, Christopher Southgate, and Francesca Stavrakopoulou (ed.) *Ecological Hermeneutics: Biblical, Historical and Theological Perspectives.* London: T&T Clark, pp. 83–93.

Daly-Denton, Margaret. 2017. *John. An Earth Bible Commentary: Supposing Him to Be the Gardener.* London: Bloomsbury/T&T Clark.

Davis, Ellen. 2009. *Scripture, Culture and Agriculture: An Agrarian Reading of the Bible.* Cambridge: Cambridge University Press.

Habel, Norman C. 2001a. (ed.), *Readings from the Perspective of Earth.* Sheffield: Sheffield Academic Press.

Habel, Norman C. 2001b. (ed.), *The Earth Story in the Psalms and the Prophets.* Sheffield: Sheffield Academic Press.

Habel, Norman C. 2009. *An Inconvenient Text: Is a Green Reading of the Bible Possible?* Adelaide: Australasian Theological Forum.

Habel, Norman C. and Vicky Balabanski. 2002. (ed.), *The Earth Story in the New Testament.* Sheffield: Sheffield Academic Press.

Habel, Norman C. and Peter Trudinger. 2008. (ed.), *Exploring Ecological Hermeneutics.* Atlanta: Society of Biblical Literature.

Habel, Norman C. and Shirley Wurst. 2000. (ed.), *The Earth Story in Wisdom Traditions.* Sheffield: Sheffield Academic Press.

Habel, Norman C. and Shirley Wurst. 2001. (ed.), *The Earth Story in Genesis.* Sheffield: Sheffield Academic Press.

Hessel, Dieter T. and Rosemary Radford Ruether. 2000. (ed.), *Christianity and Ecology: Seeking the Well-Being of Earth and Humans.* Cambridge, MA: Harvard University Press.

Horrell, David G., Cherryl Hunt, and Christopher Southgate. 2010. *Greening Paul: Rereading the Apostle in a Time of Ecological Crisis.* Waco, TX: Baylor University Press.

Horrell, David G., Cherryl Hunt, Christopher Southgate, and Francesca Stavrakopoulou. 2010. (ed.), *Ecological Hermeneutics: Biblical, Historical and Theological Perspectives.* London: T&T Clark.

McKibben, Bill. 2001. 'Where Do We Go from Here?' *Daedelus: Journal of the American Academy of Arts and Sciences*, 130:4, 301–306.

Rees, Anthony. 2015. *Voices in the Wilderness: An Ecological Reading of the Book of Numbers*. Sheffield: Sheffield Phoenix Press.

Sacred Congregation for Divine Worship. 1971. *General Instruction on the Liturgy of the Hours*. Vatican City: Libreria Editrice Vaticana.

Sacrosanctum Concilium, Liturgy Constitution of the Second Vatican Council. 1963. Vatican City: Libreria Editrice Vaticana.

The Earth Bible Team. 2002. "Ecojustice Hermeneutics: Reflections and Challenges" in Habel and Balabanski (ed.) *The Earth Story in the New Testament*. Sheffield: Sheffield Academic Press, pp. 1–14.

Tirosh-Samuelson, Hava. 2003. (ed.), *Judaism and Ecology: Created World and Revealed Word*. Cambridge, MA: Harvard University Press.

Tonstad, Sigve K. 2008. "Creation Groaning in Labour Pains" in Habel and Trudinger (ed.) *Exploring Ecological Hermeneutics*. Atlanta: Society of Biblical Literature, pp. 141–149.

Tonstad, Sigve K. 2017. *The Letter to the Romans: Paul among the Ecologists*. Sheffield: Sheffield Phoenix Press.

Tracy, David. 1981. *The Analogical Imagination: Christian Theology and the Culture of Pluralism*. New York: Crossroad.

Wainwright, Elaine M. 2016. *Habitat, Human, and Holy: An Eco-Rhetorical Reading of the Gospel of Matthew*. Earth Bible Commentary Series 6. Sheffield: Sheffield Phoenix Press.

9 Sources of authority in *Laudato Si'*[1]

Cristina L.H. Traina

"Because I said so!"

As children, we all heard this from an exasperated adult at some point. As adults, we know that the speaker was grasping at straws. Authority does not arrive by fiat but rests on reasons and justifications, even though there's no time to list them when one's daughter is about to run ahead to cross the street or has already been asked five times to brush her teeth so that she can go to bed early enough to be rested for school. Asked about the true justification for their authority, most parents would cite their responsibility for their children's welfare. When their children's welfare is truly at stake, they may need to override their children's whims. Still, the media—and some Catholics—often behave as if "Because I said so!" is an adequate explanation of the authority of papal encyclicals. After all, didn't Vatican Council I decide in favor of papal infallibility almost 150 years ago?

It did, but papal infallibility has not been exercised since 1950, when Pope Pius XII defined Mary's Assumption into heaven as an article of faith. Still, if Pope Francis's 2015 encyclical *Laudato Si'* (LS) was not infallibly declared, as the letter of the worldwide leader of the Catholic Church it nonetheless comes with a strong presumption of ecclesiastical authority. My aim in this chapter is to assess the ways in which theological authority operates within the letter: What claims support its conclusions, from what sources do they come, and how does Francis argue them? Pope John Paul II's 1995 encyclical *Evangelium vitae* (John Paul II 1995) is a good point of comparison because, like LS, it draws upon the Catholic moral tradition, including magisterial documents, scripture, theology, and science, to call society to conversion on a pressing moral issue. Here, I will argue that while Francis's citation, interpretation, and use of these authorities do not differ significantly in kind from John Paul II's, they do differ perceptibly in tone and emphasis, and Francis sets some precedents on which future popes might build.

We will begin with the documents' use of the papal and episcopal magisteria (or teaching authorities). Then, we will turn to scripture, theology, and science. The argument will emphasize scripture more heavily than other sources, for two reasons. First, both documents treat scripture as an especially important source of authority. Second, despite Vatican Council II's encouragement of a return to scripture, post-Vatican Council II encyclicals' use of scripture is rarely analyzed.

Church documents and the rhetoric of authority

Officially authoritative Roman Catholic teaching—the ecclesiastical magisterium—flows primarily from the papal magisterium, or teaching issued under papal authority: documents like papal encyclicals, declarations by the Congregation for the Doctrine of the Faith, and Vatican Council constitutions. It also includes the episcopal magisterium, or teaching by bishops. Episcopal authority is often taken to be derivative—that is, merely repeating and reframing what the Vatican has taught authoritatively. But as we will see below, LS reverses this trend, drawing some of its points from the independent documents of episcopal conferences.

Most papal social encyclicals demonstrate the orthodoxy of their novel contributions by citing some of the string of papal social encyclicals that stretches back at least to Leo XIII's 1891 *Rerum novarum* (Leo XIII 1891). Papal encyclicals also have an ecclesial—or, if you like, political—function: cultivating unity by demonstrating to their more skeptical readers that they are especially faithful to the writings of previous popes with whom those readers might feel a greater affinity than they do with the current pope. Notably, both John Paul II and Francis seem especially keen to defend their ideas by citing sources from which their opponents are likely to accuse them of departing. John Paul II's papacy followed on the heels of that of Paul VI, who had overseen most of the second Vatican Council's reforms and its subsequent interpretive documents and who has been seen mostly as a reformer. Yet John Paul II's moral theology was famously traditionalist. For instance, the theology of sexuality he articulated in *Love and Responsibility* in 1960 (Wojtyla 1960) underwrote Paul VI's only really traditionalist move, his stunning 1968 override of a pontifical commission's recommendation in favor of limited permission for birth control within marriage, which yielded *Humanae vitae*'s proscription of contraception (Paul VI 1968). And, only two years before *Evangelium vitae* (EV), John Paul II had published *Veritatis splendor* (The Splendor of Truth), which portrays Christ primarily as the strict arbiter of good, evil, truth, and falsehood and appears to dismiss several theological approaches, including liberation theology, that are self-consciously rooted in optimistic Vatican Council II visions of human society and reason. By frequently citing Vatican Council II dogmatic constitution *Lumen gentium* (Paul VI 1964) and pastoral constitution *Gaudium et spes* (Paul VI 1965), EV signals that it is adhering to the standards set by a recent reformist predecessor. It also sets out a traditionalist official hermeneutic—or interpretive framework—by which to interpret Paul VI and Vatican Council II reforms.

Similarly, Francis, viewed by many as morally permissive, cites his reputedly hard-liner predecessor John Paul II nearly 40 times and his likewise strict immediate predecessor Benedict XVI over 20 times. Conversely, he cites *Gaudium et spes*, which aligns much better with his own theology, only three times. Fascinatingly, however, Francis makes a different choice about which of his predecessors' writings to emphasize. He never refers to John Paul II's signature documents EV or *Veritatis splendor,* even though like them LS promotes respect for human life and expresses concern about the ways in which sinful self-interest erodes our ability to recognize and embrace the truth. Instead, he concentrates on John Paul II's other social encyclicals, and he cites John Paul II's occasional writings—like homilies—most frequently of all. In addition, most of Francis's citations to Benedict come from *Caritas in veritate,* Benedict's theology of love (Benedict XVI 2009). Thus, although some of Francis's choices are guided by his topic, he clearly steers readers toward some of his predecessors' works and away from others. John Paul II and Benedict XVI might not have agreed with Francis's signals about which of their writings are most relevant to Catholic ecological ethics and which are more peripheral. In this way, Francis both demonstrates fidelity to recent, demanding standards of orthodoxy and establishes a selective, reformist precedent for interpreting his more traditionalist predecessors.

Despite their shared interest in citing immediate predecessors from different theological "camps," EV and LS deploy episcopal and papal magisterial authority differently. For John Paul II, the magisterium (the charismatic teaching authority of the Church, exercised primarily by the pope and the curia) eclipses all other authorities. In EV, John Paul II cites the magisterium by name 13 times and the authority of Catholic tradition generally 14 times. He also pointedly cites the authority of the historical papal magisterium on abortion (EV 62). By contrast, he cites only one episcopal meeting, the 1991 Extraordinary Consistory of Cardinals (EV 5, 85). He acknowledges having asked bishops for help in drafting EV, and he mentions bishops in general nearly a dozen times, mainly to note that they are "in communion" with him on the question of human life. Bishops (apparently individually, not as a body) provided "valuable facts, suggestions and proposals…. [that] bore witness to their unanimous desire to share in the doctrinal and pastoral mission of the Church with regard to the Gospel of life" (EV 5). However, he does not explicitly credit any of the bishops' specific ideas, even anonymously. In addition, he pointedly subordinates the episcopal magisterium to the papal magisterium (EV 57).

Francis's rhetoric, on the other hand, is collegial rather than hierarchical. He gives the impression that the justifications for his words arise organically from many sources, and from the ground up, rather than from the top down. LS never mentions the magisterium explicitly nor cites "church tradition" as a source of moral authority. Most of Francis's citations of John Paul II, for instance, come from addresses that he gave in the global south and two-thirds world rather than from his predecessor's encyclicals. In addition, rather than referring to anonymous prelates who gave unacknowledged advice, Francis cites specific regional bishops' conference documents, mainly from outside Europe and the United States, on particular issues: usually their structural diagnoses of environmental and social problems or their accounts of the concrete harms that environmental degradation and economic predation cause in their regions.

To be sure, within the Catholic Church, a papal encyclical claims inherent authority, whether or not its author consulted widely. It is possible that the two popes consulted in very similar ways as they drafted. Still, John Paul II gives the impression of exercising his authority in isolation, and Francis gives the impression of behaving collegially. Thus, whereas John Paul II was more likely to build his arguments on established papal magisterial teachings and less likely to cite his bishops, Francis clearly wanted to create the impression of inductively embracing a global convergence of representative, independently authoritative episcopal conference statements, with a focus on regions most immediately vulnerable to the effects of environmental degradation and least equipped to influence climate policy.

Others of Francis's writings bear out this pattern, if to a lesser degree. For instance, in *Evangelii Gaudium*, Francis cites bishops' conferences over a dozen times and specifically promotes episcopal authority. He not only presents the encyclical as derivatively "reaping the rich fruits of the Synod [of Bishop]'s labours" but also promotes "sound 'decentralization'" and calls himself "Bishop of Rome" (Francis 2013: secs.16, 32).

Scripture

Both EV and LS are replete with scriptural references. Historically, Catholics have read scripture in many ways. Pre-moderns read it both literally, as history, and figuratively, for its moral, eschatological, or allegorical implications (Morrow 2016: 230). Early social encyclicals—bearing the stamp of Leo XIII's 1879 encyclical *Aeterni patris* and its mandate to return to Thomas Aquinas's distinctive moral and theological reasoning—largely avoided figurative readings, often quoting bits of literally interpreted verses at the end of a Thomistic argument, to confirm it, rather than at its beginning, to ground it (Leo XIII 1879). This proof-text style characterizes Leo XIII's influential 1891 social encyclical *Rerum novarum*, for instance. Such a reading is coherent with the Catholic belief that on matters of morals reason and revelation cannot conflict, as both are God's creation; one can get to a valid moral conclusion by either method, with the other as a check.

Since Vatican Council II, Catholic biblical scholars have pointed to Vatican Council II's 1965 Dogmatic Constitution on Divine Revelation *Dei verbum*'s invitations to theologians to reawaken patristic and medieval enthusiasm for scripture and to approach the Bible as something other than a crate of objective, redundant (because already available to reason) moral and theological norms buried in packing peanuts (Second Vatican Council 1965). As Harold Attridge has put it,

> *Dei Verbum* articulated a new and compelling way of thinking about revelation, not as the publication of a set of dogmatic propositions, but as a dynamic process of the disclosure of the reality of God, inviting humanity into an ongoing and deepening relationship....The Fathers of the Council also endorsed, at however abstract a level, critical Biblical Scholarship, ... rejecting alternatives that could have turned the clock back.
>
> (Attridge 2013: 466–467)[2]

Yet as Catholic thinkers across the theological spectrum agree, no post-Vatican Council II Catholic ethicist has "been successful in combining a credible and compelling biblical vision of the Christian life with a moral philosophy adequate to the Catholic tradition" (Murphy 2004: 121). Charles Curran put his finger on one of the challenges: critical approaches emphasize the diversity of texts and theologies in scripture, a diversity that is unfriendly to the project of creating a unified moral theology (Curran 2004: 121).

In EV and LS, John Paul II and Francis respond to this dilemma by largely eschewing critical approaches to scripture, opting instead for devotional readings that motivate the reader by painting an inspiring picture of God, humanity, and the world or a troubling picture of sin's harm to God's creatures and creation. In addition, John Paul II layers a second, more moralistic reading on top of the first, often drawing specific moral rules rather than general moral guidelines from the text.

As Curran notes, John Paul II enthusiastically embraces scripture's "dynamic process of disclosure" as a true source of spiritual inspiration rather than just as confirmation of conclusions arrived at by reason. He opts for a "homiletic and catechetical" approach that lays aside critical scholarship. Returning to the older vision of the "scripture[s] as a unified whole," he

> often develops his understanding on the basis of a meditative and even homiletic reflection on them....somewhat similar to that used by the writers in the so-called patristic age of the early church and to the practice of *lectio divina*—a meditative and contemplative reading of scripture.
>
> (Curran 2004: 121, 2005: 47)

Lectio divina (divine reading) prayer is a flexible form of private prayer that involves reading a short passage of scripture meditatively several times, first letting the message or narrative of the passage sink in slowly; then reflecting on a word or phrase that seems especially meaningful; and finally asking for inspired understanding of that passage's meaning for one's own present life. *Lectio divina* is also a common practice for preachers in search of insight for homilies. Importantly, *lectio divina* seeks a reading that is relevant to the practitioner and perhaps to their audience, not *the* definitive critical reading.

Examples of this approach in John Paul II's corpus can be found in his encyclicals *Veritatis splendor,* whose larger sections begin with homiletical meditations on biblical stories, and EV, most of whose short sections begin with a brief scriptural passage and interpretive subtitle: for instance, "'I give you thanks that I am fearfully, wonderfully made' (Ps 139:14): celebrating the Gospel of life" (EV 83). As Curran notes, typically John Paul II uses scripture to support "general responses and attitudes that should characterize the Christian life, such as discipleship, covenant, love, conversion, mercy, and forgiveness" (Curran 2005: 51). But at times—the example above is one—John Paul II seems to impose philosophical and moral commitments on scripture rather than to extract perspectives from the text on the text's own terms. This is especially the case, Curran thinks, when John Paul II tries to use scripture "to prove that Jesus saw the moral life in terms of obedience to the commandments"; for John Paul II "following Jesus today" means installing exceptionless norms.[3] In another case, Genesis 9:5—"from man in regard to his fellow man I will demand an accounting for human life"—becomes "the absolute inviolability of innocent human life" (EV 57). Curran sees these moves as examples of eisegesis, of John Paul II's projecting his own theology onto the text in ways that are meaningful for him but might not be replicated by others either in their own meditative encounters with the same passages or in historically critical readings (Curran 2004: 123). Another way to put this caution is that personal meditative readings of scripture, even a pope's, may be powerful and inspiring, but precisely because they are personal spiritual encounters with the text, they should not be thought of as automatically constituting universally authoritative readings of scripture.

Again, the flavor of Francis's approach in LS is slightly different from John Paul II's in EV. Following a political, scientific, and cultural assessment of the ecological crisis, Francis devotes paragraphs 62–100 to an extended meditation on scripture, interspersed with cultural, philosophical, and scientific references. Although like John Paul II he assumes a unified text, he deploys this assumption to make scriptural critiques of troubling scriptural interpretations. For example, he rejects the "earlier exegesis" of the dominion language in Genesis 1:28 that had been read as authorizing "the unbridled exploitation" of nature. Instead, he insists, the passage must be interpreted "in [its] context, with an appropriate hermeneutic" (67) in search of themes that will then guide moral reasoning in concrete settings. Francis argues that "the earth is the Lord's" (Ps 24:1) rather than ours, and he reads the creation narrative of Genesis 1–3 as asserting "that human life is grounded in three fundamental and closely intertwined relationships: with God, with our neighbor and with the earth itself" (66). These relationships, not "dominion," are to guide ecological ethics. In addition, LS mines scripture largely for themes, not rules: the Hebrew Bible's creation narrative, concern for living in community on the land, and praise for the creator (65–73), and the New Testament's Christologies of a fleshly, incarnate Jesus and a risen and glorious Christ who sanctifies all of creation (96–100).

Although in LS Francis certainly argues that these scriptural themes condemn current environmental and business practices, unlike John Paul II he does not tie specific moral rules to particular passages of scripture. This may be in part because detailed ecological rules relevant to our period do not exist in scripture. But it is primarily because his goal is to convert readers to a vision that will help them determine and pursue appropriate actions in specific situations. I will say more about this below. He does depart from this approach occasionally, however. For instance, in his discussion of "the relationship between human life and the moral law," he jumps several steps from the figurative Genesis guideline "observe the law inscribed at creation" to the literal particular of "masculinity or femininity": "it is not a healthy attitude which would seek 'to cancel out sexual difference because it no longer knows how to confront it'" (155) (Francis 2015: 8). Thus, it is worth exploring how both Francis and John Paul II deploy scripture in their writing on other topics.

Further exegetical differences show up in the ways in which John Paul II and Francis interpret Genesis, on which both rely heavily. Their choice of passages strongly inflects their reflections. Whereas John Paul II is particularly interested in Genesis 4—which holds God at a distance and elucidates the cascade of social and personal harm that follows even one act of jealous violence—Francis focuses on Genesis 1–3—which depict a highly involved God who lovingly fashions creation and which suggest the interdependent social and environmental consequences of both sin and grace. LS and EV would both have been very different documents if these choices had been reversed.

If EV and LS, like other social encyclicals, elect to bypass critical scholarly interpretations of scripture, what authority do they claim for their citation of it? Certainly, both explicitly revere scripture's authority as a site of God's self-revelation for the Church, and both go far beyond simple "decorative" citations of scripture to substantive argument. However, the power of their exegeses is more homiletical—hortatory and persuasive, based in their authors' devotional readings of scripture—than definitively, deductively morally authoritative. For example, Jeremiah 1:5 ("Before I formed you in the womb I knew you, and before you were born I consecrated you") anchors the section of EV in which John Paul II argues for "the value of the person *from the moment of conception*" (44–45, italics added) and therefore against the specific act of abortion. By contrast, Francis's interpretation of the same verse, citing Benedict (Benedict XVI 2005), emphasizes the equal, infinite significance of every person, *in every ecological circumstance*: "We were conceived in the heart of God, and for this reason 'each of us is the result of a thought of God. Each of us is willed, each of us is loved, each of us is necessary'" (65).

These interpretations need not be read as conflicting. They certainly overlap. The point is that neither citation makes sense as a claim about the passage's single, definitive meaning for ethics. Rather, each interpretation is an invitation to the reader to approach this remark from Jeremiah open-heartedly, with the hope of experiencing the power of the author's own prayerful encounter with the text, but without a guarantee that something else altogether, more related to one's own discernment, will not emerge instead. John Paul II's second-person invitation to "*contemplate* the One who was pierced," not merely to *reason* from scriptural accounts of Jesus (EV 50), exemplifies this approach.[4]

Consequently, unless these two popes intend to insist that their own devotional readings of scripture are *the* authoritative readings—implying that their prayerful readings trump others' apparent experiences of graced encounter with the same texts—the true authority of both John Paul II's and Francis's readings lies more in their exemplary spiritual, meditative practice than in their apparently definitive exegetical conclusions. The most we can say in the latter direction is that they impose a strong hermeneutic framework on the text, and here they open themselves to critical analysis. Both Francis and John Paul II use scripture to paint evocative and provocative moral stances that give rise to strong, specific moral norms. However, because John Paul II draws definitive moral norms directly from particular verses of scripture, we must ask whether he is practicing eisegesis—forcing a doctrine or ideology upon the text—or exegesis—drawing out meanings implicitly or explicitly present in the text and its world.

Finally, John Paul II's and Francis's devotional readings of scripture allow them to skirt important critical perspectives, like feminist, anti-racist, and de-colonial approaches to exegesis. These perspectives do not impose singular interpretations on biblical texts, but they do criticize, or even rule out, interpretations that might otherwise come up during *lectio divina* for isolated white men of privilege, like popes. These critical perspectives give us yet another reason not to accept the popes' devotional readings of scripture as definitive social teaching.

Theology

In addition to scripture and church documents, both encyclicals rely to a lesser degree on theology, primarily patristic and medieval theology. And as they do for scripture, both use theology in part to convert hearts by spinning compelling visions. For instance, in EV John Paul II marshals the poetic theological writings of Irenaeus of Lyon, Augustine, Ambrose, St. Gregory of Nyssa, Pseudo-Dionysius, and Ignatius of Antioch to paint a picture of humanity as God's crowning glory—God's image and manifestation in the world—honored and cared for in its earthly, bodily life but created for union with God (EV 34–38, 47, 80, 84; see also 52). This picture of humanity's infinite, divine value underwrites the "Gospel of life," which he obliquely admits is more accessible through spiritual contemplation and reason than (literally) in scripture (EV 2).

Likewise, in LS, Francis draws on theology primarily to support his call for "profound ecological conversion" (217), even labeling a section of his sixth chapter "Ecological Conversion." He invokes St. Francis of Assisi's "Canticle of the Creatures" to help his readers imagine the earth, the universe, and all that compose them as their siblings under God, who is their common parent (1, 11, 12). This kind of contemplation, he says, moves "our hearts...to praise the Lord for all his creatures and to worship him in union with them" (87). He finds similar sentiments in figures from St. Basil the Great, to Dante Alighieri, to Pierre Teilhard de Chardin and Paul Ricouer (77, 80, 85, 244). St. Bonaventure and St. John of the Cross help Francis cross over into a Eucharistic, panentheistic celebration of God's presence in every element of creation (233–235). He even reaches outside Christianity to the Sufi poet Ali al-Khawas (233).

Still, the flavors of moral virtue that they glean from these readings differ. Just as John Paul II is more likely than Francis to find particular, literal moral proscriptions in scripture, so he is more likely than Francis to find them in theology. He calls upon ancient and medieval theologians for his arguments for human obedience to God's law and for Christianity's original, strong adherence to particular laws. Athenagoras and Tertullian certify that "this same doctrine [against abortion] has been constantly taught by the Fathers of the Church and by her Pastors and Doctors" (EV 61); the Didache concurs (EV 54, 61); and Augustine and Thomas Aquinas converge to condemn suicide (EV 66, 71–72). For more contemporary support, John Paul II tends to rely on modern documents of the magisterium rather than on theologians. The result of this reading of theology is that John Paul II describes virtue primarily as obedience to the law, manifest in particular laws literally articulated in scripture, the theological tradition, and papal teaching, and he defines sin primarily as disobedience to them.

By contrast, as with scripture, Francis usually does not make the step directly from theology to absolute moral norms, but he also does not stop with recommending spiritual awe before God's creation. Rather, he implies that conversion yields virtue, the tendency to perform good acts and to genuinely want to do so. If one experiences the world as a "joyful mystery" (12) and feels "intimately united with all that exists" (12), then "sobriety and care will well up spontaneously" in a virtuous, radical "refusal to turn reality into an object simply to be used and controlled" (11). The point is to live "our [essential] vocation to be protectors of God's handiwork" (217). Virtue is then primarily loving and respectful care for God's creation that emerges primarily in spontaneous, contextually appropriate actions, and only secondarily in conscious, thoughtful obedience to God; and sin is then primarily a painful breach of intimate relationships, and only secondarily disobedience of divinely established laws.

In fairness, part of the difference in the way John Paul II and Francis use scripture and theology arises from their disparate projects. For John Paul II, sheer human life itself, in opposition to death, is the crucial concern (the word "life" appears nearly 800 times in EV but fewer than 150 times in LS). John Paul II is interested—not exclusively but as limit cases—in particular acts that intentionally end specific human lives: execution, abortion, and euthanasia. This sort of killing is a single act, it involves an identifiable agent and victim, and it occurs at a definite moment. Not surprisingly, despite John Paul II's inspiring vision of creation, "law" is the dominant moral paradigm (with six times as many appearances in EV as in LS).

Throughout LS, Francis is likewise concerned that human life not be attacked—he even implies that unjust use of common resources amounts to killing (95)—but his focus is mostly on the interdependent welfare of beings and ecosystems and the cumulative, systemic effects of long-term, corporate human action. Thus, alongside the "cry of the earth" (with which they are interdependent), the key criteria of injustice are variants of "poor" and "poverty," which together appear over 70 times. Of course, Francis considers poverty born of injustice to be an attack on life, but poverty admits of degrees and contexts in a way that human life, as an absolute, does not. In addition, in both society and the global ecosystem, complex effects occur over long periods, making it difficult to link and label particular agents, victims, and actions. In addition, the constellations of ecological injustices and their solutions vary by location and culture. Finally, one cannot easily develop a list of absolutely prohibited personal *acts*, even though one can identify prohibited global human *effects*, like species extinction (33).[5] This difference leads John Paul II to emphasize preservation of human life and prevention of death and Francis to emphasize promotion of human justice and the mutual flourishing of humanity and the rest of creation.

Still, both John Paul II and Francis reunite theology with contemplation in a methodological move that reminds their readers of the importance of affect, or emotion, to ethics: if one is not setting out from a place of wondering, awe-struck gratitude for creation, they imply, one will either make a moral and epistemological error by veering into the utilitarian swamp of "economic calculus" or else fail to be moved to action by one's thin, merely "intellectual appreciation" of the problem (11).

This approach raises a question about the relative weight of spiritual experience in their visions of the moral life. Despite his evocation of "our common home" in the subtitle and throughout LS, Francis frames ecological conversion primarily in Christian spiritual terms. John Paul II argues that "the Gospel of life is not for believers alone: it is for everyone....The value at stake is one which every human being can grasp by the light of reason; thus it necessarily concerns everyone" (EV 101). The question neither fully answers is whether reason and conversion take one to the same moral epistemological starting place. As James Gustafson asked years ago, what role do Christian revelation, theology, and experience play in ethics?

Does Christianity simply provide additional motivations to do what any reasonable person can judge is right? Or does it matter to the content of ethics as well?[6] Both John Paul II and Francis seem tempted to say that Christianity does matter to the content of ethics, but if it does, appeals to the general public may fail.

Science

John Paul II and Francis respect science as supplying "signs of the times" and technology as capable of providing means to make the world more humane. In EV, John Paul II points out that scientific research confirms the definitive humanity and uniqueness of human embryos (EV 60), and he lauds "the benefits of the most advanced medicine" now available, if unevenly, to the sick (EV 26). Overall, Celia Deane-Drummond argues, in LS Francis "takes the natural sciences and associated environmental questions into account in a way that is unprecedented compared to other official magisterial documents" (Deane-Drummond 2016: 414).

Although Francis never cites specific technical studies, the introduction and Chapter 1 of LS accept scientific evaluations of atmospheric and ecological degradation, projections of future decline, and elaboration of their social and economic effects. He also relies upon secular international agreements like the 1992 Rio Declaration on Environment and Development (United Nations Conference on Environment and Development 1992) and the 2000 Earth Charter (Earth Charter Initiative 2001), both developed in response to scientific assessments and predictions (see LS sections 141 and 207, respectively).

Both John Paul II and Francis also argue that the competence of science and technology is limited and that they are destructive if they are left to their own devices. John Paul II worries about "science and medicine losing sight of their ethical dimension" (EV 89); "nature itself, from being 'mater' (mother)" worthy of awe and praise "is now reduced to being 'matter', and is subjected to every kind of manipulation" (EV 22). In EV, the temptation to manipulate life seems to be mostly a product of individuals' professional hubris (EV 89).

Francis, by contrast, is concerned less about individual scientists and more about "the [cultural] tendency... to make the method and aims of science and technology an epistemological paradigm which shapes the lives of individuals and the workings of society" (107). Seizing a page from Romano Guardini, he worries about the interplay of science with the market and political power:

> The technocratic paradigm ...tends to dominate economic and political life. The economy accepts every advance in technology with a view to profit, without concern for its potentially negative impact on human beings. Finance overwhelms the real economy.
>
> (109)

Science and technology—Francis calls them "technoscience"—overstep their boundaries not just in moments of unfortunate pride or shortsightedness but whenever they intentionally, systematically put short-term profit first, transforming culture so that it does the same, and inuring people to systemic social injustice and environmental degradation. Religious ethics must resist the tendency of science and technology to become a hegemonic force, including in ethics. Even though most of the reasons for limiting the meaning-making power of technoscience and the market can be stated in secular terms, Francis, like John Paul II, believes that conversion to awe before creation is helpful for resisting their charms and fighting their pervasive social influence.

Despite Francis's greater respect for scientists' research, however, Deane-Drummond points out that he misses opportunities to engage with leading-edge scientific thinking that would bolster his case. He could have engaged scientists critical of the "technoscientific" approach who have created paradigms like the Anthropocene and others who have created frameworks like planetary boundary theory, which warns that once any one of a number of interdependent planetary systems escapes a certain normal range, all will be upset (Deane-Drummond 2016: 407–409).

He also leaves theological loose ends, failing to deal honestly with evolutionary biology's accounts of suffering and extinction. Francis leans heavily on the theology of creation and fall when incarnation and redemption might provide more complex, usable frames for reflecting on the world as it is (Deane-Drummond 2016: 410–412, 414). The same problem dogs John Paul II's EV.

Conclusion

To be sure, a fine-grained, comprehensive study of recent encyclicals' citation and interpretation of papal, episcopal, and conciliar documents as well as of scripture, theology, and science would provide a much fuller context for this suggestive analysis. Still, we can draw a few preliminary conclusions.

Despite the similarities in the sources they cite and in the authority those sources carry, there are important reasons to prefer Francis's approach in LS over John Paul II's approach in EV, even though Francis's moral vision produces moral criteria of human and environmental justice rather than clear moral rules for accomplishing them. The subtle choices Francis makes in both selection and interpretation within those sources make for a different tone and, ultimately, are more fitting to an encyclical's intended function in church and world. To account for diversity of culture and context, a papal encyclical must be universally applicable without demanding uniformity. It must be inspiring in an accessible way. It must be theological without limiting orthodoxy to a single theology and exegetical without ruling out other interpretations of scripture. It must make responsible use of science without uncritically idealizing technical solutions that are likely to benefit the wealthy in the global north at the cost of the poor in the global south. Ideally, it paints a vision rooted in scripture, theology, and the moral tradition, lays out the field on which exegetical, theological, and moral reflection happen, exhibits models of moral reasoning, and steps back to let others fill in the details at the local level.

LS largely operates in this mode, but John Paul II tends to over-determine both interpretation and conclusions by skipping steps in the analysis of his sources, implying that the authority of EV resides more in its author *per se* than in its author's reverent, responsible use of magisterial tradition, scripture, theology, and science. This is not to say that John Paul II could not have reached the same conclusions by citing the same sources; it is to say that he undercuts his own authority by setting a poor example of reading and interpretation.

As we have seen, the authority of magisterial documents operates differently in LS than in EV. Granted, the precedent Francis has set is not binding on his successors; even though he elevates episcopal sources that are normally seen as having less status than encyclicals and conciliar documents, their new status still derives from his authority as pope. Nonetheless, one can also argue that LS recognizes bishops' conferences' collegial, local theological and moral authority, an implicit claim that may set a precedent for future, collegially expressed encyclicals. Encyclicals were always addressed *de jure* to the whole church and to the whole world, but *de facto* their moral horizons and their analytical perspectives were limited initially to Europe and then to the global north. In an era in which encyclicals must comprehensively address the complex, varied effects of global phenomena in language that is respectful and accessible to people everywhere, Francis's approach is more inclusive and thus more credible.

Even LS leaves room for improvement in this regard, however. In addition to the issues raised in this article, Francis's citation of theological authorities is tone deaf in ways that undercut his inclusive intentions. Alongside scripture, the encyclical tradition, and bishops' conference documents, Francis cites male theologians, philosophers, spiritual writers, cultural critics, and even a Sufi mystic. The apparent authors of the first three groups of sources are by definition male. But nothing prevented Francis from citing women in the other categories. He could easily have found support in the work of abbess, preacher, and Doctor of the Church Hildegard of Bingen; Rilke scholar, environmental activist, and spiritual writer Joanna Macy; theologian Rosemary Radford Ruether; biologist, veterinarian, Nobel Peace Prize winner, and Green Belt founder Wangari Maathai; or any of a number of other female ecotheologians. In addition, even though human poverty is his key criterion of environmental injustice, he cites the bishops of the poor, rather than the poor themselves. In these senses, his nod to the margins is inadequate, and unnecessarily so.

Notes

1 Thanks to Hille Haker for her helpful suggestion of *Evangelium vitae* as an apt comparison and to Robert McKim, for many suggestions that improved the article. Its remaining faults are mine.
2 In addition, Attridge noted, "*Dei Verbum's* eirenic tone on issues that had long divided Catholics and Protestants [also] signalled [sic] that Biblical interpretation should be ecumenically engaged."
3 See Curran 2004: 123–125 for greater detail. EV's key demand is strict obedience to God's law, which John Paul II believes follows from the Gospel of life (e.g., EV 51).
4 Italics added. Even here, John Paul II concludes that the proper response to looking on Christ crucified is obedience; see 36, 51, and 52, for example.
5 See also LS 14, 143. Two examples among myriad may help. First, in regions with coal power, transportation by high-efficiency gasoline or diesel engines is the most climate-friendly choice; in regions that generate electricity renewably, electric motors make more sense. Second, as Rosemary Radford Ruether pointed out years ago, well-nourished Americans with plentiful food supplies may have an obligation limit themselves to vegetarian diets, but poor people in regions with limited, uncertain food access ought to eat animal protein when they can get it (Ruether 1992: 225).
6 James Gustafson asked these and other questions in Gustafson 1975.

References

Attridge, Harold W. 2013. "Reading Scripture 50 Years after Vatican II" *The Australasian Catholic Record* 90/4: 459–473.

Benedict XVI. 2005. "Homily for the Solemn Inauguration of the Petrine Ministry" Vatican website: http://w2.vatican.va/content/benedict-xvi/en/homilies/2005/documents/hf_ben-xvi_hom_20050424_inizio-pontificato.html.

Benedict XVI, Pope. 2009. *Caritas in veritate*, encyclical letter, Vatican website: http://w2.vatican.va/content/benedict-xvi/en/encyclicals/documents/hf_ben-xvi_enc_20090629_caritas-in-veritate.html.

Curran, Charles E. 2004. "John Paul II's Use of Scripture in his Moral Teaching" *Horizons* 31/1: 118–134.

Curran, Charles E. 2005. *The Moral Theology of John Paul II, Readings in Moral Theology* Washington, DC: Georgetown University Press.

Deane-Drummond, Celia. 2016. "*Laudato Si*' and the Natural Sciences: An Assessment of Possibilities and Limits" *Theological Studies* 27/2: 392–415.

Earth Charter Initiative. 2001. "The Earth Charter" http://earthcharter.org/virtual-library2/the-earth-charter-text/.

Francis, Pope. 2013. *Evangelii Gaudium*, apostolic exhortation, Vatican website: http://w2.vatican.va/content/francesco/en/apost_exhortations/documents/papa-francesco_esortazione-ap_20131124_evangelii-gaudium.html.

Francis, Pope. 2015. "Tenth General Audience on the Family" *Catechesis* (15 April 2015): *L'Osservatore Romano*, 16. Vatican website: http://w2.vatican.va/content/francesco/en/audiences/2015/documents/papa-francesco_20150415_udienza-generale.html.

Gustafson, James. 1975. *Can Ethics Be Christian?* Chicago, IL: University of Chicago Press.

John Paul II, Pope. 1995. *Evangelium Vitae*, encyclical letter, Vatican website: http://w2.vatican.va/content/john-paul-ii/en/encyclicals/documents/hf_jp-ii_enc_25031995_evangelium-vitae.html.

Leo XIII, Pope. 1879. *Aeterni Patris*, encyclical letter, Vatican website: https://w2.vatican.va/content/leo-xiii/en/encyclicals/documents/hf_l-xiii_enc_04081879_aeterni-patris.html.

Leo XIII, Pope. 1891. *Rerum Novarum*, encyclical letter, Vatican website: http://w2.vatican.va/content/leo-xiii/en/encyclicals/documents/hf_l-xiii_enc_15051891_rerum-novarum.html.

Morrow, Jeffrey L. 2016. "*Dei verbum* in Light of the History of Catholic Biblical Interpretation" *Josephinum Journal of Theology* 23/1 and 2: 227–249.

Murphy, William F. Jr. 2004. "Revisiting the Biblical Renewal of Moral Theology in Light of *Veritatis Splendor*" *Nova et Vetera* (English edition) 2/2: 403–444.

Paul VI, Pope. 1964. "Dogmatic Constitution on the Church, *Lumen gentium*" (Second Vatican Council) Vatican website: www.vatican.va/archive/hist_councils/ii_vatican_council/documents/vat-ii_const_19641121_lumen-gentium_en.html; idem.

Paul VI, Pope. 1965. "Pastoral Constitution on the Church, *Gaudium et spes*" (Second Vatican Council) Vatican website: www.vatican.va/archive/hist_councils/ii_vatican_council/documents/vat-ii_const_19651207_gaudium-et-spes_en.html.

Paul VI, Pope. 1968. *Humanae Vitae*, encyclical letter, Vatican website: https://w2.vatican.va/content/paul-vi/en/encyclicals/documents/hf_p-vi_enc_25071968_humanae-vitae.html.

Ruether, Rosemary Radford. 1992. *Gaia and God: An Ecofeminist Theology of Earth Healing*. San Francisco, CA: Harper.

Second Vatican Council. 1965. "Dogmatic Constitution on Divine Revelation, *Dei verbum*" Vatican website: www.vatican.va/archive/hist_councils/ii_vatican_council/documents/vat-ii_const_19651118_dei-verbum_en.html.

United Nations Conference on Environment and Development. 1992. "Rio Declaration on Environment and Development" www.un.org/documents/ga/conf151/aconf15126-1annex1.htm.

Wojtyla, Karol. 1981. *Love and Responsibility*, trans. H. T. Willetts. London: Collins; originally published in 1960.

10 A constructivist engagement with *Laudato Si'*

Kieran P. Donaghy

In his encyclical letter *Laudato Si'*, Pope Francis appeals "for a new dialogue about how we are shaping the future of our planet (14)."[1] He sees the "need for a conversation which includes everyone, since the environmental challenge we are undergoing, and its human roots, concern and affect us all (ibid.)." In developing his argument, which is intended to persuade a broad audience, he draws on multiple authoritative sources but especially on the social teachings of the Catholic Church, which are predicated on strong metaphysical assumptions that are not universally shared. Constructivism in ethics is the position that universal principles for guiding action in a world of multiple and diverse audiences and conflicting cultural viewpoints *cannot* be established by metaphysical arguments or religious doctrines, or discovered (empirically) in the world. Rather, action-guiding principles for a cosmopolitan audience must be constructed on the basis of plausible assumptions about agents and conditions of action that do not appeal to unvindicated ideals or particularities. Yet, constructivist ethical analyses of environmental issues can arrive at prescriptions for action that are quite compatible with those derived from religious beliefs and theological arguments. This chapter reviews a number of essential features of Francis's argument that will enable its conclusions to be compared with those of one form of cosmopolitan constructivism. Next the main lines of Onora O'Neill's constructive approach to practical reasoning are sketched. Then the chapter explores how assessments and prescriptions about human relationships with the natural environment reached through the latter approach compare with those of Francis's encyclical letter.

Introduction

In *Laudato Si'*, an encyclical letter of Pope Francis on "care for our common home," Francis urgently appeals "for a new dialogue about how we are shaping the future of our planet (14)." He sees the "need for a conversation which includes everyone, since the environmental challenge we are undergoing, and its human roots, concern and affect us all (ibid.)." While noting that the worldwide ecological movement has given rise to numerous organizations that have made progress in promoting awareness of this challenge, he remarks that efforts to solve the environmental crisis have proven to be ineffective because of opposition and a more general lack of interest. He pointedly observes that "[o]bstructionist attitudes, *even on the part of believers*, can range from denial of the problem to indifference, nonchalant resignation or blind confidence in technical solutions (ibid.)" and submits that "we require a new and universal solidarity (ibid.) [emphasis supplied]." Francis hopes that his encyclical letter, which is intended to become part of the Catholic Church's social teaching, can help others to acknowledge the immensity and urgency of the environmental challenge we face.

The encyclical comprises six chapters, beginning with a fact-based review of the present ecological crisis that draws on "results of the best scientific research available today (15)" and proceeding to a consideration of some principles of the Judeo-Christian tradition that "can render our commitment to the environment more coherent." The third chapter concerns the human roots of the ecological crisis and sets up reflections in Chapter 4 on "an approach to ecology which respects our unique place as human beings in this world and our relationship to our surroundings (ibid.)." In the fifth chapter, on "lines of approach and action," Francis "advances some broader proposals for dialogue and action which would involve each of us as individuals, and also affect international policy (ibid.)." In recognition of the need to motivate social action, the sixth chapter suggests guidelines for ecological education and human development based on Christian spiritual experience.

In his preliminary remarks, Francis alerts the reader that each of the encyclical's chapters, while addressing its dedicated subject, will also "take up and re-examine important questions previously dealt with [in the document] (16)." Among these are

> the intimate relationship between the poor and the fragility of the planet, the conviction that everything in the world is connected, the critique of new paradigms and forms of power derived from technology, the call to seek other ways of understanding the economy and progress, the value proper to each creature, the need for forthright and honest debate, the serious responsibility of international and local policy, the throwaway culture, and the proposal of a new lifestyle.
>
> (16)

In laying out his multi-part argument Francis appeals to scientific evidence, widely shared principles of environmental ethics, considerations of political viability, and religious beliefs. It is a sophisticated argument that is intended to persuade a broad audience but especially those who share his religious faith. Non-Christian readers may be less persuaded than followers of Christianity and (Abrahamic) religions sympathetic to Christianity.

Other authors have approached some of the same issues that Francis addresses but from other perspectives. One such perspective is a cosmopolitan constructivism. Constructivism in ethics is the position that universal principles for guiding action in a world of multiple and diverse audiences and conflicting viewpoints cannot be established by metaphysical arguments or religious doctrines, or discovered in the world. Rather, action-guiding principles for a cosmopolitan audience must be constructed on the basis of plausible assumptions about agents and conditions of action that do not appeal to unvindicated ideals or particularities. Yet, constructivist ethical analyses of environmental issues can arrive at universal prescriptions for action that are quite compatible with those derived from some particularist religious beliefs or theological arguments.

In this chapter, I will review a number of essential features of Francis's argument that will enable its conclusions to be aligned with those reached by cosmopolitan constructivism, sketch the main lines of Onora O'Neill's constructive approach to practical reasoning, and explore how assessments and prescriptions about human relationships with the natural environment reached through the latter approach compare with those of Francis's encyclical letter.

Essential features of Francis's argument

In reading *Laudato Si'*, one is immediately struck by how deeply a sense of *ecosystems*—natural, social, political, and economic—pervades the entire argument. This sense is manifested at the level of individual nations' economies in Francis's view of a "circular model of production and consumption (22)." Presently, a number of national economies are attempting to put this view into practice, as if it were a logical goal of efficient operation. He asserts that "[h]umanity is called to recognize the need for change of lifestyle, production and consumption [in essence, a *movement towards* a circular economy], in order to combat global warming (23)." This sense is also manifested on a global scale in his discussion of sea level rise and the potential proportion of the world's population affected (24). And he relates the basic human right of access to drinking water to the exercise of other human rights (cf. Beard et al., 2016). Indeed, the sensibility of the United Nations interlinked Sustainability Development Goals (SDGs) is discernible in much of the discussion in his first chapter, "What Is Happening to Our Common Home" (see United Nations 2015). Francis goes so far as to adopt a system-of-[ecological] systems perspective that informs many contemporary positions on sustainability when he states that "[a] true ecological approach always becomes a social approach; it must integrate questions of justice in debates on the environment, so as to hear both the cry of the earth and the cry of the poor (49)."[2]

In his second chapter, "The Gospel of Creation," Francis submits that there is much to be gained by dealing directly with the convictions of "believers," suggesting that beliefs in science and religion need not be incompatible and that "science and religion can enter into a dialogue fruitful for both (62)."[3] Moreover, he avers "[i]t is good for humanity and the world at large when we believers better recognize the ecological commitments which stem from our convictions (64)."

Francis argues that the Bible does not sanction "a tyrannical anthropocentrism unconcerned with other creatures ... Where other creatures are concerned, we can speak of the priority of *being* over that of *being useful* (69) [emphasis supplied]." That is to say that non-human creatures are to be viewed as ends in themselves and not merely as means to the achievement of human beings' objectives. More than this, he asserts

> Ancient [biblical stories], full of symbolism, bear witness to a conviction which we today share that everything is interconnected, and that genuine care for our own lives and our relationships with nature is inseparable from fraternity, justice, and faithfulness to others.
>
> (70)

He develops this theme further in the third chapter of his encyclical letter, on the "Human Roots of the Ecological Crisis," where he writes that

> [t]here can be no renewal of our relationship with nature without a renewal of nature itself. There can be no ecology without an adequate anthropology. ... Our relationship with the environment can never be isolated from our relationship with others and with God.
>
> (119)

In this chapter, Francis suggests that science itself can contribute to the ecological crisis when he states "[w]e need constantly to rethink the goals, effects, overall context and ethical limits of [science], which is a form of power involving considerable risks (131)." He singles out in particular the role that genetically modified crops can play in destroying complex ecosystem networks and, in so doing, regional economies (see also Donaghy 2001).

Francis makes the case for an "Integral Ecology" in his fourth chapter, relating the health of social and economic systems to the health of the environment. He notes that what constitutes sustainable use of any ecosystem entails consideration of its regenerative ability and this extends to social systems. He writes, "Every violation of solidarity and civil friendship harms the environment. ... Ecology ... involves protecting the cultural treasures of humanity in the broadest sense (143)." He views intergenerational solidarity as being essential to any meaningful notion of sustainable development (159), and considers the renewal of a sense of *intra*generational solidarity to be an urgent moral need (162).

In his fifth chapter, on "Lines of Approach and Action," Francis spells out what he believes is needed to address the crisis. He reaffirms "the polluter pays" principle of environmental ethics and hence the obligation of developed countries to assume their fair share of the burden of remediation.

> [T]he countries which have benefited from a high degree of industrialization, at the cost of enormous emissions of greenhouse gases, have a greater responsibility for providing a solution to the problems they have caused.
>
> (170)

But he also argues for the political requirement of an international agreement on *systems of governance* to deal with marine waste and protection of the open seas along with "the whole range of so-called global commons (174)." He sees a major purpose of political and institutional frameworks to be the promotion of best practices (177). In the spirit of Rawls 1999, however, he sees "the myopia of power politics" as being an inhibiting factor to "the inclusion of a far-sighted environmental agenda within the overall agenda of governments (178)."

Recognizing that social and moral improvisation is needed to address the ecological crisis, he suggests that

> [n]ew forms of cooperation and community organization can be encouraged in order to defend the interests of small producers and preserve local ecosystems from destruction.
>
> (180)

Some principles of subsidiarity, or leaving decision-making authority to appropriate levels of governance, may need to be observed (Cf. Williams 2005).

Going forward, Francis advocates adopting the "precautionary principle" when formulating and adopting policy responses. He does so for two reasons—the usual prudential reason and the fact that this principle "makes it possible to protect those who are most vulnerable and whose ability to defend their interests and assemble incontrovertible evidence is limited (186)." More strongly and controversially, he asserts,

> The time has come to accept decreased growth in some parts of the world in order to provide resources for other places to experience healthy growth.
>
> (193)

For decreased growth to be widely accepted, a redefinition of basic notions of progress and development will be required (Cf. Gasper 2004). Still Francis argues that "a strategy for real change calls for rethinking processes in their entirety (197)."

In closing the encyclical letter's fifth chapter and opening the sixth and final chapter, on "Ecological Education and Spirituality," Francis makes a number of keen observations on the dialogue between religion and science, and in particular what religious texts can contribute to science. He remarks that "religious classics can prove meaningful in every age; they have an enduring power to open new horizons (199)." He asks whether it is "reasonable and enlightened to dismiss certain writings simply because they arose in the context of religious belief," or at a different time or place (ibid.). Good ideas that speak to our needs may come from anywhere.

> The ethical principles capable of being apprehended by reason can always reappear in different guise and find expression in a variety of languages, including religious language.
>
> (Ibid.)

Francis comments on the instability and uncertainty that defines the current global situation, suggesting that it provides a seedbed for collective selfishness. In such an environment,

> ... social norms are respected only to the extent they do not clash with personal needs. So our concern cannot be limited to the threat of extreme weather events but must also extend to the catastrophic consequences of social unrest.
>
> (204)

To avert further environmental degradation and dangerous social unrest, Francis believes that we are challenged to examine our lifestyles. He observes that what we purchase and consume is a moral as well as an economic act.

Changes in behavior will require changes in education. For environmental education to "facilitate making the leap towards the transcendent, which gives environmental ethics its deepest meaning," Francis calls for educators to develop an ethics of ecology that, through an effective pedagogy, can help people "to grow in solidarity, responsibility, and compassionate care (210)."

He views protection of our "integral ecology" to be essential to a life of virtue and not "an optional or secondary aspect of our Christian experience (217)."

Clearly, protection of environmental and social systems entails political action. But, Francis observes,

> Not everyone is called to engage directly in political life. Society is also enriched by a countless array of organizations which work to promote the common good and to defend the environment, whether natural or urban. ... around these community actions, relationships develop or

are recovered and a new social fabric emerges. Thus a community can break out of the indifference induced by consumerism. These actions cultivate a shared identity with a story which can be remembered and handed on.

(232)

Onora O'Neill's cosmopolitan constructivism

As remarked upon above, in addition to scientific evidence, widely accepted principles of environmental ethics, and principles of political viability, Francis draws extensively upon social teaching of the Catholic Church in developing the argument of his encyclical letter.[4] In public and philosophical discourse, failure to motivate standards of judgment used in argumentation is often criticized as "appealing to a higher authority." Certainly, a problem widely shared in a "globalized" world is making and validating ethical judgments—or engaging in practical reasoning—when cultural viewpoints or, more broadly speaking, basic (including religious) values are not shared or conflict. So it is worthwhile to consider whether or not the prescriptions for action Francis issues in his encyclical letter, or ones compatible with them, might be arrived at by a different, more cosmopolitan, approach to practical reasoning. In this section, I will sketch Onora O'Neill's constructive approach to practical reasoning and suggest that it provides the basis for an affirmative answer to this question.[5]

In her book *Towards Justice and Virtue*, O'Neill is initially concerned with a problematic brought about by a crisis other than the ecological one that Francis addresses—the crisis of modernist self-justification,[6] which arises when one attempts to validate normative judgments without invoking or privileging specific religious beliefs. The problematic with which she is concerned arises in the apparent opposition between, on the one hand, approaches to ethics based on notions of justice and "the right," and, on the other hand, approaches to ethics based on notions of virtue and "the good."[7] O'Neill sees the drifting apart of sensibilities of the right and the good that used to be united (in at least some perspectives) as being due largely to the decentering of the Catholic Church as the temporal authority of belief systems (scientific and religious). To the extent these approaches appealed to realist metaphysical foundations or religious certainties that are now bracketed, they have become severed from their moorings. These approaches also differ over whether their arguments are couched in universalist or particularist terms. She remarks that it has been tempting to think of justice in universalist terms because the broad scope and cosmopolitan tasks of justice have been so important to the modern world. And it has been tempting to think about virtue in particularistic terms because other approaches seem not merely unavailable but questionable in a culturally diverse world. Convincing justifications and reasons for both justice and virtue are lacking, but both are needed. Her book is intended to address this need.

O'Neill argues that the point of practical reasoning is "to guide action whose aim is to fit the world ... to its recommendations, rather than its conclusions to the world" (pg. 42).[8] The main focus of practical reasoning is on principles of action; hence, some *abstraction* will be entailed (to define action-describing predicates and articulate principles) but not *idealization*. *Constructivism* in ethics is the claim that action-guiding principles cannot be established by metaphysical arguments,[9] or discovered in the world, but must be constructed on the basis of plausible—even if abstract—assumptions; it entails "reasoning with all possible solidity from available beginnings using available and followable methods to reach attainable and sustainable conclusions for relevant audiences" (pg. 63).

O'Neill attempts to provide a "toned-down" modal Kantian account, according to which practical reasoning relies on principles that *can* be principles for all in the relevant domain, and where the scope to which principles apply varies with the context.[10] She holds that such an account must be able to answer two questions:

1   By whom must practical reasoning be followable?
2   What does it take for practical reasoning to be followable?

The first question concerns the *scope of relevance*, whereas the second concerns *what works for people that fall within that scope*. O'Neill observes that

> although the outer boundaries of inclusive practical reasoning cannot be set with precision, they must be capacious [enough] in a world of multiple and diverse audiences who are linked rather than separated by porous state and regional boundaries, global telecommunications and interlocking and overlapping practices and politics.
>
> (pg. 54)

Once the scope is fixed, all who fall within the domain should be able to follow an ethical argument and adopt principles of action for the reasons given. Now, of course, people engage an argument from different starting points with different capacities, capabilities, and vulnerabilities.[11] So assumptions about these attributes must not be too specific. For an argument to be followable, it must be both intelligible and action guiding.

The need for intelligible descriptions of action does not mean that practical reasoning must or can avoid abstraction or that it cannot use principles. O'Neill observes that in reaching ethical judgments "we affirm not just the perceptions or appraisal of the moment, or of an in-group, but principles that may be or could be woven into and judged worth weaving into activities, lives and institutions" (pg. 88). We rely on principles and rules "to orient ourselves on a course of action or life, to navigate among existing possibilities or institutions, to chart our way to new ones or to reason with

those with whom we are not already in agreement." We also use principles and rules "to revise the very conceptions and boundaries of intelli-
gibility and the formulations of rules on which we initially rely" (pg. 89).
Action-guiding principles and rules will have a universal character—
applying to all in the relevant domain. But it is important to note that
"universal" principles need not prescribe "uniform" action.[12] O'Neill acknowledges that universal principles underdetermine action. But this

> means only that they do not provide those who adopt them with an
> auto-pilot for life, and not that they do not structure or constrain it.
> *Judgement is always needed in using or following*—and in flouting—
> [universal] *rules* or *principles*, but principles are none-the-less important.
> (pg. 78)[13]

Ethical standing: who counts?

O'Neill's constructive account of practical reasoning has three more parts.
These deal with who has ethical standing, the structure of practical reasoning, and the content and compatibility of principles of justice or virtue. Questions of standing arise for, and must be addressed by, particular
agents who need to determine to which other beings they must accord the
standing of either agent, subject, or both. O'Neill argues that what agents
need is a "justifiable procedure for fixing standing, which they can use in
acting, in taking up attitudes, and in supporting policies and practices"
(pg. 97). O'Neill takes a page from moral philosophers David Hume and
John Rawls in observing that the circumstances in which issues of justice
arise are in the first place circumstances of *injustice*. They are circumstances which generate the problems for whose resolution justice is sought.
Justice, then, *consists* (operationally) *in setting things right*. For practical
purposes, it is not necessary to have a comprehensive account of ethical
standing that covers all possible cases, but agents do need procedures that
can be deployed in circumstances they actually face in which injustices
must be rectified.

Because an *objective* account of ethical standing is lacking, one will have
to be constructed on the basis of interlocking assumptions about others on
which agents base their activities.[14] Although some of these assumptions
may be false, they have two features that make them appropriate material
for constructing an account of the scope of ethical considerations:

1   These assumptions are not arbitrary posits but are disciplined by the
    demands of acting and responding effectively in the world and they are
    corrigible (can be corrected when found to be wrong) in the light of
    improved information or understanding.
2   The assumptions on which activities are based *remain in place*: they
    cannot be assumed for the sake of taking action or in taking up attitudes

or supporting policies and relying on practices but then denied when questions of ethical propriety arise.[15]

O'Neill observes that

> ... when agents commit themselves to the assumption that there are certain others, who are agents or subjects with these or those capacities, capabilities, and vulnerabilities, they cannot coherently deny these assumptions in working out the scope of ethical consideration to which they are committed.
>
> (pg. 100)

While a constructive account of who has ethical standing cannot entirely meet concerns about the appropriateness of assumptions about others, O'Neill suggests that we can get beyond merely subjective conclusions by attending to the starting points to which agents commit themselves and by striving for reasonable coherence and adequate accuracy.

Three aspects that are particularly relevant for fixing the scope of consideration are:

1   There are others separate from the agent.
2   These others are nonetheless connected to the agent.
3   These others have limited but determinate powers.

These aspects concern *plurality, connection,* and *finitude,* and are not about states of consciousness of agents or subjects.[16]

For O'Neill,

> the most difficult cases for a practical approach to fixing the scope of ethical consideration arise when activity affects others about whom agents apparently need make no assumptions of any sort, whom they therefore seemingly need not accord ethical standing
>
> (pg. 113)

—for example, distant strangers and future generations. O'Neill believes it may be possible to fix the ethical standing of those in remote places and far future generations by considering the assumptions we actually make about them in acting.

Structure of practical reasoning: obligations and rights

The next part of O'Neill's constructive account of practical reasoning concerns its structure. O'Neill observes that practical reasoning requires that principles guiding behavior be adoptable by all in the relevant domain—all who would be affected. But to show that such principles are more than "hortatory" or advisory statements, one must show that they are linked to one another by *deontic* relationships—that is, those of *duty* or *obligation*. A constructive account of practical reasoning will help us to identify ethical requirements if it can show that there are some principles of action that *cannot be viewed as adoptable by all in the relevant domain of ethical consideration*. If we can identify such principles, there will be reason to reject them. And "if their rejection is required, a gamut of more specific principles that require, prohibit and permit certain types of activity, practice or institution for more restricted domains may also be identifiable" (pg. 126).

O'Neill suggests that we consider ethical requirements first, because "they can guide action more powerfully than other types of ethical consideration, such as those expressed in recommendations or warnings" (pg. 127). Ethical requirements link act types to act types and agents to agents in identifiable ways. The linkages are *deontic* linkages. In considering requirements, one can focus primarily either on rights (or entitlements) or on obligations. O'Neill recommends that we focus more on the latter for the reason that there are asymmetries between rights and obligations and that starting with the former may obscure the latter.[17]

O'Neill's discussion of this material is quite detailed, but the relevant distinctions may be summarized as follows. O'Neill observes that in recent accounts of justice, rights are given pride of place. Such prioritization doesn't dispense with obligations, since any right implies an offsetting obligation.[18] However, not every obligation has a corresponding right. Hence, beginning with rights may obscure some obligations.[19]

Content: principles for all

Having addressed the scope and structure of ethical reasoning, O'Neill turns her attention to its content. In taking steps toward the development of a substantive account of justice, she is not interested in looking for a complete set of ethical principles, only those that are needed to cope with problems at hand. For O'Neill, the core of justice is *the rejection of principles whose adoption would foreseeably injure some people* and she feels that the rejection of such principles can support a complex web of requirements for justice (pgs. 161–166).[20]

She remarks that

> [r]ejecting principles of injuring others will be expressed in working for and through institutions and practices which are judged relatively good at avoiding and preventing injury in *actual circumstances*, so will aim for (let alone achieve) less-than-universal non-injury.
>
> (pg. 167)

Realizing justice (to whatever degree), then, will depend in large part on there *being* institutions that promote the rejection of either systematic or capricious injury. There may be many different types of constellations of institutions that will suffice for this purpose and opting for particular constellations may entail making compromises between liberty and equality. O'Neill suggests that a criterion for choosing between alternative compromises of this sort is the adequacy with which a whole system of institutions prevents systematic and capricious injury (pg. 171). While, like Francis, O'Neill thinks that some form of subsidiarity in political decision-making is appropriate, the formation of a single global state is not.[21]

O'Neill observes that injustice can arise from injury inflicted indirectly through damage to the social fabric or the natural world. With respect to the social fabric, systematic or gratuitous deception is one form of indirect damage, which suggests a need to institutionalize transparency. With respect to the natural world, O'Neill argues damage to the natural and [human-]made environment can be unjust in two ways: promoting conditions through which others may be injured and by destroying regenerative powers, a practice that is not universalizable. Consequently, she concludes that "justice makes environmental as well as political, economic, and social demands" (pg. 177).

Realizing justice requires establishing special arrangements to supplement its "perfect obligations" (or obligations that are held by all and owed to all, offset rights not to be interfered with, and are embodied in legal and economic systems), O'Neill believes that the considerations she has offered may provide useful guidance for the following reasons.

1   [T]hey address the *range* of concerns which justice must address.
2   [T]hey do so [by] drawing only on the abstract and constructive *methods* which are available for ethical reasoning.[22]
3   [T]hey see institutional change in a down-to-earth and practical way: what may be achievable is piecemeal reform of institutions and practices rather than a utopian project of imposing an ideal constitution or of transforming "manifesto rights" [or rights which may be claimed but are not enforceable] into realities (pg. 179).

O'Neill is mindful that justice, as the rejection of direct and indirect injury, by itself may not be enough for us to lead good lives in well-ordered societies, so she turns to the pursuit of virtue. Whereas justice is a matter of perfect obligation matched by rights; virtue is not.[23] While some virtues pertain to limited spheres of activity, at least some must be inclusive principles—spanning across domains of activity—since they are indispensable for the stability of life.

> The spheres of action must be linked not only by public institutions that coordinate or subordinate them, but by continuities of character which support continuities of activity, including feeling, relationship, and community,
>
> (pg. 185)

O'Neill identifies required and optional virtues. The former include "virtues of justice," such as the rejection of injury, fairness, truthfulness, toleration, and respect for others, and "executive virtues," such as self-control, self-respect, decisiveness, courage, and endurance. "Social virtues," such as altruism and the care and concern for others, may or may not be considered as required.

In a line of argumentation similar to that employed by Francis, which may be coincidental, O'Neill offers a vindication of social virtues. She suggests that when we take into account the varied and specific ways in which particular agents and subjects are and become vulnerable to others, we come to acknowledge that justice alone is not enough (pg. 191). *The very social fabric that creates capabilities also creates vulnerabilities.* "Connected lives become selectively, variably, and sometimes acutely vulnerable lives" (pg. 192). Moreover, she observes, principles of justice take minimal account of the connectedness of lives. O'Neill suggests that, analogous to the argument that principles of justice can be derived from the requirement to reject inclusive principles of injuring, which are not universalizable, there is another argument that inclusive principles of indifference to and neglect of others also cannot be universalized.

> The underlying principles of a range of more specific required social virtues that are relevant to particular situations and at particular times can then be derived from the fact that agents have reason to reject principles of indifference or neglect.
>
> (pg. 194)

O'Neill observes that social virtues can serve as repositories of what is best about human nature, surviving in situations of social and political crises when justice fails. She identifies three "constellations" of social virtues. The first comprises traits expressed by giving and showing concern and care for others that go beyond justice (are *supererogatory*). The second "expresses the rejection of indifference and neglect less directly [than the first] by sustaining and supporting social trust and connection, so indirectly sustaining capabilities for action, communication and interaction" (pg. 202). O'Neill writes that to improve civilizing institutions, that is,

> to sustain and build confidence and trust, and with them the social fabric, we must not merely act justly, so refrain from destroying them, but help to breathe life both into current and into new practices and ways of life.
>
> (pg. 202)

The third constellation of social virtues also expresses the rejection of indifference and neglect less directly than virtues in the first constellation "in action that sustains natural and [human-]made environments on which individual lives and social fabric depends" (pg. 203).

O'Neill observes that the obligations of justice and virtue are asymmetric but complementary. Whereas obligations of justice entail the rejection of direct injury to others and of indirect injuries to the social fabric and the material basis of life, obligations of virtue entail the rejection of direct indifference and neglect to others and indirect indifference to the social fabric and material basis of life. She contrasts them as follows (pg. 205).

Obligations of justice: rejection of injury

- Rejection of direct injury to others: no systematic or gratuitous violence or coercion.
- Rejection of indirect injury:

    a   Rejection of damage to the social fabric: no systematic or gratuitous deceit, fraud, incitement to hatred, etc.
    b   Rejection of damage to the material basis of life: no systematic or gratuitous damage to natural or [human]-made environments.

Obligations of virtue: rejection of indifference and neglect

- Rejection of direct indifference to others: sympathy, beneficence, love, help, care and concern, solidarity, acts of rescue, etc.
- Rejection of indirect indifference to others:

    a   Rejection of indifference to the social fabric: selective care and support for social life and culture, expressed in toleration, participation, loyalty, social reform, etc.
    b   Rejection of indifference to the material basis of life: selective care and concern for natural and [human]-made environments, expressed in cultivation, preservation, and conservation, etc.

O'Neill observes that

> The rejection of both systematic injury and indifference and of gratuitous injury in their many manifestations, can lead *towards* just institutions and virtuous characters, but there is no point or moment of arrival at which perfect justice or complete virtue will have been achieved.
>
> (pg. 206)

O'Neill believes that the constructive approach she has elaborated provides enough material to construct "a capacious account of human obligations" and to enable an integrated account of justice and virtue to be given, even as "that account of justice and virtue will not provide complete instructions for a just social order or for virtuous lives" (pg. 210). It will, however, "provide guidelines for moving towards justice and towards virtue (ibid.)."[24]

She concludes by observing,

> At each time and place, those who hope to move towards justice and towards virtue will have to build, and rebuild, shaping the institutions, policies and practices which they find around them, and their own attitudes and activities to meet standards which, they believe, can be standards for all within the domain of their ethical consideration.
>
> (pg. 212)

Lorraine Elliott, a political scientist influenced by O'Neill and other proponents of a cosmopolitan perspective, has written more directly on the global environmental inequity brought about in large part by globalization, with which Francis is also concerned (see Elliott 2002). Elliott argues that globalization

> ... has been neither normatively neutral nor materially benign in its environmental consequences. The global politics of the environment has therefore come to be characterized by inequities in the use of resources and production of waste, in environmental impact, and in access to the structures of environmental governance at a local and global level. In effect, the lives of others-beyond-borders are shaped without their participation or consent.
>
> (Elliott 2002: 2)

Drawing on the cosmopolitan view that humanity is bound together as a single moral community with shared rights and obligations, on the Kantian view that a right violated anywhere is felt everywhere, and O'Neill's position (following Kant) that "justice is owed to all, regardless of location or origin, race or gender, class or citizenship (O'Neill 2000: 45)," Elliott argues that

> ... there are at least three conditions ... essential for an equitable and just form of global environmental governance: recognition of equal moral obligations across borders, compensatory burden sharing, and politics of consent.
>
> (Elliott 2002: 2)

Comparison of O'Neill's assessments and prescriptions with those of Francis

A comparison of assessments of our present state of affairs and prescriptions that pertain to the obligations of individuals and political entities and the natural environment by O'Neill and Francis reveals that they would appear to agree on much.

- We live within an interdependent system of ecosystems in which violations of social solidarity harm the natural environment, and vice versa.

- The world is in a state of environmental crisis that is related to a wider spectrum of social, political, and economic troubles.
- Our social nature makes us all co-dependent and vulnerable and dependent upon a robust social fabric as well as a natural environment that is able to regenerate itself.
- The ethical perspective appropriate to adopt in such a setting is universalist, act-oriented, and agent-oriented (where agents may be non-human creatures)—in Francis's words, *being* takes precedence over *being used*.[25]
- The scope of concern—who matters—includes those now living and future generations, as well as the ecosystems in which we reside.
- Considered judgment needs to be exercised in applying principles of practical reasoning—ethics is not algorithmic, cook-bookish, or catechistic.
- Justice consists largely in rejecting principles of behavior that if universally adopted will injure people, fellow creatures, the natural environment, and the social fabric and adopting constellations of principles that, if implemented, would not so injure.
- Obligations associated with justice and virtue are different and asymmetric. We need to proceed toward climate justice with virtue, rejecting indifference and neglect to harm to natural systems and cultural heritages.
- Developed countries must assume their fair share of the costs of remediating the natural environment and enabling developing countries to achieve sustainable development.
- In determining what is fair compensation and assistance, the contributions of globalization to environmental inequities must be considered.
- An international system of climate (or more broadly, environmental) governance needs to be developed and implemented but with subsidiarity of decision-making as appropriate.
- The capacities, capabilities, and vulnerabilities—and informed consent—of others affected by political decision-making need to be explicitly accounted for and respected.
- Processes need to be considered in their entirety to promote an integral ecology that is essential to life. "Social Progress" needs to be redefined and lifestyle changes adopted.
- Political action and moral and institutional improvisation are needed to respond to evolving situations.

Francis goes beyond O'Neill in tapping into resources to be found in Christian beliefs, especially in his third chapter on "The Gospel of Creation," but it should be clear from the foregoing that much of the substance of Francis's encyclical letter could be supported by even an agnostic of cosmopolitan constructivist persuasion.

Notes

1 References to *Laudato Si'* will be to sections from which text is quoted.
2 A system of systems perspective is one that views subsidiary systems that are interconnected and interdependent as components of a larger, integrated system. The human body or the infrastructure system of a modern city are examples.
3 This view is developed at length in Charles Taylor's essay, "A Catholic Modernity?" in Heft 1999: 13–38.
4 In fact, the only references given for *Laudato Si'* are previous encyclical letters and statements issued by Catholic Church authorities.
5 O'Neill is certainly not the only contemporary philosopher setting out an influential cosmopolitan constructivist perspective. Seyla Benhabib's 2006 and Kwame Anthony Appiah's 2006 volumes have also garnered much attention. O'Neill, however, was named the winner of the 2017 Berggruen Prize in Philosophy, which is awarded annually to a thinker whose ideas "have profoundly shaped human self-understanding and advancement in a rapidly changing world," in large part because of the influence on the field of moral philosophy of *Towards Justice and Virtue* (see www.nytimes.com/2017/10/03/arts/onora-oneill-berggruen-prize.html).
6 The crisis of modernist self-justification is the crisis of *not* being able to justify criteria to which we can appeal in judging behavior, conventions, and institutional arrangements *without* begging the question in favor of an otherwise unjustified normative perspective. For a book-length discussion of different views of and responses to this crisis, see Habermas (1987).
7 A virtue is an excellence of behavior in a given domain, usually a "mean" between two or more competing ends or goals (arétes). Virtues may be thought of "in terms of the act descriptions and principles that virtuous people embody in their lives and display in their action as dispositions or capacities to act, respond, and feel in determinate ways" (O'Neill 1996: 138). Subsequent references to O'Neill (1996) will be to pages in that text.
8 There are different conceptions of practical reasoning—end-oriented and act-oriented. The former take in Platonism (or action oriented by objective ends), perfectionism, metaphysical realism, and instrumentalism. Action-oriented conceptions justify actions, policies, or characters by showing that they embody certain types of principles of action and include Kantian conceptions, according to which reasoned action is informed by principles in the relevant domain all can follow, and particularist conceptions, according to which action is informed by actual norms and commitments.
9 By "metaphysical argument" is meant an argument that proceeds from first principles of ontology, or theories about the nature of being, in this case, the status of principles of right and wrong.
10 This modality is really the crux of the matter for O'Neill (as well as Kant)—what action-guiding principles *can* be accepted by all in the relevant domain. To anticipate where her argument is headed, any principles whose acceptance *would* result in harm to some *cannot* be accepted by all, and so *must* be rejected.
11 Following Amartya Sen, O'Neill takes capacities to be individual traits and talents. Capabilities are abilities to exercise capacities in institutionalized settings, and vulnerabilities are absences of capabilities.
12 An example demonstrating this point is the old socialist maxim "from each according to their ability and to each according to their need."
13 This, of course, is the point of the "Grand Inquisitor" episode in Dostoevsky's *The Brothers Karamazov*.
14 By activity O'Neill means individual acts and responses, feelings and attitudes, support for policies, and participation in practices.

15 For example, we cannot acknowledge that someone has disabilities that prohibit them from taking a job and then argue that they should be denied public assistance because they are not actively seeking employment.

16 If others separate from the agent are not affected by an action, it is not an ethical matter.

17 Nussbaum 2006 notably takes the opposite position.

18 "Unless obligation-bearers are identifiable by right-holders, claims to have rights amount only to rhetoric" (pg. 129).

19 In the interest of concision, we will not further pursue O'Neill's discussion of this material here. Her distinctions between "liberty" and "welfare" rights and "universal," "special," and "perfect," and "imperfect" duties or obligations are discussed with examples in her Chapter 5.

20 O'Neill does not argue that perfect justice is attainable and that all injury can be avoided, only that justifiable action-guiding principles will be ones that reject principles whose adoption will foreseeably injure some.

21 This view was also exposited by Kant in his essay "Towards Perpetual Peace" (Kant 1996) and by Rawls in his *The Law of Peoples* (Rawls 1999).

22 O'Neill continues, "They do not invoke either starting points or conceptions of practical reason that need unavailable metaphysical support or unavailable proof that the particularities of a given society or life are not open to ethical question" (pg. 179).

23 O'Neill observes that "[principles] of justice specify ethical requirements *and* their recipients; their observance can in principle be claimed, waived, and enforced by publicly recognized actions that can be invoked even between strangers ... Required virtues, if there are any, will also make demands that fall on all, but will not specify recipients and occasions for virtuous action" (pg. 184).

24 On a personal note, the author can state that, after teaching courses on making ethical judgments where cultural viewpoints conflict for over 20 years, students from agricultural and life sciences, engineering, humanities and arts, architecture and urban planning have found O'Neill's constructive account of practical reasoning, when applied to case-study material, to be accessible and useful.

25 As noted above, Francis goes further to observe that the Judeo-Christian tradition does not sanction a "tyrannical anthropocentrism."

References

Appiah, Kwame Anthony. 2006. *Cosmopolitanism: Ethics in a World of Strangers.* New York: W. W. Norton.

Beard, Victoria A., Anjeli Mahendra, and Michael I. Westphal. 2016. *Towards a More Equal City: Framing the Challenges and Opportunities.* Washington, DC: World Resources Institute.

Benhabib, Seyla. 2006. *Another Cosmopolitanism.* New York: Oxford University Press.

Donaghy, Kieran P. 2001. "Some Moral, Ethical, and Extra-Ethical Issues Concerning Biotechnology and How We might Deliberate about Them". *American Behavioral Scientist*, 44: 1267–1282.

Dostoevsky, Fyodor. 1953. *The Brothers Karamazov*, (trans. Alexandra Kropotkin). Garden City, NY: The Literary Guild.

Elliott, Lorraine. 2002. "Global Environmental (In)equity and the Cosmopolitan Project," CSGR Working Paper No. 95/02. Coventry: Center for the Study of Globalization and Regionalization, University of Warwick.

Gasper, Des. 2004. *The Ethics of Development*. Edinburgh: Edinburgh University Press.

Habermas, Jurgen. 1987. *The Philosophical Discourse of Modernity: Twelve Lectures*. Cambridge, MA: The MIT Press.

Heft, James L. (ed.). 1999. *A Catholic Modernity? Charles Taylor's Marianist Award Lecture*. New York: Oxford University Press.

Kant, Immanuel. 1996. "Towards Perpetual Peace," in *Practical Philosophy* (Translated and edited by Mary J. Gregor), Cambridge: Cambridge University Press, 313–351.

Nussbaum, Martha C. 2006. *Frontiers of Justice: Disability, Nationality, Species Membership*. Cambridge, MA: The Belknap Press of Harvard University Press.

O'Neill, Onora. 1996. *Towards Justice and Virtue*. Cambridge: Cambridge University Press.

O'Neill, Onora. 2000. "Bounded and Cosmopolitan Justice". *Review of International Studies*, 26: 45–60.

Rawls, John. 1999. *The Law of Peoples*. Cambridge, MA: Harvard University Press.

United Nations Resolution A/RES/70/1 adopted by the General Assembly: 9/25/15. *Transforming our World: The 2030 Agenda for Sustainable Development*. https://sustainabledevelopment.un.org/ content/documents/21252030%20 Agenda%20for%20Sustainable%20Development%20web.pdf

Williams, Bernard. 2005. "Modernity and the Substance of Ethical Life," in Hawthorn, Geoffrey (ed.), *In the Beginning was the Deed: Realism and Moralism in Political Argument*, Princeton, NJ: Princeton University Press, 40–51.

Part 4
Central concepts

11 A new anthropology? *Laudato Si'* and the question of interconnectedness

Celia Deane-Drummond

The idea of interrelatedness or interconnectedness occurs throughout *Laudato Si'* in a way that generates a fresh emphasis for theological anthropology that differs from post-Enlightenment individualism. This chapter will begin with an exploration of the role of the idea of interconnectedness in the encyclical. I then explore ways in which the encyclical is open to indigenous perspectives on the human. Further, I will argue that a convincing Catholic theological approach to what it means to be human requires engaging with anthropological research in order to fill out what interconnectedness signifies. Although traditional Roman Catholic approaches have stressed the primacy of human dignity, this chapter argues that taking proper account of interconnectedness requires a significant paradigm shift in what dignity signifies and challenges human exceptionalism.

It is clear from even a cursory reading of *Laudato Si'* that interconnectedness is a strong thread running through the text. After highlighting the contexts in which this idea appears explicitly, I will argue that interconnectedness in all its various manifestations in the encyclical represents a movement away from narrowly conceived ideas on the importance of humanity, toward indigenous ways of thinking about the world. These indigenous perspectives are associated with a much deeper sense of relationship with other beings than the Church has generally acknowledged. A strong emphasis on interconnectedness also shows up in practical applications such as alternative ways of considering what justice means. Justice is about what it means to be in *right relationships* with one another, and, according to classic traditions, *what is due* to another. But there are different ways of parsing this out. In Western traditions, where situations of injustice arise, the response is often legal and punitive. I argue that there are important lessons to be learnt from ways of conceiving what justice requires that put a much greater emphasis on the importance of maintaining interconnectedness between individuals rather than on punishment for crimes committed.

I should say at the outset that I am not trying to idealize indigenous thought in the way that has sometimes occurred in Western thought, especially in the period immediately after Darwin when anthropologists leant toward an interpretation of hunter-gatherer communities in terms of the "noble sav-age."[1] Rather, the encyclical, by stressing openness to other interpretations of what it is to be human in the world, is saying that more traditional West-ern narratives about what it means to be human that stress human excep-tionalism[2] are no longer fully adequate to the task. I am not, at the same time, suggesting that all aspects of traditional Western conceptions of what it is to be human are obsolete. Rather, a dialogue between traditions opens up new insights that are relevant as we try to understand what it means to be human in a globalized ecologically fragile world. However, any insights we may acquire in this area will not amount to universals about human na-ture and are better understood as tentative and illuminating suggestions that encourage respectful interchange between different cultures and help those from a Western tradition appreciate and understand the rich diversity in in-terpretations about what humanity signifies. This should, in turn, encourage a willingness to qualify or even modify aspects of their own tradition.

But what more precisely might that mean for Christian theology? I sug-gest that considering specific and grounded indigenous perceptions of the world opens up a fascinating window into alternative approaches to under-standing what it means to be human. Indigenous perspectives lead us away from traditional post-Enlightenment dualistic views that emphasize the separation of both nature and culture and human and animal and that as-sumed human domination and superiority. At the same time, Pope Francis needs to retain something of the traditional Roman Catholic emphasis on the special dignity of the human if his views are not going to be interpreted as simply an adoption of animist beliefs. This chapter will probe the extent to which he has navigated that tension. I also suggest preliminary ways for-ward in working out what that might mean for a theological anthropology.

The text of *Laudato Si'* itself suggests that Pope Francis has barely be-gun to navigate this tension. Instead, he has left different interpretations of what it means to be human situated somewhat uneasily alongside each other, each to some extent challenging the other. A generous reading is that this is creative theological *bricolage*, and each should be left to keep its own integrity and live in tension with the other. I suggest that, instead, the theo-logical task is to work hard to probe this issue, asking what are the limits of respectful incorporation of aspects of alternative world-views, especially in the context of Roman Catholic thought, but also wider Christian the-ology in general. I also suggest that we should edge toward an important paradigm shift within Western theological thinking about what it means to be human.

Interconnectedness in *Laudato Si*

Pope Francis draws on John Paul II for one of the most significant lines of thought in *Laudato Si'*, one that is highlighted again and again. This is the idea that the strong link between (a) concern for the individual human person in their specific dignity and (b) connection to and reconciliation of each person with God, other persons and the world provides an important way to frame what ecological conversion is all about (5). The first time that Pope Francis explicitly mentions *inter*connectedness is in relation to a summing up of all biblical faith and tradition on the integral value of creation. He also sees interconnection as important to a theological approach to the world that is concerned with right relationships in justice and that combines care for the natural world with care for oneself and care for right relationships within the human community. He writes, with reference to the stories of Cain and Abel and Noah in the book of Genesis that

> [these ancient stories, full of symbolism, bear witness to a conviction which we today share, that everything is interconnected, and that genuine care for our own lives and our relationships with nature is inseparable from fraternity, justice and faithfulness to others.
>
> (70)

However, it is worth probing the context in which this important first reference to interconnectedness appears, for it is at the end of a paragraph which begins with a discussion of the violent murder of Abel by Cain, and the tension that then arises between Cain and the earth, and of course, between Cain and God. It is a breakdown in peaceful relationships with each other, with God and with the earth that leaves a void of injustice, whereby the constant failure of humanity in one relationship impacts all other relationships. The problem, therefore, begins with humanity in its relationship with God and then spreads out to all other human relationships and thence to our relationships with other creatures and the earth. The solution, for Pope Francis, is to work toward justice and fraternity in a way that is inclusive of care for the natural world around us. The background of the earth being wounded by human sin, but then its potential healing, plays into this aspect of interconnectedness so that just as broken human relationships have repercussions that are wider than human-human relationships, right relationships and justice between people have a correspondingly wide impact.

Pope Francis does not, it seems, in this context, understand the interconnectedness *within* creation to be impacted by human sin, but only humanity's relationship with the land as such. In this sense, "renewal entails recovering and respecting the rhythms inscribed in nature by the hand of the Creator" (71). So, the interconnectedness he refers to here is that of human/God, human/human and human/land rather than that *between* creaturely kinds. The prospect that the "rhythms inscribed in nature" may actually not be recoverable does not seem to cross his mind, even though he is extremely well aware of loss of biodiversity as well as climate change (e.g. 169). It is disappointing that while he clearly recognizes the importance of each creature as a mirror of God (85) and acknowledges the worth of each living being as where the Spirit dwells (88), he does not give enough attention to a description of different creatures along with symbiotic or mutualistic relationships between them.[3]

Not only does the way human beings treat each other have repercussions for our relationship with the natural environment, but the opposite is true as well. The way we treat the natural world and its creatures also has repercussions for our treatment of one another. This becomes clear on the second occasion on which Pope Francis explicitly mentions interconnectedness, this time in the context of a discussion of universal communion and fraternity with all creatures. He says that "[it] follows that our indifference or cruelty towards fellow creatures of this world sooner or later affects the treatment we mete out to other human beings" (92). The spread of cruelty is his particular concern: "the same wretchedness which leads us to mistreat an animal will not be long in showing itself in our relationships with other people" (92). It is therefore with absolute conviction that Pope Francis can say, citing the Catechism of the Roman Catholic Church, that "[every] act of cruelty towards any creature is 'contrary to human dignity'" (92).

Unfortunately, as a number of animal welfare activists have pointed out, when it comes to practical recommendations as to what this latter connection might imply in terms of changing and challenging structural sin and individual habits of using, for example, animal products from animals that have suffered undue harm and stress, as in concentrated animal feeding operations (CAFOs), Pope Francis falls short in not explicitly drawing this out.[4] It is curious to consider why *Laudato Si'* does not explore in practical terms this structural gap between care for creatures in the Catholic tradition and the practice of consuming animals that have been reared in cruel conditions. (It is striking that Pope Francis has no difficulty linking sexual ethics with broader environmental issues.) Is this related to his cultural background in Argentina, a place where the impacts of climate change are being felt keenly, but where there is also a strong, even machismo, cultural tradition of meat eating? Citing the 1987 pastoral letter of the conference of Dominican bishops, he states clearly once again the relational aspects: "Peace, justice and the preservation of creation are three absolutely interconnected themes, which cannot be separated and treated individually without once again falling into reductionism" (92). Pope Francis becomes almost lyrical in his estimation of the importance of this dynamic, this movement of reconciliation which allows universal communion to flow from healthy and healed relationships, echoing the words of his mentor, Francis of Assisi. All creatures, he writes, are on a "wonderful pilgrimage" and are "woven together," united "by the love God has for each of his creatures and which also unites us in fond affection with brother sun, sister moon, brother river and mother earth" (92).

Interconnectedness appears next in Pope Francis's discussion of technology and the technological paradigm. He recognizes distinct problems associated with a lack of care for the earth. That lack of care becomes expressed in different ways, such as through challenges related to pollution, environmental decay, and the depletion of natural resources (111). A scientific and technological mindset will automatically take each of these challenges, isolate them and try and solve them through technical means. However, this kind of approach is inadequate according to Pope Francis, because such attempts "separate what is in reality interconnected and ... mask the true and deepest problems of the global system" (111). The deepest aspect of these problems is that we no longer care for the earth as an interconnected whole. Many scientists would actually agree with Pope Francis on this point, namely, that the challenges relate to the Earth System as a whole and not just one specific aspect of it. In Pope Francis's interpretation, the problem is at root a cultural and even moral one, so our whole perspective has gone askew. We are also obsessed with technological fixes that do not necessarily help to change our perspective. Instead, for him, a new way of thinking is required, one that encourages a fresh "way of thinking, policies, an educational programme, a lifestyle and a spirituality which together generate resistance to the assault of the technocratic paradigm" (111).

As we turn to the part of the encyclical that deals with action, his discourse on integral ecology and interconnectedness makes its appearance again. This time interconnectedness is about his new way of thinking hinted at in previous sections. So, in the first and more obvious sense, ecology is about interconnectedness. Other natural sciences also present interconnected aspects, such as time and space in physics, but importantly, physics, chemistry, and the other natural sciences are also connected. Hence, for Pope Francis,

> [it] cannot be emphasized enough how everything is interconnected. Time and space are not independent of one another, and not even atoms or subatomic particles can be considered in isolation. Just as the different aspects of the planet – physical, chemical and biological – are interrelated, so too living species are part of a network, which we will never fully explore and understand. A good part of our genetic code is shared by many living beings.
>
> (138)

Isolating knowledge into sub-parts then leads simply to forms of "ignorance" (138). Finding ways to join up these different forms of knowledge may be rather more challenging than Pope Francis imagines, not least because each has become so specialized that common language does not necessarily reflect common concepts. However, in so much as this is a vital aspect of the process of changing the way we think, it is vitally important to start new and holistic ways of thinking about problems, rather than isolating them into their separated disciplinary fragments. At the same time, lowest common denominator approaches will not work well either. Somehow the depth of each intellectual discipline needs to be retained in the dialogue, so that it is genuine, rather than superficial.

But Pope Francis is bolder yet. His notion of interconnectedness heralds and reinforces not just a new way of approaching the natural sciences, for example, by working on specific climate and other environmental challenges that are multidisciplinary in nature, but a way of joining up ecological ways of thinking with economics, the social sciences, and humanistic fields. In most academic departments, in my experience, there are examples where knowledge is divided in a way that splits off one field of study from another. Christian theology, for example, separates systematic from moral theology, or even biblical studies; or theology is split apart from religious studies or mysticism; anthropology is often split between social and biological anthropology, and so on *so that there are* multiple sub-disciplines and sub-fields. Pope Francis recommends working across disciplinary boundaries to pursue a common and shared task, in this case the most pressing challenge of our time, namely, maintaining the rich diversity of life and even our survival on our common home, the earth. In most cases, trans-disciplinarity is preferred, that is, retaining the integrity of a particular discipline while engaging in serious dialogue with others. However, in other cases, it is time to heal the fissures that have proved to be unhelpful rather than helpful. If the direction of modern scientific culture has been toward more and more specialization and fragmentation, the direction of integral ecology is directly opposite, a kind of re-annealing what has been fragmented through the fire of a cultural revolution that Pope Francis believes is necessary for lasting change.

Interconnectedness also appears toward the end of the encyclical, significantly, when Pope Francis elaborates on his thinking about the Trinity. He claims that "[everything] is interconnected, and this invites us to develop a spirituality of that global solidarity which flows from the mystery of the Trinity" (240). The Divine persons are "subsistent relations" and the world as God created it is a "web of relationships" (240). Linking the Trinity as such, or immanent Trinity, with the work of the Trinity in the world, also known as the economic Trinity, has been the task of theologians speaking about the social or ecological Trinity, such as Jürgen Moltmann, for example (Moltmann 1985; see also Deane-Drummond 2017). However, Pope Francis's association between the Trinity in itself and its action in the world seems to be looser and rather more apophatic[5] than Moltmann's more cataphatic[6] and explicit economic doctrine of the Trinity (Moltmann 1981). Pope Francis may be influenced here by a more sacramental understanding of the Trinity, hinting, as he does, at Pierre Teilhard de Chardin's understanding.[7] Pope Francis also pays explicit attention to anthropology when linking the doctrine of the Trinity to the world, so, in speaking of human persons, "they make their own that trinitarian dynamism which God imprinted in them when they were created" (240). Pope Francis, drawing on Francis of Assisi and the Franciscan tradition claims that all creatures in some sense bear the mark of the Trinity, for *"each creature bears in itself a specifically Trinitarian structure"* (239). He cites St. Bonaventure for this idea, and it seems that he thinks of this insight as a kind of intuitive knowledge that arises in prayerful contemplation. This is important, as it shows how the "web of relationships" (240) in the world is mirrored in Trinitarian relationships. However, for Pope Francis, humanity has a unique relationship with the Trinity that goes beyond this mirroring to a more active role. So, "[the] human person grows more, matures more and is sanctified more to the extent that he or she enters into relationships, going out from themselves to live in communion with God, with others and with all creatures" (40). No other creatures are described in this way, implying that human beings still have a special role in that they are in some sense mediators between God and the rest of the created world, which of course is a classic Christian view of anthropology.

Are there any potential risks in such a Trinitarian portrait of the interconnectedness of human life with all other life? Certainly, this line, or rather, better, web of thinking outlined above, drawing specifically on Trinitarian imagery, but also, I suggest, influenced by ecological thought, encourages a move away from a narrowly conceived anthropocentrism that has dominated the history of the Roman Catholic church, especially in the wake of the post-Enlightenment emphasis on individualism. The specific texts on anthropocentrism in the encyclical make this point very clear. The Bible has no place for what Pope Francis calls a "tyrannical anthropocentrism" that ignores the worth of other creatures (68). What Pope Francis means by this term is dedication to technical ways of solving problems that miss out the importance of human dimensions. Thus, he says that "[modern] anthropocentrism has paradoxically ended up prizing technical thought over reality" and has devalued the worth of the natural world and hence amounts to a loss of the "intrinsic dignity of the world" (115). Moreover, when human beings, "fail to find their true place in this world" (115) they act in a way that is damaging to themselves.

The point that Pope Francis is trying to drive home here is that we have ended up with an "excessive anthropocentrism," by which he seems to mean a breakdown of social bonds and the legacy of "Promethean vision of mastery over the world" (116). Here, too, in its place he advocates "responsible stewardship" (116), and while many scientists will agree with such a stance, stewardship is also perceived as rather too close to a managerial style of relationship with the world for many ecologically minded theologians and philosophers.[8] Further, "one cannot prescind from humanity" (118). By this, he seems to mean that paying attention to the particular value of our humanity is vitally important. And, equally critically, "[there] can be no renewal of our relationship with nature without a renewal of humanity itself" (118). Consequently, ecology and anthropology need to be combined. And ways of thinking that put technological fixes above human relationships and specialist knowledge before holistic ways of perceiving the world are both important aspects of how humanity has lost its way, leading to a "misguided anthropocentrism" (118, 119). If our anthropocentrism is misguided, this leads to a "misguided lifestyle" (122). On the other hand, moving away from misguided forms of anthropocentrism does not mean resorting to "biocentrism" (118). So the question arises: if the kind of anthropocentrism that Pope Francis objects to is tyrannical, excessive and misguided, what might be the alternatives to supplement the stewardship model he hints at?

Indigenous perspectives on the world

As we have seen Pope Francis wants to get back to a more holistic way of thinking about the world and humanity's relationships with it. It is therefore not surprising that he is open to listening to indigenous voices, not only because indigenous people are among the most vulnerable to the impacts of climate change but also because of their emphasis on interconnection with the world around them. The first time he mentions indigenous peoples is in the context of their particular vulnerability. Thus, in his section on integral ecology he remarks that it is our duty to take "special care for indigenous communities and their cultural traditions" (146). He emphasizes their close relationship with the land: for indigenous communities "land is not a commodity but rather a gift from God and from their ancestors who rest there, a sacred space with which they need to interact if they are to maintain their identity and values" (146). Agricultural and mining projects that violate the rights of indigenous peoples to their land are therefore at odds with the holistic approach that Pope Francis is calling for here. But are indigenous peoples more, in Pope Francis's mind, than rightful recipients of justice and land rights? The answer is yes, for in his affirmative discussion of cooperatives and those that work for alternative communities, he observes that

> [they] are able to instill a greater sense of responsibility, a strong sense of community, a readiness to protect others, a spirit of creativity and a deep love for the land. They are also concerned about what they will eventually leave to their children and grandchildren.
>
> (179)

And, where does Pope Francis find particularly striking exemplars of such values? His answer is that these values are "deeply rooted in indigenous peoples" (179). It is not that Western cultures lack the potential to express such values. They do so through cooperatives, for example. But indigenous peoples are able to demonstrate them more clearly, both over a longer period and in a more fulsome way.

Pope Francis therefore insists that indigenous peoples should be "principal dialogue partners" (146). Given that the majority of those living on the planet are religious believers, this should "spur religions to dialogue among themselves for the sake of protecting nature, defending the poor, and building networks of respect and fraternity" (201). The question that he has not yet addressed, however, is more precisely *how* dialogue with indigenous ways of thinking about the world could inform or even modify Western religious perspectives. Without the specificity of ethnographic research, there are some dangers in making blanket universal statements about indigenous thinking. There is a risk, too, of a naïve idealism and romanticism about what indigenous traditions might have to offer creeping in. However, given the importance of interrelationships and interconnectedness within indigenous traditions, there are, I suggest, important lessons to be learnt that can apply more universally and are of relevance to other cultures and traditions.

The anthropologist Tim Ingold offers, it seems to me, a remarkable translation of indigenous thinking into new ways of understanding the anthropological task. His research develops out of his ethnographic work in specific cultural contexts and provides important ingredients for a theological anthropology.[9] Ingold is aware that it can be misleading to portray hunter-gatherer societies as surviving exemplars of the "natural" or "original" state of humankind. I have my doubts that Pope Francis commits such an error; rather he has idealized, or rather universalized what indigenous peoples might be able to offer. Ingold proposes that the trajectory of post-Baconian thought toward control of self and environment presumes mastery as the ideal state (Ingold 2011: 62–63). Understanding humanity as transcendent to the natural world and as utterly different from the world allows that world to be viewed as raw material for human purposes. When human transcendence is emphasized excessively, it serves to contribute to the kind of tyrannical anthropocentrism that is of such concern to Pope Francis. The challenge for Pope Francis is to retain a sense of human dignity but without licensing domination or manipulation. It is significant that when Pope Francis speaks of human transcendence what he actually points to is human distinctiveness. Thus, he writes that "[our] capacity to reason, to develop arguments, to be inventive, to interpret reality and to create art, along with other not yet discovered capacities, are signs of a uniqueness which transcends the spheres of physics and biology" (81). However, the ultimate destiny of all creatures is to share in that transcendence: "all creatures are moving forward with us and through us towards a common point of arrival, which is God, in that transcendent fullness where the risen Christ embraces and illumines all things" (83). Ingold suggests that in all indigenous communities that he has encountered the environment is viewed not just as a passive container but instead as "saturated with personal powers of one kind or another" (Ingold 2011: 66). He suggests that the indigenous attitude toward that environment involves care and respect, including care and respect toward the animals and plants within it. Some measure of transcendence is anticipated in this view for human beings, but it is a non-tyrannical view that puts emphasis on shared subjectivity and personhood, rather than objectivity and manipulation.

The particular case of hunting for game includes careful use of ecological resources that are also considered to be vitally alive in addition to the personal powers associated with some natural agents. Using examples drawn from the Cree community in Canada, as well as observations from ethnographers working in other hunter-gatherer contexts, Ingold proposes that the most common perception is that there is an active decision by the hunted to yield to the hunter, so the hunted yields in a way that expresses consent. The hunter, in turn, does not try to kill more than is necessary.[10]

Ingold's work with indigenous communities is not just confined to those who practice hunting. He concludes from extensive research in the field that in general those who practice pastoralism most commonly have a very different kind of relationship with the animals that they herd, one where "animals are presumed to lack the capacity to reciprocate" (Ingold 2011: 72). It is really important to be clear about what Ingold means by the term pastoralist. He states clearly that

> the contrast I am drawing here is between hunting and pastoralism as a way of relating to animals, not between hunting and pastoral societies. It is perfectly possible for the same people in the same society to relate concurrently to different animals in quite different ways. The Blackfoot Indians of the North American Plains, for example, were hunters in relation to the buffalo, but herdsmen in relation to the horse.
>
> (Ingold 2011: 422, n. 7)

Pastoralists are, in so far as they practice pastoralism, in control of the fate of their animals, making life and death decisions about their welfare in a way that is foreign to the mindset of the hunter in hunter-gatherer communities. For Ingold, therefore, hunter-gatherers emphasize a relationship of trust, whereas pastoralists emphasize domination. Forcing another to comply with one's will undermines trust. For the hunter, the animal is given by what seems to Ingold to be a type of "revelation" by the one hunted, while for the pastoralist the relationship is much more one of control. Pastoralists still understand the animals they are herding to be agents in their own right. Hence, "[whether] the regime be one of hunting or of pastoralism, humans and other animals relate to one another not in mind or body alone but as undivided centres of attention and action, as whole beings" (Ingold 2011: 75). Ingold wishes to avoid suggesting that relationships of trust are morally or intrinsically better than those of domination or even *vice versa*. A basic stance of trust is also commonly associated with risk, tension, and ambiguity, including at times chronic anxiety and suspicion. It is important to note that he resists the idea that pastoralists were, in shifting their relationship to one of domination, somehow on the path to modernity or in an *alienated* relationship with the natural world. The point of raising this here is to give rather more texture to thinking through what precisely it might mean to consider indigenous ways of being in the world and take their very diverse views of interconnectedness with other creatures more seriously.[11]

While Ingold holds back on making judgments as to which type of interaction with animals is morally superior, he does come to the judgment that when hunter-gatherer societies speak about subjective agency in the world, it is not in the metaphorical, personified sense that is most common in Western cultures. Anthropologists have often presupposed that such indigenous propositions are not true to what is "actually" the case, since according to Western traditions, especially following Kant, the difference between humans as agents and other beings in the world who are assumed to lack subjectivity is a matter of fact, rather than something disputed. Instead, given the ecological crisis that speaks to the radical disengagement of humans from the world of nature, it is time to listen to those who have for centuries concerned themselves with care for, being with, and attentiveness to the creaturely others that exist in their world. Both hunters and herdsmen can, in view of this, "offer some of the best possible indications of how we might proceed" (Ingold 2011: 76).

The language of trust and domination that Ingold uses remains normatively and ethically charged in a way that is bound to make the former seem more positive than the latter, and his attempts to avoid that impression are not entirely convincing. Further, Native American nations have found ways to live in between two worlds (their world and that of Western society) while employing specific forms of social relationships that are still broadly in tune with their native cultures. The extent to which such cultures have become enculturated to Western influences varies depending on their relative isolation but a common consensus among ethnographers is that even relatively isolated communities are influenced in some way.

Another interesting example of the difference between Western and indigenous traditions in terms of how the idea of interconnectedness is appropriated practically that I will consider briefly here is how *justice* is perceived in a Native American community. While a survey of all the different kinds of justice systems in their specifics across different indigenous communities is outside the scope of this chapter, the following example highlights how when connectedness across human relationships is given priority this has a significant impact on the practical and societal structures that inform community function. Justice in Navajo Native American conceptions is concerned with restoring relationships and establishing the common good. It is very different from a procedural or contract model of offence then punishment characteristic of dominant Western justice systems. Interestingly, the Navajo model of justice resonates with Pope Francis's emphasis on interconnectedness, though he does not work out ways in which this might inform different kinds of justice systems in the encyclical.

Concluding remarks: revisiting human dignity

Affirming human dignity, as one might expect, is critically important for Pope Francis. Its importance stems from the essential aspects of the Christian tradition that speak of God's love for all people. Pope Francis says that "[those] who are committed to defending human dignity can find in the Christian faith the deepest reasons for this commitment" (65). At the same time, the special dignity that God gives to all people also confers a particular responsibility to care for the earth, so one of humanity's tasks is to "recognize that other living beings have a value of their own in God's eyes" (69). Here, we find reference to another kind of anthropocentrism, namely, a "distorted anthropocentrism" (69) that fails to recognize that each living creature reflects "a ray of God's infinite wisdom and goodness" (69).

Finding ways to affirm human dignity, recognize our interconnectedness with other living beings, respect the dignity of all life, and recognize the important insights arising from the lifeways of indigenous communities is no easy task. There are tensions in combining such different sets of knowledge and understanding. It is important to recognize those tensions, without giving up on a search for a holistic multifaceted approach to care for the earth. Pope Francis encourages Catholic thought to revisit ancient traditions that were rather better at recognizing humanity's embeddedness in the natural world. That does not, it seems to me, mean giving up on human dignity, but finding other ways of appropriating its meaning. One potential way this might be done is through recognizing that human history has been richly informed and even shaped by our relationship with other animals. Hence, the different aspects of what have traditionally been thought of as being unique characteristics of humanity in Christian theology are then qualified by recognition of important aspects of their presence in many other social animals as well.[12] Another potential line of research would be to explore a scientific understanding of mutualism in the biological world as a way of informing what mutualism might mean between human communities, or in multispecies communities. A third area of research would be to modify or challenge justice systems in the Western world so that they take more account of the need for reconciliation rather than punishment. A fourth area is theological animal ethics that spells out the gross injustices in current dominant systems of animal use, such as in food production, that impact negatively on the lives of vulnerable humans and animals. There are likely to be many others that are related to the importance of qualifying the limits of what human dignity might signify. None of these suggestions need involve a compromise in acknowledging the importance of human dignity. The steps, it seems to me, that need to be taken will always involve respectful dialogue across cultural differences and appreciation for new insights arising from that dialogue, rather than simple fusion of cultures and denial of differences.

Notes

1 There is a delicate balance to be struck here. For while on the one hand hunter-gatherer societies demonstrate important insights about the possibilities for human culture living in close connection with other creatures, to presume that such groups are thereby closer in evolutionary terms to early hominins or represent a more "primitive" form of humanity or, on the other hand, an "ideal" humanity, is a mistake born out of neo-colonial and potentially racist

presuppositions. Indigenous communities, like all other human communities, have had a very long evolutionary history of change. For a very thoughtful interpretation, see Baynes Rock 2017: 47–67.

2 I am defining exceptionalism here as a particular stress on the moral importance of the human compared with the moral worth of other creatures.

3 For an article that discusses the theological importance of symbiosis see Deane-Drummond, forthcoming.

4 As taken up in David Clough, "Rethinking Our Treatment of Animals in Light of *Laudato Si'*" this volume. See also Clough 2019, an important new volume that provides an extensive treatment of different aspects of animal ethics from a Christian theological perspective.

5 The apophatic tradition is about that which is related to what God is not, or the mystery of God.

6 The cataphatic tradition is about what can positively be claimed about who God is in systematic or dogmatic terms.

7 Pope Francis mentions Teilhard's thinking only once (Footnote 53) and this is in relation to his understanding of Christology as the "measure of all things." However, his discussion toward the end of the encyclical of the Eucharist as "the living centre of the universe, the overflowing core of love and of inexhaustible life" (236) hints at Teilhard's thinking, though these remarks also hint at themes embraced by the Eastern church that he references in the previous paragraph (235).

8 For a discussion of this point, see Deane-Drummond 2004: 44–45.

9 I discuss Tim Ingold's work in much more detail in Deane-Drummond 2019.

10 For discussion of Cree and their relationships with animals, see Ingold 2011: 10, 13–14, 24–26, 48–52, 142, 424.

11 Elsewhere I have critiqued the ways in which Tim Ingold's language of "domination" and "trust" carries moral overtones, in spite of his protestation that such terms are morally neutral. See Deane-Drummond 2019, in press.

12 I have written a monograph on this topic, Deane-Drummond 2014.

References

Baynes Rock, Marcus. 2017. "In the Minds of Others" in Celia Deane-Drummond and Agustin Fuentes (eds.) *The Evolution of Human Wisdom*, pp. 47–67. Lanham: Lexington Press.

Clough, David. 2019. *On Animals: Volume 2: Ethics*. London: Bloomsbury.

Deane-Drummond, Celia. 2004. *The Ethics of Nature*. Oxford: Wiley/Blackwell.

Deane-Drummond, Celia. 2014. *The Wisdom of the Liminal: Evolution and Other Animals in Human Becoming*. Grand Rapids, MI: Eerdmans.

Deane-Drummond, Celia. 2017. *Ecology in Jürgen Moltmann's Theology*, 2nd edn. Eugene, OR: Wipf and Stock.

Deane-Drummond, Celia. 2019 *Theological Ethics through a Multispecies Lens: Evolution of Wisdom Volume One*. Oxford: Oxford University Press.

Deane-Drummond, Celia. "Symbiotic Wisdom: Recovering a Memory of Deep History" forthcoming in *Theology and Science*.

Ingold, Tim. 2011 [2000]. *The Perception of the Environment: Essays on Livelihood, Dwelling and Skill*. London: Routledge.

Moltmann, Jürgen. 1981. *Trinity and the Kingdom of God*, translated by Margaret Kohl. London: SCM Press.

Moltmann, Jürgen. 1985. *God in Creation*, translated by Margaret Kohl. London: SCM Press.

12 "Realities are more important than ideas"

The significance of practice in *Laudato Si'*

Gretel Van Wieren

In November 2013, Francis issued the first apostolic exhortation of his papacy, *Evangelii Gaudium* (The Joy of the Gospel), calling Catholics to engage in a "new evangelization" that focuses on social inclusion of the poor and peace and public dialogue.[1] Buried half way through the 51,000-word document is the phrase after which this chapter is titled: "realities are more important than ideas." The expression reappears in *Laudato Si'* in chapter three, "The Human Roots of the Ecological Crisis," which appears to be a direct response to Lynn White, Jr's famous 1967 essay, "The Historical Roots of Our Ecologic Crisis" that blamed Christian anthropocentrism for the current environmental crisis. Unlike White, however, Francis focuses in the encyclical on the types of social structures and systems that he perceives as most responsible for Earth's degradation. Additionally, *Laudato Si'*'s consideration of a wide variety of social ecological practices that may help to restore Earth's systems is distinctive among religious treatments of climate change. Such a focus on practice and the notion that norms and ideas are often best understood as emerging from actual lived experiences—from confronting realities rather than from contemplating ideas—warrants further examination, for it represents an approach that has been neglected in the study of environmental ethics, including religious treatments. This chapter thus proceeds as follows. It begins by giving an overview of environmental ethical thought, noting how practice *has* come to be considered in the field, if only recently. Next, it details the range of environmental problems and practices that are emphasized in *Laudato Si'*, suggesting that its focus on agriculture makes it especially distinctive among religious climate statements and that it may yield new insights about the human relationships to land. The chapter's final section further examines the role of agriculture in the encyclical, noting how it explicitly connects current global agricultural and food practices and planetary warming.

The call for practice in environmental ethics

The term "environmental ethics" refers nowadays to a field of study initially developed in the early 1970s by professional philosophers and religion scholars in response to the environmental crisis.[2] The publication of Rachel Carson's *Silent Spring* (1962) as well as the Sierra Club campaign against the proposed damming of the Colorado River in the Grand Canyon National Park (1965–68) had generated widespread public concern about ecological degradation. Additionally, historian White's 1967 essay prompted questions regarding the crisis's underlying roots. These writings and events, in turn, prompted philosophers and religion scholars to begin asking fundamental questions about the moral dimensions of the human relationship to nature.

Although theorists initially focused on questions of nature's value and the need to develop a new, nonanthropocentric—nonhuman centered, in other words—ethic, additional topics discussed within environmental ethics today range from conceptual issues regarding nature's meanings and the relationship between environmental science and practical experience to practical issues addressing biodiversity, habitat loss, climate change, wilderness, deforestation, ecosystem management, toxics and pollution, social justice, sustainability, new urbanism, agriculture and food, and ecological restoration. Within the nexus of topics considered under the heading "environmental ethics," some authors believe that it is most important to focus on theoretical issues regarding the moral status of nonhuman nature, whereas others emphasize the need for analysis of the political and economic system and the underlying logic of domination that have given rise to the environmental crisis in the first place. Still other environmental ethicists have focused on the human experience of nature and the ways in which these experiences may form ecological values and virtues in relation to natural lands and civic communities.

Some authors have understood the human relationship to nature and environmental ethics as a whole in religious terms.[3] According to these perspectives, the environmental crisis is viewed not only as a moral crisis but also, fundamentally, as a spiritual crisis. Although the roots of the crisis may (or may not) lie in a religious (Christian) worldview as White argued, its solution for some environmental ethicists, nevertheless, requires a religious response.[4] An environmental ethic requires spiritual or sacred grounding according to this understanding, for deep and lasting change to occur. Scientific understandings may be able to tell us what to do with respect to ethical environmental concerns, but religious understandings, these authors believe, can tell us why we should take this or that action.

Scholars who think that environmental issues have a religious aspect emphasize a variety of methods and topics. Some scholars, for example, draw primarily on the sources of specific religious traditions (e.g., sacred texts, theological doctrines) in order to critique, retrieve, or reconstruct these traditions' moral worldviews in ways that elevate ecological concern. Representative of this approach is the work of Mary Evelyn Tucker and John Grim, conveners of the Forum on Religion and Ecology (FORE) and editors of the Harvard Center for the Study of World Religions' ten-volume book series, *Religions of the World and Ecology* (see, e.g., Hessel and Ruether, eds. 2000). Building on the thought of cultural historian and ecological theologian Thomas Berry, Tucker and Grim's work emphasizes the need to expand "the growing dialogue regarding the role of the world's religions as moral forces in stemming the environmental crisis."[5] In doing so, they also encourage the global religions to tap their traditions for sources of wisdom that may help spiritually narrate the new scientific universe story of cosmic and Earth evolution, to use their terms.

Other religion scholars look to sources outside institutional religion, citing the ways in which nature-based activist or recreational groups often link understandings of nature's sacred value with an environmental ethic of respect and care. Most notable is the work of Bron Taylor, founder of the International Society for the Study of Religion, Nature, and Culture (ISSRNC) and editor of the multivolume *Encyclopedia of Religion and Nature* (ERN) (see, for instance, Taylor 2009). The ERN was conceived to remedy "the lacunae in the inherited [from Tucker and Grim] 'religion and ecology' field," states Taylor in its introduction (Taylor 2005, 1375). The lacunae run along two interrelated lines, according to Taylor: first, marginal or boundary-crossing nature-based spiritual experiences have been neglected and, second, methods appropriate for examining them have been ignored. To correct these oversights, Taylor and others have focused their "religion studies lens" on the lived-nature religions of those who follow a radical environmental or "dark green" worldview.[6]

Among the deepest disagreements in the study of environmental ethics are these: whether a unified, nonanthropocentric theory of value should be developed or a plural approach should be embraced; the extent to which our concerns should be anthropocentric or nonanthropocentric (or both); and the role of experience in deciding how to act. In philosophical environmental ethics, these disagreements are evident in the debate between intrinsic value theorists (e.g., J. Baird Callicott, Holmes Rolston) and environmental pragmatists (e.g., Eric Katz, Andrew Light).[7] Intrinsic value theorists argue that if we could just get our thinking right about nature (e.g., that nature in itself has moral value, quite apart from its value to humans), environmental ethical action would be done. Pragmatists, on the other hand, suggest that we do not need a new ethical system for valuing nature, rather, we need to accentuate the good cultural values about nature that already exist, and work to develop positive processes to decide how best to act environmentally.

These philosophical debates are reflected similarly in religious environmental ethics (see, e.g., Peterson 2007, 45–62). Anna Peterson, for example, argues that the link between how we think about ourselves in relation to nature and what we do or who we are in relation to nature may not be as unidirectional as many environmental ethicists have assumed for the past four decades. Environmental ethics, according to Peterson, should "abandon the idealist assumption of a simple and unidirectional relationship between ideas and practice, in which practice is always derivative or secondary to ideas and which believes that if we get the ideas right, then the practices will follow" (Peterson 2007, 57). It is not that theorists should discontinue the task of clarifying and redefining ideas, writes Peterson; rather, they should reorient the task and method of environmental ethics to pay more attention to lived environmental experience.

There are a number of reasons that authors such as Peterson argue that it is important to look to practice for ethical insights. One is that an expanded treatment of lived environmental practices may yield additional sources for understanding the plurality and diversity of experiences that shape moral decision-making. This is the argument that some feminist philosophers and theologians make with regard to the need to explicitly consider women's experiences of environmental degradation and restoration when it comes to developing moral (and technical) responses (see, e.g., Ruether, ed. 1996). Another reason for looking to practice for ethical insights relates to the idea that acts transform people. The idea that practices shape how we think about ourselves and the world is, of course, not a new one. Aristotle and, later, Aquinas wrote about the concept in relation to their virtue theories and, in particular, in relation to how people acquire moral virtues through the habituated performance of this or that activity. Finally, looking to practice for ethical insights helps to underscore the role that embodied, affective experiences may have in shaping environmental values, virtues, and norms. This is the idea stressed in theories of biophilia that stress that contact with the natural world is integral to the development of human health and well-being and more sustainable environmental cultures.[8]

Francis appears in *Laudato Si'* to take seriously the call to elevate the role of actual practices and experiences—and the problems that form the lived contexts for concretizing them—in our thinking about how to act in relation to the natural world.[9] Four of the encyclical's six chapters (one, three, five, and six) focus explicitly on environmental realities and the material practices and experiences that are intertwined with them, while the other chapters (three and four) pay significant attention to such phenomena. Chapter one ("What Is Happening to Our Common Home") opens with a quotation resonant with Peterson's above:

> Theological and philosophical reflections on the situation of humanity and the world can sound tiresome and abstract unless they are grounded in a fresh analysis of our present situation, which is in many ways unprecedented in the history of humanity.
>
> (17)

The encyclical goes on to detail a wide range of problems associated with global climate change, all of which can be attributed to what Francis calls the process of "rapidification"—the state whereby the speed and intensity of human activities outpace the "naturally slow pace of biological evolution" and fail to promote a broader concern for the common good and sustainable human development (18). Five main problem areas form the basis of Francis's concern.

Problems, practice, and experience in *Laudato Si*

Pollution and climate change

Pollution is the first environmental problem that the encyclical addresses, focusing on how atmospheric contaminants negatively affect human health, especially for the world's poorest populations. Emphasizing corporate-driven technological approaches to, say, alleviating poor air quality, writes Francis, may, in turn, cause additional problems, for such approaches are "incapable of seeing the mysterious network of relations between things" (20). Toxic pollution also results from the hundreds of millions of tons of waste that is produced each year, much of which is non-biodegradable. Chemical waste that results from industrial and agricultural production contributes to bioaccumulation in organisms, where toxicity levels are magnified at each level of the food-chain. A "throwaway culture" is mostly to blame, states *Laudato Si'*. Industrial culture has not modeled itself on how natural ecosystems work in terms of the cyclical process of death, growth, and reproduction. Instead, the huge volume of unrecyclable items and materials produced are turning our earth into "an immense pile of trash" (22).[10] Add to this the fact that non-biodegradable products that accumulate in landfills and waterways emit warming gasses that contribute to climate change. "The climate is a common good, belonging to all and meant for all," writes Francis (23). "Humanity is called to recognize the need for changes of lifestyle, production and consumption, in order to combat this warming or at least the human causes which produce or aggravate it" (23).

The warming effect on the carbon cycle "creates a vicious circle which aggravates the situation even more," states the encyclical (24). The destruction of ecosystems for the extraction of fossil fuels and development of large-scale industrial farming purposes, for example, leads to declines in forest-, wet-, and peat-lands, which serve as naturally occurring carbon-sinks. The melting of polar ice caps and increased decomposition of organic material caused by increased temperatures in high-alpine areas contribute to the release of warming methane and carbon dioxide gasses. The worst of climate change's impacts will be felt by the world's poorest countries and people, many of whom continue to rely on a direct connection to the land for their subsistence. When the land becomes no longer arable, people are forced to migrate, without recognition by international conventions or legal protection. In the face of this, the encyclical states, "[many] of those who possess more resources and economic or political power seem mostly to be concerned with masking the problems or concealing their symptoms, simply making efforts to reduce some of the negative impacts of climate change" (26). Note how for Francis the problem of pollution is inherently "bound-up" with the felt experiences of the world's poorest communities and countries, and how this serves as a basis for the development of normative action steps to be performed by wealthy and powerful individuals and societies. Additionally, the section's focus on production and consumption, corporate agriculture, and migration accentuates the significance of actual material practices.

The issue of water

Water degradation and depletion is the second environmental problem area noted in *Laudato Si'*. Where water supplies were once relatively constant in human history, large-scale extraction of water for industrial agricultural and production purposes has led to water scarcity and drought in many parts of the world, further exacerbating the conditions of poverty and habitat loss. The contamination of water sources due to industrial farming, mining, and production practices is particularly felt by the poor, who experience a disproportionate mortality rate due to unsafe water-related diseases and illnesses such as cholera and dysentery. Where fresh water remains, global corporations are increasingly buying land in order to privatize water, treating water as if people did not have the right in question. Again, notice how the encyclical focuses heavily on the lived experiences of the poor in analyzing the problems associate with the world's water crisis, and how, as it does, the specific practices of corporate farming, mining, industrial production are also underscored as especially pernicious and in need of reform.

Loss of biodiversity

Species and ecosystem loss is the third area of concern listed in the encyclical. Interestingly, this is the longest of the sections devoted to environmental problems. "The earth's resources are also being plundered because of short-sighted approaches to the economy, commerce and production," begins this section (32). Potential future food and medicinal sources, as well as new scientific discoveries, are lost through the destruction of plant and animal species. Plant and animal species also have "value in themselves," states *Laudato Si'*, and thousands of them are going extinct each year because of human activities (33). "Fungi, algae, worms, insects, reptiles and an innumerable variety of microorganisms" are also being decimated with the destruction of ecosystems (34). Human intervention to respond to such losses often further aggravates environmental problems, such as when synthetic agro-toxins kill off certain insect and bird species which are helpful in other regards in the ecosystem, and whose loss must then be compensated for through another intervention.

"Caring for ecosystems demands far-sightedness, since no one looking for quick and easy profit is truly interested in their preservation" (36). Biodiversity is typically not assessed when evaluating the environmental impact of infrastructure, industrial, and agricultural development, the encyclical points out; but it should be. Few countries, for example, show concern for creating biological corridors where animals can continue to migrate and roam freely when their natural habitats are broken up by highways, dams, or fences. Areas richest in species number, variety, and rarity such as the Amazon and Congo basins should be shown extra protection for how they help safeguard the global ecosystem and other forms of life. Threats to the world's oceans from uncontrolled or selective fishing practices and pollution from industrial waste and agricultural runoff represent a serious threat to the planet's water supply and to the habitat of an immensity of living creatures, particularly its most fragile of organisms. Here, Francis focuses on the material realities faced by nonhuman organisms, and the types of social ecological practices that may help to reverse their decline. New norms for production and agriculture must be adopted, according to the encyclical and, as such, are elevated in the document's environmental ethical schema.

Decline in the quality of human life and the breakdown of society

While the above topic areas include mention of the negative impacts of the climate crisis on humans, particularly the poor, so too is significant attention paid to nonhuman organisms and systems. This is interesting from a conceptual and methodological perspective insofar as it represents an attempt to develop an ethic centered on the needs and well-being of life on earth as a whole, rather than primarily on human beings, which is in contradistinction to White's claims about Christian anthropocentrism. The next two sets of environmental problems articulated in *Laudato Si'* focus mainly on human beings and communities.

At just two and a half pages, section four is the shortest in length of the five sections in the encyclical devoted to environmental problems. It emphasizes the environmental decline of urban centers and the alienating influences of a hyper-technological society. Cities have become "excessively wasteful of energy and water," states the encyclical (44). Often poorly planned, they tend to be chaotic, unruly and polluted, physically and aesthetically, with little green space. "We were not meant to be inundated by cement, asphalt, glass and metal, and deprived of physical contact with nature," it contends (44). Places that do afford green space, rural and urban, are often made private and purchased and used only by the wealthy, rather than accessible to "the disposable of society" (45). The digital world and media have created a culture of information overload, which threatens humanity's capacity for learning from the great sages of the past in terms of cultivating true wisdom, dialogue, and inner examination. Today's technology, *Laudato Si'* acknowledges, does present exciting possibilities, though with it can arise "a deep and melancholic dissatisfaction with interpersonal relations, or a harmful sense of isolation" (47). The practices of urban design and media technology are emphasized as especially significant in this section. It suggests that the experiences of direct contact with the natural world and interpersonal relationships are integral to promoting positive environmental change.

Global inequality

The final environmental problem and associated lived experiences examined in the encyclical focuses on the environmental injustices faced disproportionally by the most vulnerable and excluded persons. Ecological and social degradation go hand in hand, states *Laudato Si*:

> we have to realize that a true ecological approach always becomes a social approach; it must integrate questions of justice in debates on the environment, so as to hear *both the cry of the earth and the cry of the poor.*
>
> (49)

Those in power in urban areas often lack direct contact with people who "remain at the bottom of the pile" (49). Development policies are wrongly focused on reproductive health and population growth as an environmental solution, rather than on reducing consumerism and waste by the global minority of the wealthiest in the world.

Further, the encyclical states, social inequity affects not only individuals and local communities but also entire countries and even continents in the form of "ecological debt" between the global north and south:

> ...developing countries, where the most important reserves of the biosphere are found, continue to fuel the development of richer countries at the cost of their own present and future. The land of the southern poor is rich and mostly unpolluted, yet access to ownership of goods and resources for meeting vital needs is inhibited by a system of commercial relations and ownership which is structurally perverse. The developed countries ought to help pay this debt by significantly limiting their consumption of non-renewable energy and by assisting poorer countries to support policies and programmes of sustainable development.
>
> (52)

It is the globalization of the "dominant technocratic paradigm" that underlies such problems, with its logic of unlimited economic growth and its belief in an infinite supply of earth's resources (101). The issue is not technology itself, states the encyclical, rather it is "the way that humanity has taken up technology and its development according to an undifferentiated and one-dimensional paradigm," which wrongly sees technological solutions and the current market economy as the cure-all for today's environmental problems (106). Moreover, the kind of "super-development" that characterizes the technocratic paradigm promotes maximum consumption and wastefulness while at the same time failing to meet the basic needs of the world's poor.

Notice how Francis's insights here about the logic and beliefs associated with the dominant technocratic paradigm emerge by first focusing on the actual problems and lived realities being experienced at the hand of the current climate crisis. Francis also provides a critique of modern anthropocentrism and what he calls an "inadequate presentation of Christian anthropology" for how it misrepresents the human relationship to nature and promotes a "Promethean vision of mastery over the world" (116). He does so, nonetheless, only after detailing the environmental problems and practices already described. This returns us to the methodological point made at the chapter's outset—ideas and norms should be understood as largely derivative of material problems, practices, and experiences, and should be treated as such in conceptualizing environmental ethical frameworks.

Francis's focus on agriculture

Laudato Si' pays a significant amount of attention to agriculture, a focus that is unique in comparison with other religious statements on climate change and in the environmental ethical scholarship more generally.[11] Spotlighting it here will allow us to continue the process of looking to practice for insights about the human relationship to the natural world and noting how the encyclical explicitly incorporates actual practices and lived experience in its environmental ethic. Especially in the past decade, questions related to food production and consumption have intensified as biotechnological developments related to agricultural practices have exploded. The use of recombinant DNA techniques for transforming the genetic basis of agricultural plants and animals has posed significant environmental and ethical questions about which types of alterations are or are not permissible. Questions related to the potential health risks and ecological consequences of genetically modified organisms (GMOs) are now being coupled with debates about intellectual property rights (IPRs) and whether genetically modified (GM) seeds and animals are patentable. Ethical issues of equity and justice are increasingly raised in relation to issues of food access where populations do not have access to healthy and nutritious food, often due to the social organization of food systems.

Global environmental issues such as climate change, topsoil and fisheries depletion, land and water pollution, and public health, we are fast learning, are significantly linked to agriculture. Increased global interdependence introduces vexing ethical questions when it comes to analyzing trade-offs related to food's production and consumption, for at times benefits to farmers living in one part of the globe, means losses for poor people living in another part of the world. All of this makes for a dramatically different landscape for exploring questions about food and eating and the moral life than we have encountered in the past.

Yet the field of environmental ethics has been slow to see the issues of agriculture and food as topics worthy of analysis. Moreover, where agriculture and food *have* been considered in environmental ethics, religious and spiritual dimensions have been overlooked.[12] This is surprising, particularly when one considers that the academic study of environmental ethics is considered to have formed largely in response to the work of Aldo Leopold and Rachel Carson, both of whom focused on the moral and spiritual implications of industrial agricultural practices in the 1930s and 1960s, respectively. Furthermore, the topic of food ethics has become increasingly popular in broader society, including among religious communities, making it even more curious that environmental ethicists whose work has a focus on religion have largely neglected the topic.

Perhaps this neglect arises from the fact that the professional study of environmental ethics is relatively new, with scholars only being able to cover so many topics in the four decades since its inception. But it may be more than that. Wild nature has long been favored in environmental thought, leaving some scholars and activists skeptical about the status of agriculturalized land. Further, questions have been raised about whether the very activity of agriculture is adequate for fostering a healthy and durable relationship between people and the natural world, and, more so, whether agricultural civilizations, including the religions that grew out of them, such as the Vedic and Abrahamic, are in a fundamental way responsible for creating the current disconnect between humans and land.[13] These are valid concerns and ones that should be taken seriously in my mind. Yet I would still argue that agriculture provides an especially interesting example of how values and ideas about the human relationship with nature may be shaped by actual practices.[14]

Among religious climate statements, *Laudato Si'* provides the most comprehensive treatment of the social and ecological problems associated with current agricultural practices. The encyclical's length (80 pages/45,000 words) could be part of the reason for this, yet I suspect that it also has something to do with the fact that Francis's home country of Argentina has over the past two decades witnessed dramatic shifts in the agricultural landscape, including, most notably, the expansion of large-scale multinational corporate farming operations. Chapters one ("What Is Happening to Our Common Home") and three ("The Human Roots of the Ecological Crisis") deal most explicitly with agriculture's climate interface. Francis writes that the "vicious cycle" of global warming affects

the availability of essential resources like drinking water, energy and agricultural production in warmer regions, and [is] leading to the extinction of part of the planet's biodiversity... Things are made worse by the loss of tropical forests which would otherwise help to mitigate climate change.

(24)

An entire section is dedicated to the issues of water, including how the increasing lack of fresh water impedes much agricultural activity while industrial agricultural activities on the other hand cause a lot of water pollution. Later in the encyclical, when discussing the problem of human intervention in ecosystems, agriculture is cited as an example: "many birds and insects which disappear due to synthetic agro-toxins are helpful for agriculture: their disappearance will have to be compensated for by yet other techniques which may well prove harmful" (34).

Francis calls for greater analysis of "[the] replacement of virgin forest with plantations of trees, usually monocultures," which "can seriously compromise a biodiversity which the new species being introduced does not accommodate. Similarly, wetlands converted into cultivated land lose the enormous biodiversity which they formerly hosted" (39). Highly biodiverse areas need greater global protection, states *Laudato Si'*. These include the Amazon and the Congo basins, for "when these forests are burned down or levelled for purposes of cultivation, within the space of a few years, countless species are lost and the areas frequently become arid wastelands" (38). The encyclical critiques overfishing which leads to "a drastic depletion of certain species" and the destruction of coral reefs as a result of pollution from deforestation and agricultural monocultures is also noted (40).

Laudato Si' does not consider GMOs to be inherently morally problematic, though it does raise concerns about how the expansion of GM crops by "oligopolies" negatively impacts small farmers and destroys complex ecosystem networks and seed biodiversity (134). It calls out multinational corporations for doing things in the developing world that "they would never do in developed countries or the so-called first world," including contributing to local agricultural decline. The alternative paradigm proposed in *Laudato Si'* is one of "integral ecology" which respects the interrelated character of earth, including the human and social dimension (137). Here, Francis notes the importance of privileging the "cultural ecology" of indigenous peoples whom he views as "not merely one minority among others" but "principal dialogue partners, especially when large projects affecting their land are proposed" (145). Francis also strongly critiques the hyper-consumption of some in rich countries for how it negatively impacts the world's poorest areas, particularly in Africa where droughts are devastating farmers.

Action items in the document are weak on agriculture, though there is a call for international dialogue that could lead to planning for a sustainable and diversified agriculture (164). Recommendations about how agriculture should be reformed include the adoption of more participatory forms of decision-making about the use of public land and the development of smaller-scale, localized farming operations. Additionally, Francis suggests that collectives of small producers may provide a different model for agriculture, one that emphasizes community and a non-consumeristic way of life. Small-scale farming is also mentioned in relation to the need to promote a diverse economy and business creativity. Francis calls on civic leaders to support the expansion of these types of diversified food production systems. So too there is a need for dialogue about new national and local policies and transparency in decision-making, suggesting that political activity on the local level could be directed at

> protecting certain species and planning a diversified agriculture and the rotation of crops. Agriculture in poorer regions can be improved through investment in rural infrastructures, a better organization of local or national markets, systems of irrigation, and the development of techniques of sustainable agriculture. New forms of cooperation and community organization can be encouraged in order to defend the interests of small producers and preserve local ecosystems from destruction. Truly, much can be done!
>
> (180)

The final chapter on spirituality is surprising weak on agricultural and food dimensions, particularly since it advocates for a "new lifestyle" marked by simplicity and sobriety (203). Instead, the encyclical focuses on reducing other consumeristic behaviors such as buying and spending, rather than on making climate friendly food choices. One could imagine that an emphasis on modifying eating practices would be part of the encyclical's call to educate the church about the covenant between humanity and creation, which includes

> avoiding the use of plastic and paper, reducing water consumption, separating refuse, cooking only what can reasonably be consumed, showing care for other living beings, using public transport or car-pooling, planting trees, turning off unnecessary lights, or any number of other practices.
>
> (211)

Nonetheless, even the document's final section on the sacraments of the Eucharist and Sabbath rest—both practices which are ripe for agricultural interpretation as they center on breaking bread in community—food is only mentioned in a mystical, cosmic sense. *Laudato Si'* still provides the most significant current example of a religious document on climate change that specifically addresses the consequences of industrial agriculture on warming planetary conditions and, conversely, its role in promoting social ecological sustainability. Moreover, it emphasizes the environmental ethical and social justice issues pointed up by today's agricultural system, even as it surprisingly neglects food and farming's spiritual dimensions.

To conclude, *Laudato Si'* provides an instructive example of how concrete problems and lived practices may form the basis for a religious-oriented environmental ethic. There are, it must be noted, important issues that it neglects, including the ones regarding food and agriculture just noted, as well as the practice of ecological restoration, I would argue. Yet overall

Laudato Si' may be the most comprehensive practice-oriented religious environmental ethical statement that has thus far been written. "Realities are more important than ideas" is a concept that it takes seriously rather than one to which it merely gives lip service.

Notes

1 An apostolic exhortation is a papal document that focuses on significant pastoral matters of the church. It is viewed by the Church as less important than an encyclical or apostolic constitution, but more important that other ecclesiastical letters. Exhortations are typically written in response to a meeting of bishops.
2 For more on this discussion, see Van Wieren 2013: 6–12.
3 On the history and emphases of different religious approaches to environmental issues, see Jenkins 2007.
4 According to White, the Christian interpretation of the dominion texts in the Hebrew Bible (e.g., Genesis 1:26), as well as its transcendent view of God and otherworldly view of salvation, led to an instrumental, anthropocentric, and disenchanted view of the natural world. This view wedded well, White argues, with the mechanized, static understanding of nature, with man as its superior and active conqueror, which developed through the Middle Ages and sixteenth- and seventeenth-century scientific revolution and the Protestant Reformation in Europe. It is this nexus of Western science and technology motivated by a Christian anthropocentric worldview that led to the current environmental crisis, according to White. See White 1967. For more on White's wide-ranging influence in the study of environmental attitudes and behavior, see the following publications: Taylor 2016; Taylor, Van Wieren and Zaleha 2016.
5 Mary Evelyn Tucker and John Grim, "Series Foreword," in Hessel and Ruether 2000.
6 The global religious traditions, or certain segments of traditions, are not precluded from Taylor's understanding of nature-based religion. However, he is skeptical of Tucker and Grim's claim that the world's religions are in fact directly contributing to the emergence of an environmental ethic on a global scale. See Taylor 2016.
7 See Callicott 1989; Katz and Light 1996; Rolston 1988.
8 See, for example, Kellert and Wilson 1993.
9 Likely this relates to Francis's Latin American upbringing and the influence on his thought of liberation theology, which emphasizes critical analysis of socioeconomic and political structures for how they affect the lived experience of oppressed and marginalized communities. Relatedly, during the writing of this book chapter, Francis canonized Oscar Romero which previous popes refused to do. For an essay on how Francis's liberationist theology relates to his environmental ethic, see Iheka 2017.
10 I use small "e" for earth in the discussion that follows because that is what the encyclical uses. For an interesting discussion on the use of "earth" rather than "Earth" by the Roman Catholic Church, see his discussion of the debate that ensued over its use during the process of adoption of the Earth Charter in Taylor 2009: 194–195.
11 For more on this discussion, see Van Wieren 2018.
12 Consider the topics addressed at the annual meetings of the two largest professional societies dedicated to the scholarly study of agricultural and food

ethics—the Agriculture, Food and Human Values Society (AFHVS) and the European Society for Agricultural and Food Ethics (EURSafe). Of the hundreds of papers given at the 2014–15 meetings, both of which I attended, only one or two related in any way to the topic of religion or spirituality.

13 See, for example, Shepard 1973 and 1998.

14 For more on this idea, see Piso, Werkheiser, Noll and Leshko 2016.

References

Callicott, J. Baird. 1989. *In Defense of the Land Ethic: Essays in Environmental Philosophy*. Albany, NY: SUNY University Press.

Hessel, Dieter and Rosemary Radford Ruether, eds. 2000. *Christianity and Ecology: Seeking the Well-Being of Earth and Humans*. Cambridge, MA: Harvard University Press.

Iheka, Cajetan. 2017. "Pope Francis' Integral Ecology and Environmentalism for the Poor," *Environmental Ethics* 39(3): 243–259.

Jenkins, Willis. 2007. *Ecologies of Grace: Environmental Ethics and Christian Theology*. New York and Oxford: Oxford University Press.

Katz, Eric and Andrew Light. 1996. *Environmental Pragmatism*. London and New York: Routledge.

Kellert, Stephen R. and Edward O. Wilson, eds. 1993. *The Biophilia Hypothesis*. Washington, DC: Island Press.

Peterson, Anna. 2007. "Talking the Walk: A Practice-based Environmental Ethic as Grounds for Hope." In *Ecospirit: Religions and Philosophies for the Earth*, eds., Laurel Kearns and Catherine Keller. New York: Fordham University Press, 45–62.

Piso, Zachary, Ian Werkheiser, Samantha Noll and Christian Leshko. 2016. "Sustainability of What? Recognising the Diverse Values that Sustainable Agriculture Works to Sustain," *Environmental Values* 25: 195–214.

Rolston, Holmes. 1988. *Environmental Ethics: Duties to and Values in the Natural World*. Philadelphia, PA: Temple University Press.

Ruether, Rosemary Radford, ed. 1996. *Women Healing Earth: Third World Voices on Ecology, Feminism and Religion*. Maryknoll, NY: Orbis Books.

Shepard, Paul. 1973. *The Tender Carnivore and the Sacred Game*. New York: Scribner.

———. 1998. *Coming Home to the Pleistocene*, ed., Florence R. Shepard. Washington, DC: Island Press.

Taylor, Bron. 2005. "Introduction." In *Encyclopedia of Religion and Nature*, ed., Bron Taylor. London and New York: Continuum, vii–xxvi.

———. 2009. *Dark Green Religion: Nature Spirituality and the Planetary Future*. Berkeley: University of California Press.

———. 2016. "The Greening of Religion Hypothesis (Part One): From Lynn White, Jr. and Claims that Religions can Promote Environmentally Destructive Attitudes and Behaviors to Assertions They are Becoming Environmentally Friendly," *Journal for the Study of Religion, Nature and Culture* 10(3).

———, Gretel Van Wieren and Bernard Zaleha. 2016. "The Greening of Religion Hypothesis (Part Two): Assessing the Data from Lynn White, Jr., to Pope Francis," *Journal for the Study of Religion, Nature and Culture* 10(3).

Van Wieren, Gretel. 2013. *Restored to Earth: Christianity, Environmental Ethics, and Ecological Restoration*. Washington, DC: Georgetown University Press.

———. 2018. *Food, Farming, and Religion: Emerging Ethical Perspectives*. London and New York: Routledge.

White, Lynn, Jr. 1967. "The Historical Roots of Our Ecologic Crisis." *Science* 155: 1203–1207.

13 Opposing the "technocratic paradigm" and "appreciating the small things"

Robert McKim

Introduction

Pope Francis begins his critique of what he calls the "technocratic paradigm" by complaining about "the way that humanity has taken up technology and its development *according to an undifferentiated and one-dimensional paradigm* [that] exalts the concept of a subject who, using logical and rational procedures, progressively approaches and gains control over an external object" (106; italics in original).

The Pope is not opposing technology as such.[1] Thus, he says that technological development that leads to a better world and an "integrally higher quality of life" is welcome (194). He remarks that "[we] must be grateful for the praiseworthy efforts being made by scientists and engineers dedicated to finding solutions to man-made problems" (34). He writes enthusiastically about numerous beneficial technologies and the "possibilities they continue to open up for us," remarking that "science and technology are wonderful products of a God-given human creativity" for which we cannot but feel gratitude and appreciation (102; also 131). And he observes that technological innovations that would facilitate a "circular model of production"—with maximally efficient uses of resources, recycling, and minimal waste—are desirable just as are technological innovations in the area of energy storage (22, 26).

Moreover, *liberation* from the technocratic paradigm can be found in appropriate uses of technology:

> We have the freedom needed to limit and direct technology; we can put it at the service of another type of progress, one which is healthier, more human, more social, more integral. Liberation from the dominant technocratic paradigm does in fact happen sometimes, for example, when … technology is directed primarily to resolving people's concrete problems, truly helping them live with more dignity and less suffering. …
>
> (112)

Pope Francis says that the problem, or at least a central part of the problem, is that "our immense technological development has not been accompanied by a development in human responsibility, values and conscience" (105). So technological development is unproblematic when it is accompanied by, and guided by, an appropriate sense of responsibility, appropriate values, and an appropriate operation of conscience. The question is what these would consist in.

In any case, it is clear that technology, as such, is not the main problem. Rather, it is "the way in which humanity *has taken up* technology and its development" (106, my italics). Explaining what this means and what the technocratic paradigm amounts to requires discussion of central themes in *Laudato Si'*.

Paying "renewed attention to reality and the limits it imposes"

To be in the grip of the technocratic paradigm is to treat everything around us as if it were "something formless, completely open to manipulation" (106), "an insensate order, ... a cold body of facts, ... an object of utility, ... [and] raw material to be hammered into useful shape" (115).[2] To so treat the world around us is to disregard "the message contained in the structures of nature itself" (117). It is to "lay our hands on things, attempting to extract everything possible from them while frequently ignoring or forgetting the reality in front of us. Human beings and material objects no longer extend a friendly hand to one another; the relationship has become confrontational" (106). *Laudato Si'* advocates instead being "in tune with and respecting the possibilities offered by the things themselves" (106). Pope Francis says, "[the] time has come to pay renewed attention to reality and the limits it imposes" (116).

What does this talk of treating the world as if it were "formless [and] completely open to manipulation," of "possibilities offered by the things themselves," of paying "renewed attention to reality and the limits it imposes," and of "the message contained in the structures of nature itself" amount to? A central part of the answer is to be found in the following area. The Pope's view is that we need to take into account the value of various things that have value. Thus, Pope Francis says that *each human being has a* "unique dignity," (43) an inalienable dignity and worth (30, 119, 136), and indeed an "immense" and "infinite" dignity (65). He talks about the consequences of "[failing] to acknowledge as part of reality the worth of a poor person, a human embryo, [or] a person with disabilities" (117).

Pope Francis also says that other living things have value in God's eyes and we must respect the goodness of each creature (69). The spirit of God lives in every creature and each creature reflects something of God and has a message to convey to us (88; also 221, 246). Moreover, every creature has its own value and significance (76); "must be cherished with love and respect" (42); is "the object of the Father's tenderness, who gives it its place in the world" (77; also 96); and sings "the hymn of its existence" (85). He writes approvingly of the attitude of his namesake Saint Francis of Assisi, according to whom "each and every creature was a sister united to him by bonds of affection" (11). He calls for a new reverence for life and he appears to mean life in all of its forms (207). All of life is also to be loved and respected (213).

The Pope says that *other species* have value in themselves and we have no right to destroy them (33). He describes the value that is involved when other species are destroyed or seriously harmed as "incalculable" (36)—which I take to entail that it is very great. Entire ecosystems too are "good and admirable" in themselves and their regenerative ability requires our consideration (140). Finally, the world, as such, has an "intrinsic dignity" (115), which is a remark that seems to have implications for every landscape and ecosystem, and indeed for everything in the world.

What is prohibited therefore is dealing with other humans, other animals, other species, ecosystems, and the entire world around us, in ways that ignore the value such things have in virtue of being the sorts of things they are. To do so is to ignore various limits to how things may be treated that arise from their value. On the other hand, to recognize this value is to refuse "to turn reality into an object simply to be used and controlled" (11). It is clear that protecting *human* dignity is central to the Pope's thinking and equally clear that his concerns extend far beyond this. The value of other things (other living things, species, ecosystems, etc.) is not just a matter of their value to humans; such things have value in themselves and should be responded to as such.

Now the sort of failure to take account of the value of things that the Pope is opposing might not involve deploying sophisticated modern technology of any sort. For example, ignoring a poor person or being dismissive of the interests of a person with disabilities or being cruel or indifferent to particular animals or wantonly cutting down trees and destroying the habitat they provide need not require much in the way of technology. A subsistence farmer who works the earth with basic tools might be cruel to his chickens or might totally fail to treat his dog with love and respect or might derive enjoyment from cruel "sports" in which animals are tormented or injured or killed for entertainment. Or he might eliminate the local habitat of a threatened species without a second thought.

What is obvious though is that current technologies make it possible to cause harm of these and other sorts on a larger scale and more quickly. Thus, industrial chicken farming has magnified greatly the scale on which harm can be caused to chickens. Indeed, this entire system of farming may be cruel with its indifference to the plight of the individual chicken and no one to pay attention to its miserable and unnatural life, its suffering, and its desperate cries as it is slaughtered. And farmers, developers, and others whose activities have a direct impact on the earth have access to machinery, herbicides, pesticides, and so on that have a huge impact on other forms of life. Global supply chains, with their vast technological and financial resources, combine with the appetites of consumers to eliminate habitat for entire forms of life in the blink of an eye.

Failure to live within appropriate limits is central to the technocratic paradigm. As we saw in the first passage quoted in this chapter, the technocratic paradigm is criticized in the encyclical for "[exalting] the concept of a subject who, using logical and rational procedures, progressively approaches and gains control over an external object" (106). But suppose the "external object" is Ebola or cancer or the island of plastic in the Pacific or climate change. Technologies that will enable us to "gain control" of such conditions or phenomena in the specific sense of enabling us to eradicate them appear to be just what is needed and using *all* available procedures to gain control over, and indeed eradicate, such "objects" is exactly what we should do. Maybe the problem is partly a matter of taking this approach to *everything*, which is to say wanting to control everything. But the question arises of what we are trying to accomplish when we set out to take control. If future humans were to take control of many aspects of life that are currently beyond our control but generally did so with a view to promoting whatever values they should be promoting while doing so, there would be no problem in this area.

The real problem is our "[becoming] enthralled with the possibility of limitless mastery over everything" (224). *Limitless* mastery is control that is without restraint; in particular, it is not guided or restricted by the relevant values or norms. So what is problematic is not exactly a matter of gaining control over external objects; nor is it exactly a matter of expanding the range of matters over which we have control though expanded control comes with increased risks.

The key issue is instead the purpose with which we gain control, what we are setting out to accomplish when we do so, and—crucially—the normative framework within which we are operating. What is problematic is attempting "to extract every thing possible" from things around us and setting out to exercise "absolute dominion" (75; also 117), "absolute domination" (67), and "tyrannical and irresponsible domination" (83; also 68)—all of which bespeak an unwillingness to operate within appropriate limits. The problem has to do with behaving like "masters, consumers, ruthless exploiters, unable to set limits to their immediate needs" (11). The problem is "technology severed from ethics" (136). Anthony Annett nicely captures this central aspect when he remarks that the technocratic paradigm "regards creation as an external object to be manipulated, mastered, and controlled, with no concern for its inherent value or limits" (Annett 2017: 163).

More on "paying renewed attention to reality and the limits it imposes"

The Pope's opposition to treating the world as if it were "formless [and] completely open to manipulation" and the concomitant emphasis on "possibilities offered by the things themselves," and on "paying renewed attention to reality and the limits it imposes" has what appears at first glance to be a rather different dimension. Remarks such as these seem to point to, or at least hint at, what we might characterize as a "teleological" or "goal-directed" approach to the physical world. What I mean by this is just the idea that things are intended to be used in some ways and not in others.[3] To think in this way is to oppose the thought that we can do as we please with the world around us and everything in it, using it in ways that happen to suit whatever purposes we happen to have.

But how are we to tell what are the possibilities offered by "things themselves" and what are its "natural potentialities"? What limits would operating within such "possibilities" and "potentialities," and paying additional attention to reality in the relevant sense, impose on how we may use and what we may do with, say, a type of material? Consider wood, for example. It strikes most people today as natural and in accordance with the "possibilities offered" by wood to use it for making furniture or in building a house. But what about making plywood by cutting very thin sheets of wood and gluing them together? What about turning wood into plastic? What about developing a titanium-strength wood-derivative for use in construction? (For discussion of the latter two possibilities see *The Economist* of June 16, 2018.) Where do we cross the line from conforming to "possibilities offered by the [thing itself]" and from "[paying appropriate] attention to reality and the limits it imposes" to *not* conforming to those possibilities and to *not* paying appropriate attention to reality and the limits it imposes? Who is to say?

Needless to say, the use of wood for making furniture or for building houses is something that required a history of discovery and that developed over time. *Those* uses did not announce themselves to our ancestors when they first encountered wood. There is no reason to think that uses for wood or anything else that are well established by now, and that consequently now strike people as natural and fitting—as in accordance with its "natural potentialities"—are definitive of its uses for all time. There is no reason to think that history has come to an end in this particular respect. Often it is only when new technology permits a new use of a type of material that a relevant potentiality becomes apparent; naturally, this applies to technologies that are *yet to be* developed. So it is difficult to know what limits this entire line of thought would put on how you can modify something and what you can use it for.

Or at least this is so unless we interpret the relevant limits in terms of the values and norms mentioned in the last section. Consider again the case of wood. Wood-derived plastic would be more environmentally friendly than oil-based plastic just as a titanium-strength derivative of wood would be more environmentally friendly than alternatives currently used in construction. A very reasonable approach to take here is to say that technological developments and ways of using whatever materials we have access to that are environmentally friendly are to be encouraged.

Correspondingly, environmentally harmful uses—and of course uses that would be harmful in any other way—are to be discouraged and may be unacceptable.

To take this approach is to focus less on the nature of the material, or thing, itself and more on the use to which it might be put, the consequences of that use, and especially on the values and norms to which that use should conform. To take this approach is also to cash in the above terminology that looked as if it was about potentialities that are built into things in terms of using those things in ways that comport with all the values mentioned in the last section, and of course with whatever other relevant values or norms there may be. This reading is consistent with the encyclical as a whole and amounts to a plausible proposal though it requires for its further elucidation a more thorough analysis of the relevant norms. I said in the first sentence of this section that the discourse under discussion—"possibilities offered by the things themselves," "paying renewed attention to reality and the limits it imposes," and so on—has *what appears at first glance* to be a rather different dimension, one that goes beyond the discussion of values in the last section. What I am now suggesting, in effect, is that this appearance is misleading and that the best way to interpret this discourse is in terms of the values in question, or at any rate in terms of the broader relevant normative framework.

The influence of Romano Guardini

Bishop Robert Barron has probed an important aspect of the background to the idea of *limits imposed by reality* in a short reflection on the influence of the work of the German theologian Romano Guardini on *Laudato Si'*. Guardini's work was the focus of the doctoral studies of Jorge Mario Bergoglio—later Pope Francis—in Germany in the late 1980s.

Bishop Barron focuses in his reflection on some letters written by Guardini in the 1920s while he was on holiday near Lake Como in Italy and later published in English as *Letters from Lake Como* (Guardini 1994).[4] While the influence of these letters on *Laudato Si'* is clear, some of the key ideas in the encyclical actually serve as a corrective to parts of what Guardini is saying, and exploring some aspects of the relationship between these letters and the encyclical illuminates further the idea of limits imposed by reality. Bishop Barron comments as follows on these letters.

> [Guardini] was enchanted ... by the physical beauty of the area, but what intrigued him above all was the manner in which human beings, through their architecture and craftsmanship, interacted non-invasively and respectfully with nature. When he first came to the region, he noticed, for example, how the homes along Lake Como imitated the lines and rhythms of the landscape and how the boats that plied the lake did so in response to the swelling and falling of the waves. But by the

1920's, he had begun to notice a change. The homes being built were not only larger, but more "aggressive," indifferent to the surrounding environment, no longer accommodating themselves to the natural setting. And the motor-driven boats on the lake were no longer moving in rhythm with the waves, but rather cutting through them indifferently.

(Barron 2015)

Guardini was lamenting the disruption of a particular type of humanly inhabited and humanly shaped landscape (Guardini 1994: 5). The old ways that were being disrupted involved a measure of mastery over nature while still permitting closeness to nature and being "fully integrated into nature" (Guardini 1994: 13). Guardini was troubled by what he regarded as the replacement of an appropriate and acceptable way in which humans had lived in, and had shaped, nature with a way of living in and shaping nature he regarded as excessive and inappropriate.

In what he considered the earlier *acceptable* stage, nature and culture were two different things but in this stage these "two notes [rang] out harmoniously together" (Guardini 1994: 68). Guardini comments as follows on the disquieting world he saw emerging.

[There is a] new desire for mastery [that] does not in any sense follow natural courses or observe natural proportions. Indeed, it treats them with complete indifference. ... ... What holds sway is not a vital and sympathetic power, an ability to follow the inner course of reality and to shape it accordingly. Instead, mechanistic laws are present that have been established once and for all and that anyone can manipulate. Materials and forces are harnessed, unleashed, burst open, altered, and directed at will. There is no feeling for what is organically possible or tolerable in any living sense. ... On the basis of a known formula, materials and forces are put into the required condition: machines. Machines are an iron formula that directs the material to the desired end. ... Everything is mass produced, nothing individual. ... Standardization is the way to go.

(Guardini 1994: 45, 46, 58)

So, according to Guardini, there is, on the one hand, relying on and using nature and modifying it to an extent but all the while going with the flow in the sense of cooperating with nature. And there is, on the other hand, the quest for domination and mastery and the types of interaction with nature these encourage. There is a strong anti-industrial, anti-machine, and anti-mass production dimension to these letters from Guardini. He writes about the "terrible," even "barbarian," sight of a factory or a smokestack intruding upon and threatening the finely tuned rural setting in which humanity and nature had lived in relative harmony (Guardini 1994: 7, 17).[5]

Some of the remarks I made in the last section bear on Guardini's talk of what fails to "follow natural courses or [to] observe natural proportions," what fails to "follow the inner course of reality," and what goes beyond what is "organically possible." In particular, I would reiterate here the difficulty of attaching any clear meaning to these terms other than the normative one proposed above. Consider these remarks in which Guardini is lamenting the loss of what he considered an example of a finely cultivated traditional relationship with nature:

> In older Italian houses, especially in rural areas, you will always find the open hearth. ... [Nature] is put to human use, and an element of human existence is achieved. ... [Nature] is still close at hand. We still have here a flaming fire that people have kindled and keep burning. ... But note how we have left all that with our coal stoves ... or with our steam heating, which completely anonymously keeps the house at a certain temperature by means of a boiler. Or think of heating by electricity, in which nothing burns at all, but a current comes into the house and gives warmth in some way. The manifestation of culture has gone, the link with nature has been cut, a totally artificial situation has been created.
>
> (Guardini 1994: 14–15)

An obvious problem is that open hearths are notoriously energy inefficient, with most of the fuel's energy going up the chimney. Modern stoves are much more efficient and new technologies permit yet more efficient uses of energy. Indeed, the correct response to this aspect of what Guardini is saying is readily available in the encyclical. As noted, liberation from the technocratic paradigm is said to be available through deploying "technology [that] is directed primarily to resolving people's concrete problems, truly helping them live with more dignity and less suffering" (112). More efficient and less polluting ways of heating our homes are just this sort of technology. We also read that liberation from the technocratic paradigm occurs when "cooperatives of small producers adopt less polluting means of production, and opt for a non-consumerist model of life, recreation and community" (112). The question arises: what about *large-scale* producers who adopt less polluting and more efficient techniques to make products that are also less polluting and that become widely available, thereby solving some of the deepest social problems. The answer is obvious.

There is in addition a combination of sentimental attachment and aestheticism at play in Guardini's thinking.[6] The obvious problems in this area include the fact that sentiments differ and sentiments change, and the same goes for aesthetic tastes. What pleases one person displeases another. And what one person thinks out of place in a natural setting seems entirely appropriate and in place to another. More to the point, people may be sentimentally attached to, or aesthetically pleased by, what is environmentally harmful. Consider, for example, the manicured, over-fertilized, highly managed lawns of the American Midwest with their inhospitality to biodiversity. Unfortunately, there are people who feel that such lawns are pleasing to the eye. Once again, the best approach to take on these matters actually fits with the overall orientation of the encyclical. As Sandra Lubarsky puts it, Pope Francis is calling for "the reintegration of aesthetics into our way of thinking and a reconnection of aesthetics with ethics" (Lubarsky 2015: 92). What is needed is an aesthetic sense, and a sense of attachment, that is guided by or inspired by or gives expression to the relevant ethical considerations or that at least operates within parameters that reflect those considerations.

In any case, the overall stance of LS is that the development of more and more technology within the limits provided by the relevant norms, and especially developments that aim to promote those norms, are to be *welcomed*.

To sum up, we have identified some aspects of the technocratic paradigm. And we have seen that various values and norms are central to Francis's response to what he finds problematic about this paradigm. Next, I want to probe further both what he finds problematic and his response to what he considers problematic.

A deeper grasp of the problem

Actually, it is striking how many additional dimensions there are to the target that Pope Francis has in his sights when he opposes the technocratic paradigm. I will next identify some additional elements in this paradigm, or elements associated with it.

"Where profits alone count"

The first such element has to do with the relentless pursuit of profits. Francis is very critical of the way in which any and all technological developments, whether beneficial or harmful, are embraced in modern economies, provided they are profitable for business: "The economy accepts every advance in technology with a view to profit, without concern for its potentially negative impact on human beings" (109). He writes that "[when] your only aim is to make profits, the destruction of the natural environment, and its systems and societies, is not considered" (109; also 56, 187, 190).

He does not object to making a profit (129). His view is that the pursuit of profit is legitimate provided it stays within the limits imposed by the relevant norms. Indeed, Francis writes approvingly of "more diversified and innovative forms of production which impact less on the environment" and that are also profitable (191). The problem arises when the pursuit of profit is your *only aim* and when the pursuit of profit is *unrestrained*. The problem arises when "technology is not consciously created and morally designed, but only executed, in a technocratic fashion with a sole focus on economic growth and profitability" (Edenhofer and Flachsland 2017: 185). Anthony Annett also hits this nail squarely on the head:

> [A] blinkered focus on profit maximization discounts the harm done to the environment, the rhythms of nature, and biodiversity and ecosystems. It leads business to ignore the effects of their actions on the earth and future generations, because they do not pay the full costs of using up shared environmental resources – only when they do so, says Pope Francis, can their actions be deemed ethical (195).
>
> (Annett 2017: 170)

Technology as a law unto itself

Another aspect of the technocratic paradigm takes us in a different direction though it is closely related to the critique of technology without limits and without restraint. This is the idea of technology as master, as a law unto itself, as all-dominating, as aiming for "lordship over all," and as "a self-perpetuating system with no controlling center" (Hanby 2015). This idea of all-dominating technology is spelled out here:

> The idea of ... employing technology as a mere instrument is nowadays inconceivable. The technological paradigm has become so dominant that it would be difficult to do without its resources and even more difficult to utilize them without being dominated by their internal logic. ... Technology tends to absorb everything into its ironclad logic, and those who are surrounded with technology "know full well that it moves forward in the final analysis neither for profit nor for the well-being of the human race", that "in the most radical sense of the term power is its motive – a lordship over all". As a result, "man seizes hold of the naked elements of both nature and human nature".
>
> (108)[7]

This idea of all-dominating technology is rather different from the idea of an all-dominating market that dictates the direction that technology will take and how it will be used. Here, we are talking about technology dictating *its own* direction.

"Technological solutionism"

Here is a closely related but distinct concern. This is the idea of "[making] the method and aims of science and technology an epistemological paradigm which shapes the lives of individuals and the workings of society" (107). In the same section Francis says that

> technological products ... create a framework which ends up conditioning lifestyles and shaping social possibilities along the lines dictated by

the interests of certain powerful groups. Decisions which may seem purely instrumental are in reality decisions about the kind of society we want to build.

A few lines later we read this: "Life gradually becomes a surrender to situations conditioned by technology, itself viewed as the principal key to the meaning of existence" (110).[8]

This is another aspect of the idea that technology "tends to absorb everything into its ironclad logic": it provides a framework through which everything is seen and within which the idea of what constitutes a problem and what would constitute its solution is understood. I take the term "technological solutionism" from Vincent J. Miller who nicely presents the key idea here as the thought that technological products "train us in a narrow, exploitative vision of the world whenever we use them" (Miller 2017: 24).

Surely though what needs to be said here is that technological products and developments are problematic *insofar as* they "train us in a narrow, exploitative vision of the world." For some problems have technological solutions that are environmentally constructive, culturally enriching, and so on. So perhaps what we have here is a danger associated with technology. And we can agree with Francis that it is a mistake to think that technology as such can solve the problems to which our misuse of technology has given rise. The solution lies in a proper appreciation of the relevant norms and *these* may legitimately guide us in the deployment of technological solutions.

Fragmentation and "reductionism"

Part of what is involved in technological solutionism is thinking that whatever solution a problem may have, it will be a technological solution to that particular problem. The worry is that this blinds us to cases in which a particular problem is best understood as part of an interconnected set of problems with the solutions being correspondingly broad. Pope Francis writes that

> [the] specialization which belongs to technology makes it difficult to see the larger picture. The fragmentation of knowledge proves helpful for concrete applications, and yet it often leads to a loss of appreciation for the whole, for the relationships between things, and for the broader horizon, which then becomes irrelevant.
>
> (110)[9]

This is also what Francis has in mind when he mentions "a reductionism which affects every aspect of human and social life" (107).

As with some other elements mentioned, we might question what exactly the problem is. What is wrong with reducing a problem to its components? Indeed, isn't that sensible when there are components that can be tackled independently? Probably the key, again, is to see what is under discussion here as a *danger* of technology: that it will obscure complexities and relationships and the full picture, encouraging a focus on a narrow technical fix.

The blindness to complexity that is under discussion seems to be associated in the encyclical with another theme, namely the belief that an increase in technological power means progress on numerous other important fronts—"as if reality, goodness and truth automatically flow from technological and economic power as such" (105).

Technological interventions that create new problems

Not only is "[technology] ... linked to business interests ... incapable of seeing the mysterious network of relations between things," it "sometimes solves one problem only to create others" (201). This is different from "fragmentation" though, again, there is a close connection between the two. The problem here is that "a vicious circle results, as human intervention to resolve a problem further aggravates the situation" (34). For example, in destroying pollinators, we create a need for a new mechanism for pollination; and introducing *that* mechanism may well create new problems we have not foreseen.

"The interests of certain powerful groups"

The mention of technology *linked to business interests* draws attention to another aspect of the technocratic paradigm, one that was already mentioned in passing. This is the idea of empowering some while disempowering others. There are "new power structures based on the techno-economic paradigm" so that those with the economic resources to use them become dominant over others and over the entire world (53, 104). So there is a "minority who wield economic and financial power" (203). On the other hand, the majority, being in the grip of the technocratic paradigm "believe that they are free as long as they have the supposed freedom to consume. But those really free are the minority who wield economic and financial power" (203).

Interestingly, Pope Francis also says that even those who wield economic and financial power suffer from a loss of "genuine freedom" (108). He writes that

> [our] freedom fades when it is handed over to the blind forces of the unconscious, of immediate needs, of self-interest, and of violence. In this sense, we stand naked and exposed in the face of our ever-increasing power, lacking the wherewithal to control it.
>
> (105)

Part of his point here seems to be that real freedom requires "human responsibility, values and conscience" (105). So, even the privileged and powerful are diminished: relative to those over whom they wield power there is a sense in which they are free but in another sense they too are in bondage—a point that recalls the idea of technology as aiming for "lordship over all."

Possible additional elements in the technocratic paradigm

We have identified some central aspects of what Pope Francis means to oppose when he criticizes the technocratic paradigm. However, there are additional themes that also merit a mention in this context, some of which have already been hinted at in passing. For instance, Francis writes that "the new power structure based on the 'techno-economic paradigm' may overwhelm not only our politics but also freedom and justice" (53). So there are associated political and cultural dangers. He also says that the confrontational approach to nature that this paradigm involves

> has made it easy to accept the idea of infinite or unlimited growth … [which] is based on the lie that there is an infinite supply of the earth's goods, and this leads to the planet being squeezed dry beyond every limit.
> (106)

Hence the illusion of endless growth is relevant too.

There is an element of selfishness involved. Francis explicitly associates the technocratic paradigm with the idea that "everything [is] irrelevant unless it serves one's immediate interests" (122; also 123, 204). He warns against approaching the world around us in such a way that "efficiency and productivity are entirely geared to our individual benefit" (159) Compulsive consumerism is also associated with the technocratic paradigm. It is mentioned as an example of how the techno-economic paradigm affects individuals (203).

Cultural homogeneity, or a loss of the cultural variety that is "the heritage of all humanity" (144) is also associated with the technocratic paradigm. There are forces at work that "make us all the same" (108). The result is that humans are deprived of local cultural resources that may be essential for solving local problems (144). Indeed, "[the] disappearance of a culture can be just as serious, or even more serious, than the disappearance of a species of plant or animal" (145).

Celia Deane-Drummond introduces another element into the mix when she writes that

> [it is the] unbridled use of technologies that Pope Francis wants to resist most strongly, along with *the cultural allure of technologies that threaten to undercut face-to-face human relationships*. It is not so much that new technologies are sinful, but *when their use undercuts human dignity and relationships* they have the potential to become idols.
> (Deane-Drummond 2016a: 13, my italics)

Here, the emphasis is on destructive consequences for relationships. Deane-Drummond mentions another theme when she traces the Pope's concern with "technological solutionism" (as I call it above) to the idea that empirical science provides, or could provide, a complete explanation of life (Deane-Drummond 2016b: 400) (The latter idea is mentioned, or hinted at, in Section 81). And Vincent J. Miller mentions the idea of a strong separation between humans and nature as central to the technocratic paradigm.

So we have a long list of elements. Some certainly are constituents or aspects of the technocratic paradigm. Some are perhaps better understood as consequences of living in the grip of this paradigm or as features that are normally associated with it or that typically accompany it or to which it is conducive. Some may be problems that are exacerbated by it. Some may be factors that partially give rise to it, contributing to its occurrence. As mentioned, some are probably best understood as *dangers* associated with the technocratic paradigm.

What we have in the technocratic paradigm, in any case, is a multi-faceted and somewhat open-ended idea. I think that the relationship between it and other ideas in *Laudato Si'*, such as the types of anthropocentrism that the Pope also decries, is sometimes a bit unclear, as are some of the relationships among its components. What is very clear though is that Francis is most concerned to oppose exploitation of the world around us that is solely focused on profit and that rides roughshod over the relevant norms and values so that we cause damage without a second thought, using and abusing what should instead be approached with respect or even reverence. And he is right.

A deeper grasp of the solution

In spelling out various dimensions to the technocratic paradigm, I have mentioned what the Pope has to say about the normative framework that should govern how we deal with the world around us, starting with the value that various things have in themselves. I noted above that the things that are said to have value include other humans, other animals, other species, and ecosystems.) If the technocratic paradigm is a central part of the problem, a central part of the solution is "to recover the values and the great goals swept away by our unrestrained delusions of grandeur" (114).

Actually, it is striking how many additional aspects there are to the relevant normative framework that emerges from the encyclical. Like the aspects of the problem, the aspects of Francis's proposed solution are connected to each other in many ways and in explaining one we sometimes invoke others. Moreover, in this area too, the relationships among the relevant elements are at times a little unclear though the big picture is both clear and compelling. Next, I sketch the additional normative elements mentioned in the encyclical. To do so is actually to illuminate further the character of the technocratic paradigm: it does so by casting light on the manifold ways in which this paradigm is said to lead us astray.

Common good

The common good must be promoted. "Common good" is used in this context to refer to what is good *for humans*. As Vincent J. Miller notes, there is an emphasis on

> goods that can only be achieved by humans together in society ... [and that cannot] be achieved privately. ... [The common good] concerns matters that affect all and require the contribution of all members of society in order to be achieved.

(Miller 2017: 20)

This focus on all members of society goes hand in hand with special attention to the situation of the poor and vulnerable; they have a right to everything that is essential for human survival (30). There is also a focus on future generations of humans (36, 67).

A focus on promoting the common good requires attention to the consequences of our actions. As we have seen, technology that "is directed primarily to resolving people's concrete problems, truly helping them live with more dignity and less suffering" (112) is desirable, which is again to think in consequentialist terms. More broadly, there is a moral imperative "[to assess] the impact of our every action and personal decision on the world around us" (208), which suggests that the relevant consequentialist evaluation needs to attend to many factors. So the normative picture that emerges from the encyclical certainly has consequentialist elements.

Ecological sensitivity

Pope Francis welcomes the ecological sensitivity that is developing in some countries though he also laments that it is not reducing consumption. He observes that we must respect "the delicate equilibria existing between the creatures of this world" (68). The idea of being ecologically sensitive—like the aforementioned ideas of being environmentally friendly and avoiding actions that are environmentally harmful—does not interpret itself. For example, someone might think that to be ecologically sensitive is to retain some space, however diminished, for indigenous forms of life so that they are not entirely wiped out. What being ecologically sensitive requires is of course a highly contested matter and I cannot pursue the matter in detail here; by way of illustrating what might be meant I will just mention two approaches I find congenial.

One such approach combines the ideas of ecological health and ecological integrity.[10] *Ecological health* is present when two conditions are met. First, processes of nature, such as water purification, nitrogen fixation, soil stabilization, nutrient retention and recycling, and the production of clean air, are operating normally, with the result that many "ecosystem services"—such as clean air, potable water, flood control, and crop pollination—are provided. Nature continues to provide such functions as these—and not just for people. A second element in a healthy ecosystem is resilience, or the ability to cope with disturbance. Ecological health is to be preserved everywhere: it is a level below which we should aim not to fall anywhere. *Ecological integrity*, on the other hand, is preserved when there is ecological health as just described and, in addition, the historic species composition of the biotic community is maintained or restored. So here we go beyond *functioning* to make reference to *composition*. Advocates of this combination of ideas think of ecological integrity as being especially relevant in set-aside biodiversity preserves. This combination of ideas provides one outline of how to begin to think about what ecological sensitivity requires.

An alternative reading of ecological sensitivity would take it to endorse the ideas of the eminent biologist Edward O. Wilson in his book *Half Earth: Our Planet's Fight for Life*. Wilson suggests that humans should set aside roughly 50% of the planet as a sort of permanent preserve, undisturbed by human activity.

> I propose that only by committing half of the planet's surface to nature can we hope to save the immensity of life-forms that compose it. ... The Half-Earth proposal offers a first, emergency solution commensurate with the magnitude of the problem[.] ... A biogeographic scan of Earth's principal habitats shows that a full representation of its ecosystems and the vast majority of its species can be saved within half the planet's surface. At one-half and above, life on Earth enters the safe zone. ... [It] is entirely reasonable to envision a global network of inviolable reserves that cover half the surface of Earth.
>
> (Wilson 2016: 3, 4, 209)

It might be proposed that *this* is what ecological sensitivity requires.

Interrelatedness and intimate unity with all that exists

Responding appropriately to the interrelatedness of all things is central to the encyclical. This has many aspects and many implications. The interrelatedness of things has implications for how we see individual members of other species. For example, as Vincent J. Miller puts it,

> [we] can see wild animals as more than predators, nuisances and potential game. We can attend to their myriad ecological interconnections upon which we depend. ... All things around us – soil, trees, bees – ... are so much more than that simple object that meets our eye. They are interconnected in ways that have profound importance for our lives.
>
> (Miller 2017: 17, 15)

Healing our relationship with the earth is said to be intimately related to healing all fundamental human relationships (119; also 118). One implication is that an adequate response to the "cry of the earth" requires an adequate response to the "cry of the poor." Also it is contrary to human dignity to cause animals to suffer or die unnecessarily (130) so these factors too are intimately connected. Moreover, a sense that we are intimately related to everything around us will in turn elicit various responses from us: "if we feel intimately united with all that exists, then sobriety and care will well up spontaneously" (11).

Needs rather than wants

What is permitted is taking from the world what we need. Going beyond that to satisfy whims and consuming for its own sake are prohibited. Francis is critical of "the disordered desire to consume more than what is necessary" (123). He says that "[each] community can take from the bounty of the earth whatever it needs for subsistence ..." (67) and that everyone has a right to what they need to survive (30, 94).

Living simply

Closely related to the focus on needs rather than wants is an emphasis on the importance of living simply. "Less is more" is the apt phrase used to express this idea (222, 223). Francis advocates a "simplicity which allows us to stop and appreciate the small things, to be grateful for the opportunities which life affords us, to be spiritually detached from what we possess, and not to succumb to sadness for what we lack" (222).

Sobriety, care, sacrifice, generosity, a spirit of sharing, humility

Next, there is a set of attitudes and dispositions we should exhibit in our dealings with the world around us. We have already seen that Francis mentions "the sobriety and care" that will well up spontaneously... [when] we feel intimately united with all that exists" (11). He reports approvingly that the Ecumenical Patriarch Bartholomew has urged people "to replace consumption with sacrifice, greed with generosity, [and] wastefulness with a spirit of sharing" (9). Francis also says that people need environmental education that will help them to grow in "solidarity, responsibility and compassionate care" (210). He says that "sobriety and humility" are among the "great values" we should promote (224).

Awe, wonder, fraternity, a friendly hand, and a sense of place

There are also what are, I think, best understood as a set of dispositions, attitudes, and responses that, Pope Francis is saying, we should exhibit *toward* the world around us. These include awe, wonder, and a fraternal attitude:

> If we approach nature and the environment without this openness to awe and wonder, if we no longer speak the language of fraternity and beauty in our relationship with the world, our attitude will be that of masters, consumers, ruthless exploiters, unable to set limits on their immediate needs.
>
> (11; also 85 and 225)

And Francis mentions the importance of developing a sense of place, which is to say an attachment to the landscape and natural setting in which you have grown up (84). In addition, building on the idea of interdependence, Pope Francis advances the inspiring proposal that people who live in a particular place should set out to protect all forms of life that share that place (42).

Serene attentiveness and becoming painfully aware

Two other attitudes toward the world around us are emphasized repeatedly. Francis recommends "an attention full of fondness and wonder" (97). This "serene attentiveness" enables us to be completely present to everyone and everything (226). It makes us more sensitive to the value of things around us and to their interconnections (Miller 2017: 16, 17). Closely related to this idea of attentiveness is the idea of "cherishing each thing and each moment" (222).

Douglas E. Christie highlights another dimension when he observes that what is involved here is a loving awareness "that we are deeply bound to, dependent upon, and responsible for all of creation ... [and this] means *becoming vulnerable to all that we behold*" (Christie 2017: 124, my italics). We should "dare to turn what is happening to the world into our own personal suffering and thus to discover what each of us can do about it" (19). This idea of becoming painfully aware of damage to the world around us, and of allowing ourselves to be vulnerable to it, is powerfully expressed in *Laudato Si'* in this quotation from another church document: "God has joined us so closely to the world around us that we can feel the desertification of the soil almost as a physical ailment, and the extinction of a species as a painful disfigurement" (89).

Mystical meaning, divine presence, and beauty

Various normatively significant features of objects in the world around us also need to be mentioned. For example, "there is a mystical meaning to be found in a leaf, in a mountain trail, in a dewdrop, in a poor person's face" (233). Francis says in the prayer at the end of the encyclical that God is "present in the whole universe and in the smallest of creatures." Whatever exactly is involved in the presence of mystical meaning or in God being present everywhere, either would seem to provide reason not to treat things around us casually or as to be used in any way we want. Also, we must learn to stop and admire things that are beautiful (215). Indeed, a route to liberation from the technocratic paradigm is made available "when the desire to create and contemplate beauty manages to overcome reductionism through a kind of salvation which occurs in beauty and in those who behold it" (112).

Appreciating the small things and "little daily actions"

The Pope's emphasis on the individual, the small, and the local, and on what individuals can accomplish wherever they may find themselves and whatever their circumstances, are among the potentially most fruitful ideas in *Laudato Si'*. The living things in our experience, however small and inconspicuous they may be, are deserving of our attention, care, empathy, and consideration. We are to attend to such particular things though always with an eye to their interdependence (86). We need to "experience what it means … to enjoy them" (223). As noted above, living simply "allows us to stop and appreciate the small things" (222).

There is also "a nobility in the duty to care for creation through little daily actions" (211). While Francis recognizes, naturally, that major policy initiatives and technological breakthroughs are needed, each of us can contribute through "simple daily gestures which break with the logic of selfishness, violence, [and] exploitation" (230; also 231). This emphasis on the individual, the local, and on what we can each do here and now, is empowering and relevant to everyone everywhere. We do not need to wait for powerful institutions to change their course or for others to "get their act together."

Additional normative elements

This by no means exhausts the normative elements introduced in *Laudato Si'*. Here are some others. Francis says that we should cultivate sound virtues (211) and this probably should be taken to involve more than the various elements I have mentioned—for example, generosity and humility—that are reasonably classified as virtues. He advises us "to live wisely, to think deeply and to love generously" (47). He advocates "responsible stewardship" (116), which is a term that, like "ecological sensitivity," requires interpretation. (Indeed, the same interpretations might be considered, by way of example, in this case.) Just as cultural homogeneity is associated with the technocratic paradigm, cultural diversity seems to be understood to be part of the solution. Hence, respect must be shown for the cultural riches of others, including their spirituality (63). Francis says that every *government* has a responsibility to preserve its country's environment (38) and this is, in effect, to open up another area of inquiry, namely the different responsibilities of different institutions. And in a remark that suggests some policies that would issue from his normative perspective, he says that the full cost of environmental harm should be borne by those who profit from it (195).

Combining the various normative elements

As with the interpretation of the sort of problem provided by the technocratic paradigm, we have seen that when it comes to solving the problem, there are once again many elements to consider. And many of these need clarification and explanation; for example, what is it about individual organisms and individual ecosystems that makes them valuable beyond their value for us? How is this idea to be understood? A great deal could also be said about the extent to which the elements mentioned overlap with each other or are in tension with each other.

Naturally, the question arises of what these normative elements add up to. And the first thing to say about this is that what we have before us is not exactly a normative framework but rather elements that such a framework might include. And there is no formula for uniting seamlessly all of these factors. There is no way to avoid difficult questions about their relative importance. As Eric T. Freyfogle observes, the Pope introduces a large number of normative considerations but he says little about how they are to be combined (Freyfogle 2017: 91, 104, 109). While Francis mentions "the need to promote and unify all the great values" (224), he also observes that it is "difficult to reach a balanced and prudent judgement on different questions, one which takes into account all the pertinent variables" (135; also 141). One could not easily exaggerate the relevant complexities. Even the task of combining the values mentioned near the start of this chapter would be a Herculean one. Just by way of example, there are much discussed perplexities about how to reconcile a concern for ecosystems with a concern for individual animals.[11] And surely "mystical meaning" and beauty, for example, are relevant in some way to the value of things that possess them; but how exactly? And so on.

Second, much of the time we do not need to combine such elements into a coherent whole. We should reject the unrealistic idea that we are somehow disempowered till we have systematically thought through all of the key elements of our normative framework and all the relations among them. (I also think that attempts to combine such elements into a coherent whole will be arbitrary in all manner of ways.)

What we can say for sure though is that taking to heart even a subset of the normative elements to which Pope Francis has drawn attention will be transformative for many people. He has provided a challenge to other religions, to secular institutions, and to humanity as a whole.

Notes

1 There are some sentences in the encyclical that suggest otherwise and I later comment on their meaning. See Notes 7–9.
2 Here, the encyclical is quoting Guardini 1956: 74.
3 This idea also seems to be hinted at near the end of 78.
4 Guardini's reflections of three decades later in his book *The End of the World* are acknowledged in *Laudato Si'* and have received attention from commentators but the earlier letters are at least as relevant to the encyclical.
5 Guardini's distinction between earlier acceptable ways of intervening in nature and current problematic ways of doing so is clearly reflected in these remarks in the encyclical:

> Men and women have constantly intervened in nature, but for a long time this meant being in tune with and respecting the possibilities offered by the things themselves. It was a matter of receiving what nature itself allowed, as if from its own hand. Now, by contrast, we are the ones to lay our hands on things, attempting to extract everything possible from them while frequently ignoring or forgetting the reality in front of us. Human beings and material objects no longer extend a friendly hand to one another; the relationship has become confrontational.
>
> (106)

Francis also seems at times somewhat enamored of Guardini's opposition to mass production and machine-based production. (I have 203 in mind in particular.) But the clear message of the encyclical is that production should be assessed in large part by virtue of its environmental implications; whether it involves mechanized mass production is beside the point.

6 Incidentally, I do not propose to try to give a comprehensive account of Guardini's views in this area. Such an account would recognize that he gave some thought to new ways of being human that would in effect adapt successfully to the technological age (e.g., Guardini 1994: 81–83, 85, 92, 93).
7 This is a complex passage with a number of strands, one of which is the idea I am referring to as "technology as a law unto itself." Actually this is an example of a part of the encyclical where technology *as such* may appear to be characterized as the problem. Here, the *technological* paradigm, the "ironclad logic" of technology, and the "internal logic" of the resources of the technological paradigm are mentioned as problematic. Francis even appears to say that technology aims for its own empowerment: "in the most radical sense of the term power is its motive – a lordship over all." However, the main thrust of the encyclical, as I say at the start of this chapter, is that technology as such is not the problem and that technological development is unproblematic and even to be welcomed when it reflects an appropriate sense of responsibility, appropriate values, and an appropriate operation of conscience. Maybe the parts of section 108 that seem to suggest that technology per se is the problem are not really about technology as such but about technology that is being deployed in accordance with the technocratic paradigm. Or maybe what is under discussion here is a *danger* of technological innovation. Incidentally, the parts of the quoted passage that are in quotation marks are from Guardini 1956: 74.
8 This is another point at which the finger of blame might seem to be pointed at technology as such. In response, I would just reiterate my points in Note 7.
9 Here too the finger of blame might seem to be pointed at technology as such.
10 Here, I draw on these papers: Callicott and Mumford, 1997 and Callicott, Crowder, and Mumford, 1999.
11 There is a vast literature on this topic. Some seminal discussion can be found in Callicott 1980 and Jamieson 1998.

References

Annett, Anthony. 2017. "The economic vision of Pope Francis" in Vincent J. Miller (ed.) *The Theological and Ecological Vision of Laudato Si': Everything Is Connected*, London: Bloomsbury, 160–174.

Barron, Robert. 2015. "Laudato Si and Romano Guardini" posted June 23, 2015. www.wordonfire.org/resources/article/laudato-si-and-romano-guardini/4808/

Callicott, J. Baird. 1980. "Animal Liberation: A Triangular Affair" *Environmental Ethics* 2 (4), 311–338.

Callicott, J. Baird and Karen Mumford. 1997. "Ecological Sustainability as a Conservation Concept" *Conservation Biology* 11 (1), 32–40.

Callicott, J. Baird, Larry B. Crowder, and Karen Mumford. 1999. "Current Normative Concepts in Conservation" *Conservation Biology* 13 (1), 22–35.

Christie, Douglas E. 2017. "Becoming painfully aware: Spirituality and solidarity in Laudato *Si*'" in Vincent J. Miller (ed.) *The Theological and Ecological Vision of Laudato Si': Everything Is Connected*, London: Bloomsbury, 109–126.

Deane-Drummond, Celia. 2016a. "Pope Francis: Priest and Prophet in the Anthropocene" *Environmental Humanities* 8 (2), 256–262. https://read.dukeupress.edu/environmental-humanities/article/8/2/256/8143/Pope-FrancisPriest-and-Prophet-in-the-Anthropocene

Deane-Drummond, Celia. 2016b. "*Laudato Si'* and the Natural Sciences: An Assessment of Possibilities and Limits" *Theological Studies* 77 (2), 392–415.

Edenhofer, Ottmar and Christian Flachsland. 2017. "Laudato Si': Concern for our global commons" in Vincent J. Miller (ed.) *The Theological and Ecological Vision of Laudato Si': Everything Is Connected*, London: Bloomsbury, 177–191.

Freyfogle, Eric. 2017. *A Good That Transcends: How U.S. Culture Undermines Environmental Reform*. Chicago, IL: The University of Chicago Press.

Guardini, Romano. 1956. *The End of the Modern World: A Search for Orientation*. Translated by Joseph Theman and Herbert Burke. Edited with an Introduction by Frederick D. Wilhelmsen. Chicago, IL: Henry Regnrey Company.

Guardini, Romano. 1994. *Letters from Lake Como: Explorations in Technology and the Human Race*. With an Introduction by Louis Dupré; translated by Geoffrey W. Bromiley. Grand Rapids, MI: Eerdmans. (First published in German as *Die Technic und der Mensch: Briefe vom Comer See*. 1981. Mainz: Matthias-Grünewald-Verlag).

Hanby, Michael. 2015. "The Gospel of Creation and the Technocratic Paradigm: Reflections on a Central Teaching of Laudato Si". www.communio-icr.com/files/42.4_Hanby_website.pdf

Jamieson, Dale. 1998. "Animal Liberation Is an Environmental Ethic" *Environmental Values* 7 (1), 41–57.

Lubarsky, Sandra. 2015. "That we may sow beauty" in John B. Cobb and Ignacio Castuera (ed.) *For Our Common Home: Process Relational Responses to Laudato Si'*, Anoka, MI: Process Century Press, 92–94.

Miller, Vincent J. 2017. "Integral ecology: Francis's spiritual and moral vision of interconnectedness" in Vincent J. Miller (ed.) *The Theological and Ecological Vision of Laudato Si': Everything is Connected*, London: Bloomsbury, 11–28.

Wilson, Edward O. 2016. *Half-Earth: Our Planet's Fight for Life*. New York: Liveright Publishing Corporation, A division of W. W. Norton & Company.

Index

Note: Page numbers followed by "n" denote endnotes.

Abidin, Z. 5, 11, 15
abortion 98, 154, 158, 160–1
academic fragmentation 194
aesthetic taste 224–5
Aeterni patris 155
Afrasiabi, K. 53
agriculture, industrial 13
Akbari, R. 53, 54
Alexander, G. 36n8
Alexander VI, Pope
Al-Khawas, Ali 160
Alperovitz, G. 36n16
Amazon rainforest 122
Ambrose 159
Ammatoans 54
Amstutz, M. R. 93n8
animals 13, 16, 95–104; as objects of
    affection 95–6, 102, 104; biomass
    of domesticated 99–100; care and
    respect toward 197; consequences of
    killing 101; eating animals 192, 200;
    human domination over 190, 197–9;
    intensive animal agriculture 100–3;
    sacrifice of 54; trust between humans
    and 198–9; used for human food
    99–102; wild 3, 99–100, 102–3
animism 41, 44, 47, 51–2, 54
Annett, A. 220, 226
Anthropocene, the 49, 112, 121
anthropocentrism 13, 42, 50–1, 65, 96,
    97, 104, 138, 141, 195–7, 200, 202,
    204, 210, 214n4
Appiah, K. 183n5
Aquinas, Thomas 155, 160, 205
Aristotle 205
Asosiasi Masyarakat Adat
    Nusantara 48

Athenagoras 160
Atkinson, J. 46
Attridge, H. 156, 165n2
Augustine 159, 160
authority, sources of in *Laudato
    Si'* 152–66; ecclesiastical source
    152–5; episcopal source 153–5,
    164; scriptural source 152, 155–9;
    theological source 152, 159–62;
    science as a source 152, 162–3

Bagir, Z. A. 47, 48, 55
Balabanski, V. 138
Barron, Bishop Robert 222–3
Basil the Great, Saint 160
Bauckham, R. 84
Baynes Rock, M. 201n1
Beard, V. 169
Becker, L. 36n9
Benedict XVI, Pope 154, 158
Benhabib, S. 183n5
Bennett, T. 36n3
Berry, T. 204
Berry, W. 26
Bible 13; environmental reading of the
    109–11, 133n7, 137–51
biocentrism 50–1, 196
biodiversity 60, 72, 95, 123,
biodiversity, loss of 3, 61
biophilia 205
birth control 76, 91; in Brazil 80–1
Bonaventure, Saint 160, 194
borders 12, 78, 79, 86; open 85–6,
    89–91
Brennan, C. 109, 126–7, 129, 132,
    134n21
Buitendijk, T. 130

Busch, J. 39
Butt, S. 48
Byrne, B. 150n6

Cafaro, P. 77
Cahill, K. 35n2
Callicott, J. B. 204, 214n7, 237n10, 237n11
Camosy, C. 98
capitalism 108, 117
Care packages 88, 90
Caritas in veritate 154
Carson, R. 203
Carter, A. 63
Carver, T.N. 93n4
Catechism of the Roman Catholic Church 97, 112, 192
Catholic Church 13, 94n9, 114, 120–8, 131–2, 152, 155, 173, 195
chance, metaphysics of 84
cheap-labor policy 90, 92
Christianity 11, 39, 40, 44, 47, 50, 51, 52–3, 83, 162
Christie, D. 234
Clough, D. 7, 13, 201n4
Cobb, J. 77
common good 11, 23–5, 28–30, 33, 231
concentrated animal feeding operations 192
consequentialists 86–7, 94n9
consumerism 106, 109, 111, 118, 125, 229
constructivism (in ethics) 15, 167, 169
contraception 76, 80, 119–20
conversion 49–51
Cotton-Purdue bill 91
Crean, Bishop William 127
creation care 76, 77, 78
Crowder, L. 237n10
cruelty 192
cultural diversity 235
cultural homogeneity 229
Curran, C. 156, 157, 165n3

Daly, H. 7, 12, 77, 79, 93n3, 94n10
Daly, L. 36n16
Daly-Denton, M. 13, 133n7, 150n4, 150n5
Dante Aligheri 160
Day of Prayer for Creation 124
Deane-Drummond, C. 15, 162–3, 194, 201n3, 201n8, 201n9, 201n11, 201n12, 229–30

DeWitt, C. 77
Dei verbum 155, 156
demographic transition 80, 82–3, 93n4
deontic relationships 177
deontologists 86–7, 94n9
Department of Agriculture (Ireland) 115
Department of Communications, Climate Action and Environment (Ireland) 115
Dillard, A. 112
divestment from fossil fuels 119, 127–8
Doctrine of Discovery 43–4
domination 15, 99, 102, 104, 144, 190, 197–9, 201n11, 203, 223
dominion 13, 25, 43, 97, 102, 108–11, 138, 140–4, 214n4, 220
Donaghy, K. 14, 170
Doran, R. 40, 50, 52, 53
Dostoevsky, F. 183n13
Dworkin, R. 64

earth: as a common home 35; as a gift to human beings 6, 23; care for the 25, 193, 200; cry of, the 12, 60–75, 145, 161, 233
Earth Bible Commentary 138
Earth Bible Team 138
Earth Charter 106, 162
ecological conversion 11, 38, 39, 49–51, 56, 95, 104, 142, 160, 161, 191
ecological debt 12, 60, 69
ecological footprint 81
ecological health 231–2
ecological hermeneutics 14, 133n7, 137–40, 142, 148, 149
ecological integrity 231–2
ecological restoration 108, 117–8
ecological services 61, 93n6
economic growth 82, 88, 94n9
ecosystems 5, 16, 33, 61–2, 72, 117, 134n11, 161, 169, 181, 182, 206–7, 212, 219, 230, 236
Ecumenical Patriarch Bartholomew 77
Edenhofer, O. 226
electricity consumption 68
Elliott, L. 181
endangered species 97
environmental education 120, 123, 172, 233
environmental ethics 202
environmental justice 43
Epstein, R. 36n7
Erwin, A. 131–2

Eucharist 124
evangelical Christians 93n7, 106, 109
Evangelii Gaudium 155, 202
Evangelium vitae 14, 152–65
extinction 61, 62, 63

Fachsland, C. 226
Feehan, John 123
Fisher, C. 56n9
forests: protection of 38; converted to
	agriculture 48
fossil fuel consumption 68
Francis of Assisi, Saint 95, 160,
	194, 218
Franciscan tradition 194
fraternity with all creatures 192
Freyfogle, E. 6, 11, 36n5, 36n6, 36n9,
	36n12, 36n13, 36n15, 36n17, 36n18,
	36n19, 36n22, 236
future generations 25, 28, 32, 176, 182

Garber, P. 3
Gaudium et spes 153, 154
genetically modified organisms 210
George, H. 36n15
Georgescu-Roegen, Nicholas 93n2
Global Catholic Climate
	Movement 129
global response 128–32
global supply chains 219
Godden, L. 36n3
Gregory of Nyssa, Saint 159
Grim, J. 203–4, 214n5, 214n6
Gross, R. 4
Grossi, P. 36n10
Growth: decreased 171; unlimited 229
Guardini, R. 42, 142, 162, 222–4,
	237n2, 237n4, 237n5, 237n6, 237n7
Guiding Ecojustice Principles 138
Gustafson, J. 161, 165n6

Habel. N. 138, 143
Hackett, R. 46
Haker, Hille 165n1
Hanby, M. 226
Haq, N. 53
Hardin, G. 86–7
Hauser-Schäublin, B. 48
Heaney, S. 112
Hefner, R. 47
Heft, J. 183n3
Hessel, D. 139, 203
Hidayah, S. 46

Hildegard of Bingen 164
Hofsvang, E. 38
Horrell, D. 139. 150n5, 150n6
human development 67–9, 71, 73, 74
Human Development Index 67
human dignity 189, 190, 197,
	199–200, 218
human exceptionalism 189, 190, 201n2
human nature 15
human uniqueness 195, 197, 200
Humanae Vitae 119–20, 122, 131, 153
Hume, D. 175
Hunt, C. 139, 150n5, 150n6
hunter-gatherers 190, 198, 200n1
Hurd, E 46
Huxley, A. 112

Ignatius of Antioch 159
Iheka, C. 214n9
Ilgunas, K. 36n17
immigration 12
incarnation, Christian doctrine of 98
indigenous communities 38–59, 196–7;
	Indonesian 38, 40, 44, 45; rights of
	39; diversity of 41
indigenous perspectives 11, 15, 189,
	190, 196–9
indigenous religions 11, 38–59
indigenous traditions 197
industrial chicken farming 219
Ingold, Tim 197–9, 201n9, 201n10,
	201n11
integral ecology 137, 170, 172
interconnectedness 15, 189–200
interdependence 235
interfaith dialogue 38, 39
Interfaith Rainforest Initiative 38,
	41, 55
International Society for the Study of
	Religion, Nature, and Culture 204
intrinsic value 62, 65, 74, 75
intrinsic value theorists 204
Irenaeus of Lyon 159
Islam 11, 39, 40, 47, 50, 51, 52–3, 55

Jamieson, D. 237n11
Jenkins, W. 214n3
John of the Cross, Saint 160
John Paul II, Pope 49, 152, 154,
	156–65; *see also* Karol Wojtyla
Joireman, S. F. 36n21
Jordan, Barbara 91
Jordan, Bill 124, 133n5, 134n15

Jordan Commission 91
Jubilee year 24
justice 173, 175–82, 184n23;
    obligations of 180, 182
justice 189, 199

Kant, I. 181, 183n10, 184n21
Katz, E. 204, 214n7
Kellert, S. 214n8
K'iche' people 46
Kolimon, M. 56n7

land, fertility of 31
lectio divina 156–9
Leo XIII, Pope 153, 155
Leopold, A. 4, 26, 106
Leshko, C. 215n14
Li, N. 131
liberation theology 120, 122, 153,
    214n9
Liberti, S. 36n14
lifeboat ethics 86–7
Light, A. 204, 214n7
limitless mastery 220
Linklater, A. 35n2
Lonergan, B. 50
Lubarsky, S. 225
Lumen gentium 153

Maarif, S. 41, 47, 54–5
Maathai, Wangari 164
Macron, President 106
Macy, J. 164
Major, A. 56n6
Malthus, T. 79
market forces 32
Marshall Plan 88, 90
Martiam, N. 55
Marx, K. 73, 76, 79
Masuzawa, T. 46
Mathiessen, P. 117
McDonagh, Sean Fr. 106, 121–6, 129,
    132, 134n13, 134n14
McKibben, B. 10, 149
meat, eating 125
Merrill, C. 117
migration 88
Mill, J. S. 66
Miller, V. 227, 230, 231, 232, 234,
Moellendorf, D. 7, 12, 64, 69, 70,
    71, 72
Moltmann, J. 77, 84, 194
moral value 24
Morrow, J. 155

Mostert, H. 36n3
Mulla Sadra 53–4
Mumford, K. 237n10
Murphy, W. 156

Nasr, S. 52–3
nature: intrinsic value of 12, 60, 72;
    fragmentation of 26; market value of
    26; mastery over 223; moral status
    of 203; personal powers in 197;
    perspectives on 111–3; reverence for
    40; theology of 123;
natural capital accounting
    108, 115–7
new creation 145
non-anthropocentrism 63, 65, 204
Noll, S. 215n14
Noonan, J. 76
Nostra aetate 52
Nugroho, S. 56n7
Nussbaum, M. 184n17

Oliver, M. 112
Ompusunggu, M. 48
O'Neill, N. 167, 173–83
other species 61, 148; intrinsic value of
    93n6; value of 61, 62, 63, 219
O'Neill, O. 15,
Ormerod, N. 40, 49–51, 52
Ostrom, E. 36n4
overpopulation 12, 13, 77–8, 82,
    113–4, 122
Özdemir, I. 53

papal authority, use of to promote
    Laudato Si' 118–21
papal infallibility 152
pastoralists 198
Paul VI, Pope 79, 153
Pearce, F. 36n14
perennial philosophy 53
Peterson, A. 204–5
Philippines, logging in 121
Picard, M. 47
Piso, Z 215n14
Pius XII, Pope 152
plants, human use of 61
Polanyi, K. 36n20
Polkinghorne, J. 84
polluter pays principle 116, 171
poor, the: cry of the 12, 60–75,
    209–10, 233; justice for the 106;
    needs of the 30–1; preferential
    option for 91, 149

population 12, 76–94 108, 113–5;
  population growth 76, 78, 85, 92;
  population policy 85–92
poverty, eradication of 66–70, 73–5
practical reasoning 173, 174, 182,
  183n8
practice, role of 202–14
precautionary principle 171
private property 11
private property 21–37; as a cultural
  institution 26, 35; social limits on
  23–4; social purpose of 27–31
profit, pursuit of 16, 225
property rights 23, 28
Prophet Muhammad 55
Pseudo-Dionysius 159
Putri, P. 45

Qur'an 53, 55

Rawls, J. 171, 175, 184n21
redemption, Christian doctrine of 98–9,
  102, 104
Rees, A. 138
refugee resettlement 88, 90
Rerum novarum 153, 155
reverence for life 219
religion 46–7
religious communities, accomplishments
  of 8–9
religious practices and rituals 9
religious traditions: accomplishments
  of 7–8; as sources of inspiration
  7; environmentally constructive
  teachings of 5–7; environmentally
  obstructive teachings of 5–7
Ricoeur, Paul 160
Right to Sustainable Development 67,
  69–71
Rio Declaration on Environment and
  Development 162
Ruether, R. 139, 164
Ruskin, J. 81
Ryan, A. 36n9

Sacrosanctum Concilium 142
Sapiie, M. 48
Saraswati, A. 45
Scott, W. 36n11
Season of Creation movement 124
Second Vatican Council 123, 142
Sedulur Sikep 44, 45, 48
selfishness 229
Sen, A. 67, 183n11

sentimental attachment 224
serene attentiveness 234
Setiadi 45
Seymour, F. 39
Shepard, P. 215n13
Sierra Club 203
Singer, J. 36n8
sixth great extinction 123
slavery 149
Smith, W. C. 46, 47
Snodgrass, J. 41, 42
Soeharto 47, 48
Soekarno 47
solidarity: intergenerational 170;
  intragenerational 170
Sorondo, Bishop Marcel Sánchez 129
Southgate, C. 139, 150n5, 150n6
Stavrakopoulou, F. 139
steady-state economy 77, 87
stewardship 97, 109, 111, 138,
  141–2, 195
Stevens, C. 38, 39
subsidiarity, principle of 32, 33, 79,
  171, 178, 182
Suhkdev, P. 115
sustainability 83
sustainable development 12, 67, 69;
  Right to Sustainable Development
  69–71
Sustainability Development
  Goals 169
Sweeney, John 123, 129
syncretism 47
system-of-systems perspective 169

Taylor, B. 10, 204, 214n4, 214n6,
  214n10
Taylor, C. 183n3
T'boli people 121–2
technocratic paradigm 16, 39, 42–4, 97,
  108, 120, 144, 209, 217–38
technology 42, 217, 219, 225, 227,
  231, 237n7
Tedje, K. 41, 42
Tehan, M. 36n3
Teilhard de Chardin, P. 160,
  194, 201n7
Tennyson, A. 65–6, 112
Tertullian 160
theological anthropology 189,
  190, 197
Tonstad, S. 138, 150n6
Tracy, D. 140
Traina, C. 7, 14

Trinity, the 194–5
Trócaire 122, 127
Trudinger, P. 138
Tucker, M. 203–4, 214n5, 214n6
Turkson, Cardinal Peter 122

US Conference of Bishops 128

Van der Walt, A. J. 36n9
Van Wieren, G. 15, 214n2, 214n4, 214n11
Vanin, C. 40, 49–51, 52
Vatican Council I 152
Vatican Council II 153, 155, 156
Veritatis splendor 153, 154, 157
virtue 173, 178–82, 183n7; obligations of 180, 182

Wainwright, E. 138, 139
Wenger, T. 46
Werkheiser, I. 215n14
Wetangterah, L. 56n7
White, L. 202, 203, 214n4
Williams, B. 171
Wilson, E. O. 10, 60–1, 72, 93n6, 214n8, 232
Wisdom of Jesus Son of Sirach 147
Wisdom of Solomon 146–7
Woodworth, P. 7, 10, 133n11
Wordsworth, W. 112
World Council of Churches 122
Wojtyla, K. 153; *see also* Pope John Paul II
Wurst, S. 138

Zaleha, B. 214n4